KU-515-143

POETRY NOTEBOOK

Also by
CLIVE JAMES

POETRY NOTEBOOK

Reflections on the
Intensity of Language

CLIVE JAMES

Liveright Publishing Company
a division of W. W. Norton & Company
NEW YORK • LONDON

Copyright © 2014 by Clive James
First American Edition 2015

First published in Great Britain under the title POETRY NOTEBOOK: 2006–2014

All rights reserved
Printed in the United States of America

For information about permission to reproduce selections from this book, write to
Permissions, Liveright Publishing Corporation, a division of W. W. Norton & Company, Inc.,
500 Fifth Avenue, New York, NY 10110

For information about special discounts for bulk purchases, please contact
W. W. Norton Special Sales at specialsales@wwnorton.com or 800-233-4830

Manufacturing by Courier Westford
Production manager: Louise Parasmo

Library of Congress Cataloging-in-Publication Data

ISBN 978-1-63149-027-9

Liveright Publishing Corporation,
500 Fifth Avenue, New York, N.Y. 10110
www.wwnorton.com

W. W. Norton & Company Ltd.,
Castle House, 75/76 Wells Street, London W1T 3QT

1 2 3 4 5 6 7 8 9 0

To Adam Gopnik

How oft when men are at the point of death
Have they been merry! Which their keepers call
A lightning before death . . .

Romeo and Juliet

Contents

Introduction

This book got started early in 2006, when I had lunch in London at an open-air restaurant near Holborn, on an unusually sunny winter's day. My companion was Christian Wiman, editor of the magazine *Poetry*. Operating from its base in Chicago, *Poetry* magazine has always been a force in the world of poetry, even for those of us who believe that a poem should get beyond the world of poetry if it can, and get itself heard in a wider world. I was pleased to discover that Wiman held the same belief.

I was even more pleased when he suggested that I might write my opinions about poetry down, and publish them from time to time in his magazine, in the form of a Poetry Diary. Or perhaps a better title would be Poetry Notebook, to obviate the impression that I was thinking about nothing except poetry every day. Even if I were, it would surely be better to let the daily thoughts accumulate into proper arguments, as long as I kept them short. Brevity would be the watchword; as, indeed, it is for poetry; or anyway it ought to be. Right there was one of the many opinions that I would have the chance to focus on and perhaps clarify, or even, as gracefully as possible, admit to have been wrong. Whichever poem or piece of a poem was in question, if it had vitality then all other considerations would be trumped. I could already hear the book's tone of voice in my head: always a good sign with any writing project.

No, Poetry Notebook would be the right title. Having settled that matter, we talked on: mainly about poetry in Britain, poetry in America, and the function of the Atlantic Ocean in coming between the two. If Robert Frost had not first secured his British reputation, would he ever have risen to supremacy in America? We discussed whether Seamus Heaney – still alive at the time – could possibly have enjoyed reading all those poetic offerings from his students at Harvard, or whether even he, who had the patience of a saint, might not have prayed for release. All we could be sure of was that he had never written a poem about it. His manners were too good. Perhaps there needed to be a revival of bad manners, on the scale of Auden trashing any spare room he was ever allowed to stay in, or Verlaine expressing his feelings about Rimbaud by putting a bullet into him.

I remember that by the time we got to the coffee we were agreeing that the later Wallace Stevens spent too much time writing in his own manner. To speak on such a theme – instead of falling silent, as if the CIA might have the table bugged – was a testimony to Wiman's moral courage, because for an American editor it is a bold thing to question, even in part, the achievement of an American poetic giant. But it was clear that Wiman was a brave man all round. Fine-drawn with a close haircut, he looked like a more than usually sensitive astronaut. He was, however, carrying a vicious form of bone cancer. It was inspiring to hear so young a man – so young and so cruelly stricken – making such a point of being clear about how poetry ruled his mind, even at a time when his body was putting him on notice that the years ahead would be tough sledding.

A few years later I fell ill myself; but I had already published, in *Poetry*, a few chapters of my Poetry Notebook that treated time as if it were running short. Only occasionally did I still feel inclined to write a longer piece about poetry. I was getting old, and the concentration necessary for writing a long piece seemed better reserved for writing poems, when they came. After I fell ill, I quit writing longer pieces altogether, although I still wrote the occasional short book review when I thought, perhaps foolishly, that the poet had a right to my continued acknowledgement: Michael Longley, Stephen Edgar, Les Murray and Wiman himself. But two or three brushes with death left the thought of any extended prose excursion looking overly ambitious, and even after my leukaemia went into remission I was short of energy. My translation of the *Divine Comedy* still required a lot of attention: the verse-writing was complete, but there were introductory pages of prose that still needed to be written, and my share of the editorial scrutiny was a hard task. Put it all together and it was no longer likely that I would get many critical articles even started, let alone finished. Critical ideas, however, still thronged in my head, as they always had. Now more than ever they tended to be ideas about poetry, and now more than ever they tended to be conclusions about poetic bedrock: the intensity of language that marked the real difference between poetry and prose. But a lifetime of thinking about the subject had not left me with an aesthetic system to convey. It had left me with a thousand thoughts. To register them, a Poetry Notebook was the ideal form.

One of those ideas will be found to rule this book. The favourite question of any editor of a literary page, anywhere in the world, is: 'What is a poem?' Your answer is meant to be short, snappy, quotable, bloggable. One answer, which I devised and published years ago, is that a poem is any piece of writing that can't be quoted from except out of context. I still find that idea serviceable as an epigram. A better question, but one that you will never be asked, is: 'How do you recognize a piece of writing as a poem?' There are trick answers. One of them is to point out that if you have to ask, then already it is not a poem. But the best answers are not tricks. They are registrations of what we feel and think when we encounter a stretch of language that transmits the thrill of human creativity by all its means, even by the means with which it is put together.

Declaring itself to be a poem is one of the main things a poem does. But such a declaration takes a good deal of management: the poet has to have mastered the mechanics of what he is doing, even as he strives to make the result seem inevitable. In my active years as a critic I made it a rule, when talking about poetry, to confine myself to practical points that I felt professionally qualified to discuss, having long been engaged in writing poems of my own. With due allowance for scale, I wanted to stay in the territory that Dr Johnson, himself a great critic, retroactively marked out for Dryden, our first great critic: the poetry criticism of a poet. Thus I steered well clear of theory, although there was always a possibility that there was a theory behind my approach: the theory that concentrated meaning should be what any poet was after.

But all too often, and especially if they stemmed from recent times, the poets made it clear – it was often the only thing they made clear – that they were less interested in meaning than in just sounding significant. In pursuit of significance, they would say anything, apparently in the belief that they were saying everything. Bits of their poems, as if driven to their isolated positions by no impulse except the random fidgets, would appear all over the page, like the manufactured evidence of an explosion that had never taken place. About such poetry, I seldom had anything to say. On both sides of the Atlantic, and in Australia, the creative writing schools churned forth slim volumes by the thousand, all of them supposedly full of poetry but few of them with even a single real poem in them. Spreading to cover the whole of the English-speaking world, this long eruption of unspecific stuff had one sole merit: nobody could praise it, analyse it or teach it without inadvertently proving that it was fake. There were exceptions of course; real talent can survive anything, even encouragement; and you could pick up the occasional creative writing collection in which the writing really was creative. But all too often there was only the claim, and never the deed. With so much tosh on the loose, the real thing looked more real than ever.

Better to say that it sounded more real than ever. One hears the force of real poetry at first glance. There is a phrase, something you want to say aloud. Sometimes the phrases link together into a whole line. Perhaps there is a stanza of these lines, a memorable unity. Very occasionally, there is a whole poem: a stand-alone unity that insists on being heard entire, and threatens never to leave one's memory. Even if you don't set out to memorize a real poem, it somehow seems to be memorizing itself for you. This authoritative audible presence, I believe, is an indispensable connection between the reader and the thing read. If that connection does not form, there is no real poem.

These and other matters are discussed at greater length in the following chapters; but always, I hope, they are discussed as tersely as possible. In the later part of life, and especially after I fell ill, I became convinced that the notes I had been putting into the margins and endpapers of poetry books for so many years were the basic stuff of what my critical response to poetry had always been; but that if I published those notes in paragraph form, the chain of argument should be kept brief, and precisely because poetry mattered to me so much. It had always mattered: but now it had become so vital to me that I didn't wish to insult it, or its readers, by manufacturing swathes of prose to convey my reactions. So I composed my chapters for *Poetry* magazine out of miniature essays. Occasionally there were other outlets or institutions which wanted me to write something about poetry – the *Wall Street Journal, Quadrant,* the Poetry Archive – but with those assignments, too, I could proceed only by prior agreement that I would keep things terse and particular. The same agreement applied when I wrote a farewell Notebook piece, which I place here at the back of the book, as a kind of finale. Christian Wiman having moved on from *Poetry* magazine, it was time for me to stop anyway; but Alan Jenkins of the *TLS*, visiting me where I was convalescing in Cambridge, kindly suggested that if I wanted to write one more chapter, he would consider it for his pages.

In that last chapter, as in the first, and in all the others in between, my critical arguments were sometimes not much more than a single paragraph long. Sometimes, because the habit dies hard, the paragraphs joined up; sometimes a single topic dominated the whole piece; but most of the pieces were not, at that stage, trying to be a book. Perhaps now, so late in the day, they are. If so, it is a book which can be guaranteed not to treat poetry as anything less than the occupation of a lifetime: except that, for those attuned by their nature to poetry's great mystery, the lifetime can begin very early on, with the first enthralled realization that a single sentence, or even less, is like nothing else they have ever heard.

Cambridge, 2014

Acknowledgements

For most of the notes in this *Poetry Notebook*, Christian Wiman of *Poetry* (Chicago) must have my thanks for providing a resplendent first home. I should also thank Alan Jenkins of the *TLS* for agreeing to print the Notebook's last chapter. Near the end of the book, before that last chapter, I have placed a sheaf of commissioned pieces that I have written in recent years. I am grateful to the editors concerned. The pieces are not strictly in note form, but one of my role models, Randall Jarrell, never minded mixing various types and formats of essay, as long as they fitted his view of poetry; and anyone who reads Jarrell's *Poetry and the Age* today might soon decide that nobody's view was ever more coherent, as if poetic quality were a world in itself.

My thanks to Prue Shaw, to Deirdre Serjeantson and to David Free for reading the manuscript. Prue Shaw, in addition to several other crucial comments, employed scholastic means to prove that an apparently rogue apostrophe in a line by Marvell actually belonged there; and Deidre Serjeantson reminded me that Milton might not necessarily have thought he was doing an unpoetic thing when he unloaded a classical library into the Garden of Eden. Martin Amis also spoke well in praise of Milton. My daughter Claerwen James designed the book's cover for the British edition. My assistant Susanne Young played a crucial role in assembling the working manuscript: in our cybernetic era there are so many ways of laying out a poem on the page, and almost all of them are wrong. The *Wall Street Journal*, the Poetry Archive and the Reading for Life organization deserve my thanks for encouraging the idea that I should try to pack as much judgement as possible into a small space, at times when I felt that a short piece might not just be best, but all I could do.

I should also thank the editors of publications in Britain, the USA and Australia that asked me for book reviews and for articles about poetry: the *New York Times Book Review*, *Standpoint*, the *Monthly*, the *Spectator*, *Prospect* and the *Financial Times*. Don Paterson, in his role as poetry editor of Picador, commissioned the chapter on Michael Donaghy and also, in his usual generous fashion, edited the initial manuscript of this book. Watching from New York, Robert Weil of Liveright was inspiringly determined to get a transatlantic edition published, even though, in present-day America, the issue of permissions makes it so expensive in time and trouble for the critic of poetry to quote what he is criticizing. Robert Weil also suggested the possibility that there might be some linking interludes to help students conclude that I was not deliberately being elliptical about a subject sufficiently elliptical already: a suggestion that Don Paterson endorsed. So really I had two editors, and I am grateful to both of them; but the opinions are all mine, although here and there, for the sake of narrative logic, I have modified the chronological order in which I wrote them down.

PART I
NOTES ON POETRY

LISTENING TO THE FLAVOUR

Almost fifty years ago, Hart Crane was one of my starting points as a reader of modern poetry. He still is. But my admiration for him always led to a quarrel, and it still does. By now, I hope I can do a better job of framing the quarrel as an argument, instead of as one of those impatient snorts we give when we are drawn in but not convinced, put off but can't let go. The argument starts like this. If 'Voyages', one of the stand-out pieces in *White Buildings*, had maintained its show of coherence all the way to the end, it would have been a successful abstract poem sequence. It didn't have to make sense, but it did have to keep up its confident, even if drunkenly confident, tone: and it didn't. Or, to put Hart Crane back into the present tense which is his due, it doesn't. The show breaks down in section IV, where the second stanza seems to be beginning with its second line, a first line having apparently gone missing.

> All fragrance irrefragably, and claim
> Madly meeting logically in this hour
> And region that is ours to wreathe again,
> Portending eyes and lips and making told
> The chancel port and portion of our June –

A textual crux that Crane might have designed specifically to help give his future scholars tenure, the phantom first line could have been a surmountable anomaly. (Plainly the narrative syntax is a put-up job throughout the poem, so any ellipsis is a hole in a mirage.) But the credibility drops to zero when we encounter 'Madly meeting logically'. In the first three sections of the poem there have been plenty of adverbs as self-consciously fancy as 'irrefragably'; and the main reason 'The chancel port and portion of our June' rings dead, apart from the exhausted wordplay of 'port and portion', is that we have met too many similar structures previously ('In these poinsettia meadows of her tides'). But 'Madly meeting logically' is too much. We might have forgiven the stanza's cargo of leaden echoes if the mad logical meeting had not forfeited our attention, as when a barroom war hero piles on that fatal implausible detail too many.

After this sudden and damaging loss of pressure in section IV, you don't, for the rest of the poem – two and a half more numbered sections – hear much that doesn't remind you of what you have heard before. The structures of phrases and sentences are made more recognizable because the content they had earlier in the poem has not been equalled, so that they stand out like ribs in a starved chest. 'The bay estuaries fleck the hard sky limits' is new and strangely gorgeous, but precious little else is, whereas the first two thirds of the poem, up to the point of breakdown, glitter with fragments that you can't forget. I first read 'Voyages' in Sydney, a city in which you can taste the ocean in the summer air, and I can still remember the first thrilling impact of such moments as 'The waves fold thunder on the sand', 'The bottom of the sea is cruel', 'Of rimless floods, unfettered leewardings / Samite sheeted and processioned . . .' (but I thought 'Laughing the wrapt inflections of our love' was painfully weak), '. . . the crocus lustres of the stars', 'Adagios of islands, O my prodigal' and the catchily florid, neo-'Adonais' lines near the end of part II:

> Hasten, while they are true – sleep, death, desire
> Close round one instant in one floating flower.

Feeling tolerant, at the time, about preciousness if it sounded sufficiently compressed, I was much taken by that floating flower, and also, of course, by the killer line at the very end of that same section:

> The seal's wide spindrift gaze towards paradise.

For several days I practised a wide spindrift gaze myself, until it occurred to me that I might look like a seal in search of a mate. But the embarrassment didn't stop me writing nonsensical sequential poems on my own account. In several unfortunate instances I managed to get these published by student magazines. Not very many years later, I started having nightmares in which I featured as a fireman from *Fahrenheit 451* vainly searching for any copies of those magazines that I had not yet incinerated. The nightmares stopped when I was at last able to see how unlikely it was that anyone had ever remembered a line I had written. And anyway, like abstract painting, abstract poetry extended the range over which incompetence would fail to declare itself. That was the charm for its author.

But even the most dull-witted author was obliged to realize that his freely associating work of art – proudly meaningless, although really meaning everything – would have no readers unless it had its moments. Whether in a formal poem or an informal one, everything depended, and still depends, on the quality of the moment. Formality and informality are just two different ways of joining the moments up. The question will always be about which is superior, and the 'always' strongly suggests that neither of them is. Whatever kind of poem it is, it's the moment that gets you in.

Just lately I was granted a powerful demonstration of this when I started rereading Robert Frost, something that I have done every ten years or so throughout my adult life. I would never stop reading him if there were not something talkatively smooth about him that allows me to convince myself he is not intense. Then I pick him up again and find that his easy-seeming, usually iambic, conversational forward flow is a deception, a way of not just bringing show-stopping moments to your attention but of moving them *past* your attention, so that you will form the correct impression that he has wealth to spare and does not want the show stopped for such a secondary consideration as brilliance. Take a poem like 'At Woodward's Gardens'. For more than half its length, the monkeys in a cage could be characters in a prose narrative that just happened to possess an iambic lilt. But after the monkeys steal the boy's burning-glass, suddenly you get this: 'They bit the glass and listened to the flavour.' The moment is so good that the way it serves the poem to perfection is only part of its appeal: once we know about the monkeys and the burning-glass, the line becomes memorable on its own. And I think we could all give examples, from our memories, of how a poetic moment can put the poem it comes from in the shade. Without going to the bookcase, I can write down one of the first lines by Empson that ever bowled me over. 'And now she cleans her teeth into the lake.'

And it *was* a first line, of a poem that has always seemed dark to me after that first magnesium flash. As a diehard formalist myself, I don't like to admit that the unity of a poem, its binding energy, might not be the most important of its energies. But there are clearly cases where this is so. Take 'Good Friday', Amy Clampitt's wonders-of-the-biosphere poem that starts in the Serengeti and does a pretty good job of getting evolution into a nutshell. For its knowledgeable precision, Marianne Moore and Elizabeth Bishop would both have recognized a worthy acolyte. But the poem would hold together better if there were not an isolated burst of lyricism tearing it apart. The second stanza, the one about the cheetah, is the one you remember, and even then only for its first three lines:

> Think how the hunting cheetah, from
> the lope that whips the petaled garden
> of her hide into a sandstorm, falters . . .

After which, the narrative falters too. Rhythm doesn't concern Clampitt very much. The syllabics of Marianne Moore are probably somewhere in the background, but not even that system for manufactured unpredictability means much to her. She is just out to avoid the iambic pulse, as Pound once advised, confident as he was that it was creatively exhausted. Clampitt writes poetry shorn of almost every formal effect. But we see the consequences when a moment stands out like the alteration of the cheetah's coat. Not even the rest of the stanza can keep that up, let alone the rest of the poem.

Defenders of the formal poem could plausibly say that it has a better, not a worse, chance of joining the moments up, so that its ability to contain them, and intensify them with a symmetrical framework and a melodic structure, becomes a satisfaction in itself. Frost did so, many times: 'The Silken Tent' is not only wonderful throughout, it is especially wonderful *because* it is wonderful throughout. In whatever form he chose, writing a poem, not just writing poetry, was what Frost was after. (As Frost wrote to Wallace Stevens after they dined together in Key West, 'our poetry comes choppy, in well-separated poems'.) And most of us would not have much trouble in compiling a list of well-separated poems that we keep complete, or almost complete, in our heads: Shakespeare's Sonnet 129, Marvell's 'The Definition of Love', Keats's 'Ode on Melancholy', Dowson's 'Vitae Summa Brevis', Yeats's 'An Irish Airman Foresees His Death', Cummings's 'You shall above all things be glad and young', Stevens's 'The Emperor of Ice-Cream', MacNeice's 'The Sunlight on the Garden', Auden's 'Lay Your Sleeping Head, My Love', just to name some of the poems I could at one time or other in my life recite from memory. (In the old Australian school system, you had to get poetry by heart or they wouldn't let you go home.) There are poets who mainly write poetry but still write the odd poem that gets an extra dimension from being poised like a silken tent: Dylan Thomas's 'In my sullen craft or art', for example. We don't necessarily have to remember the whole poem. (We might not *want* to learn it. Even though I can recognize and place almost any line from Larkin's collected poems, I have never set out to learn one of his poems by heart, because somehow, I find, they frown on that activity.) But we can always remember that it struck us as being all of a piece.

Frost made that his aim. Even in his longer poems, the aspiration to self-containment was always there. His often-stated ideal 'the sound of sense' was meant to be a unifying element. Sometimes the dialogue passages in the longer poems got too high above that unifying tonal range. In 'Snow', the hero, Meserve, is meant to be naturally eloquent, but anyone talking about him becomes eloquent too, so exchanges crop up that sound like nothing ever spoken since the Elizabethan theatre was in flower.

'He had the gift
Of words, or is it tongues I ought to say?'
'Was ever such a man for seeing likeness?'

It isn't that Frost's dialogue isn't good. It's too good: too good for the otherwise well-separated poem. But you'd hardly call the fault characteristic. It comes from a high, indeed hieratic, ambition; and his more usual ambition, the more demanding ambition, was the genuinely humble one of 'lodging a few poems where they will be hard to get rid of'. There is no need to think that he was poor-mouthing himself when he talked like that. He knew very well that the poem that could be remembered as a whole, and not just read through, was the hardest target to aim at. And he hit it dozens of times. If some nervous graduate recites 'Stopping by Woods on a Snowy Evening' at a commencement ceremony, that isn't a sign of how Frost played the grizzled wiseacre, although he sometimes did: it's a proof that he attained his object as a poet.

When they knew each other back in England before the First World War, Ezra Pound – excellent critic that he was, when not in the grip of mania – could see the essential strength of the early Frost's diction. For one thing, it was so classically schooled. (Even today, when so much biographical and critical work on Frost has accumulated, it is often forgotten that it was Frost, and not Pound or Eliot, who really knew Greek and Latin.) But Pound wanted modern poetry to go in a less formal direction, in which a poem could be sustained by its moments – a direction in which a long poem made of fragments might be possible. (In fulfilling that plan some of Pound's later imitators were to be more convincing than he was: Galway Kinnell with *The Avenue Bearing the Initial of Christ into the New World*, Christopher Logue with his *War Music*.) We have to make our own minds up whether the evidence of the short poems in *Personae* proves that Pound was really such a master of set forms he could afford to abandon them, but what matters is that he did so, and was prepared to back those who did the same. One of them was Eliot, who really was a formal master: but his informal poems, especially

Prufrock and *The Waste Land*, changed everything, and deserved to, because the moments were many and unforgettable. Alas, one of the side effects was to create the impression that anyone could do it, and that everything could be said by saying anything.

Frost had a keen and worried eye for trends. He was never as nastily jealous of his turf as his most influential later biographer, Lawrance Thompson, made out. But Frost did have a roost to rule, and he felt it threatened by the runaway vogue for poetry that made a virtue of lacking discipline. How could his concealed discipline be a merit in a field where discipline itself was held to be an inhibition? By the late 1930s, lecturing at Amherst or at Harvard or just dropping funny remarks at any whistle-stop in his endless tour through the poetry-reading circuit that he invented, he was ready to trash Pound's name: politely, but decisively. But Frost the patriarch was all too aware that his lifelong emphasis on craft had become an anachronism, if poetry were to be measured by the sheer number of people writing it. A great Frost poem like 'The Axe-Helve' (even Baptiste's ethnically flavoured dialogue fits it exactly) was a metaphor for the poet's pride in skilled work. Pride in unfettered expression was a different kind of pride, and looked, to him, awfully like unfounded self-approval.

At this distance, Frost's celebrated gibe about formless poetry – tennis without a net – rings hollow, and not just because it has been repeated too often by solemn traditionalists. Too many poems without rhyme, without strict shape, without ascertainable rhythm – without almost everything – have been unarguably successful. But within an informal poet's work, I think, even those successful poems mainly add up to poetry. Few of them are the choppily well-separated thing. Craig Raine's *History: The Home Movie* passes every test for the brilliant moment. It is a universe of brilliant moments. But are its constituent individual poems really self-contained? He might answer that they aren't trying to be, and indeed there is no compulsion any more to try any such thing. (There is still an inner, instinctive compulsion, perhaps: take the way that someone as modest as U. A. Fanthorpe, whose poems are usually shaped by nothing but her unspectacular powers of argument, suddenly writes a lulu like 'Not

My Best Side' – still formless, but vital in every line.) But if the scope has opened further for the highly talented, it has not done so without making far too much room for the talentless, who are no longer easily recognizable. Apart from the encouragement offered the poetaster to become more productive than he has ever been in history, there is the even more reprehensible encouragement offered such a gifted poet as John Ashbery, in his later career as an arts factory, to turn out a continuous emission of isotropic mincemeat. Still, you can always say that about hamburger: it's as American as apple pie.

In another instalment, if I don't get lynched for this one, I would want to mention the famous 1960 Grove Press anthology *The New American Poetry* (edited by Donald M. Allen), which was instrumental in spreading the American abstract poem across the Atlantic to Britain, and indeed across the Pacific to Australia. Pound (along with William Carlos Williams) gave Charles Olson's poetry the courage to be born, and Olson did the same for a generation of freedom-loving bards not just in America but in the entire English-speaking world. Pound had argued – and Eliot had helped him prove – that a poem could be sustained by memorable moments. Olson proved that it could be sustained by unmemorable ones, provided that the texture of the accumulated jottings avoided the sound of failed poetry, which it could do if the pentameter were rigorously eschewed. Buttressed by the widely shared opinion that his ungovernable output had to be poetry because it wasn't prose, Olson acquired imitators wherever in the world English was haltingly spoken. If Hart Crane had lived to see the day, he would have looked for another ship and thrown himself off the back of that.

As for Frost, he had already foresuffered all, like Tiresias: his streak of paranoia was actually a perception. In post-war America, there would be hold-outs against temptation: Richard Wilbur, Anthony Hecht. In Britain, the dazzling example of Auden's formal virtuosity was to hold the advancing blob at bay for a long time, all the way to Larkin and beyond. By now, however, the game has irreversibly lost its net: you have to *pretend* the net is still there. But let there be no doubt that Olson's influence was liberating. The question is about what it liberated. I quote from *The New American Poetry*. Here is the entirety of the sixth of 'The Songs of Maximus':

> you sing, you
> who also
> wants

That's all, folks. I can't believe it was very hard to do. No wonder so many young poets of the future felt inspired. Perhaps that was a kind of freedom, but I still think I might have chosen a better course in emulating Hart Crane, who at least required that his epigones should plausibly echo the slurred volubility of dipsomania.

Interlude

When I wrote 'Listening to the Flavour' for *Poetry* (Chicago) and thus inaugurated my Poetry Notebook, I was gripped by the notion that I might use this approach to sum up my own lifetime of poetry reading, which I had begun by working my way through the constantly varying stack of slim volumes on my cafe table at Sydney University. But it also occurred to me that the world had changed, and that young beginners of today might think differently about those slim volumes. They might not even have seen any. Even with such a literary subject as poetry, you can nowadays get a long way without taking your eyes off the computer screen. Hart Crane's mysteriously lovely poem 'North Labrador', for example, is available at a single click on the PoemHunter site, if you don't mind dodging a preliminary advertisement on video. But for the young literary enthusiasts that I personally know, the book is not yet dead. I hope that stays true, for their sake; because I remember too well the thrill of buying those slim volumes second-hand. When the *Wall Street Journal* asked me to nominate my five favourite modern poetry books, my first reaction was to ask myself why a serious newspaper was behaving like a blog. (Five Favourite Modern Poetry Books; Five New Teenage Celebrities Forgotten Since Last Week.) But I soon saw an opportunity beckoning: to transmit, for a new generation, my gratitude for the neatness and the concentration of the slight volume densely packed with memorable meaning. A big 'collected' volume can overwhelm you: you might bounce off. The slim volume allows you to feel straight away that you might be getting somewhere. Having reached that conclusion, I had to admit that it didn't apply to Robert Frost, whose slim volumes had always appealed to me less than the big collected volume, getting bigger all the time as he grew older. Nor did it apply to Yeats, whose work, in my beginning days, was available only in the forbiddingly chubby Macmillan collected edition. So really I had two opinions on the matter, even after so long a time. Anyway, I did my list, and tried to enjoy the tacit contract that anything I said had to fit into a tiny space, like one of the microdots of old-fashioned espionage.

FIVE FAVOURITE POETRY BOOKS

W. B. Yeats, *The Tower* (1928)

Every separate collection of Yeats's poems from *Responsibilities* (1918) onward is tremendous, but *The Tower* is my favourite. 'That is no country for old men. The young / In one another's arms . . .' Not a bad start. I'm lucky enough to own a copy of the book – bought long ago as part of a job lot in an Oxford antiquarian bookshop on its way out of business – but I wouldn't fancy even the most determined enthusiast's chances of finding a hardback copy second-hand today. It can be found easily, though, in the *Collected Poems*, where the groupings of the original individual volumes are sensibly preserved. (This is a good rule, often broken by misguided scholarly editors who restore the chronological order that the poet himself once carefully avoided in favour of something more interesting.) The only threat that Yeats's *Collected Poems* offers is that the beginning reader might get caught up in the Celtic fairyland of the great man's winsome early days. Cut straight to *The Tower* and you're in the middle of his full-blown achievement, with masterpieces arriving one after the other: 'Sailing to Byzantium', 'Nineteen Hundred and Nineteen', 'Leda and the Swan', 'Among School Children' and (last poem in the book, and one of the greatest poems written in the twentieth century) 'All Soul's Night'. In everyday life Yeats stayed young and foolish too long, but in the full maturity of his art he got such a rich music out of seemingly ordinary speech that the language found and kept its ideal speaker.

Robert Frost, *Collected Poems*

Frost's individual collections are useful to have, but the full *Collected Poems* is the book that matters, because his masterpieces, which were seldom of more than medium length at most, are scattered evenly throughout his long and fruitful career. The trick with the *Collected Poems* is to avoid the longer poems until the shorter ones have taken over your mind. The longer poems have good things in them, but the self-contained showpiece poems give you his essence, and his essence is one you should learn to recognize before watching him distribute it over the framework of an extended edifice. In his case, familiarity breeds reverence: never dodge a Frost lyric just because it is famous. 'The Gift Outright' isn't any less of an achievement because Frost thought it elementary enough for him to recite at JFK's inaugural. A public life is one of the things Frost wanted for his poetry. The idea of obscurity for its own sake repelled him. Though he could play the part of cracker-barrel philosopher, his reputation for folksiness was largely foisted on him by those who had a vested interest in the oblique and wanted poetry to be taught rather than remembered. Frost wanted it to engage the reader straight away, even when the appeal was subtle. He sets out (the present tense seems more and more appropriate) to get his lines into your head, and with a short but perfect achievement like 'The Silken Tent' he can get a whole poem into your head, even though, because of the intricacy of its construction, readers will find it almost impossible to memorize what they can never quite forget.

W. H. Auden, *Look, Stranger!* (1936)

Already a giant in his lifetime, Auden has been treated after his death to the monumental splendours of a pharaonic entombment. The posthumous books with his name on them are so big that you would swear he was occupying his own equivalent of the Valley of the Kings. It would be churlish to begrudge all this scholarly effort (Edward Mendelson is a learned, tactful and often necessary editor) but the original slim volumes are the form that Auden should be read in, if you can find them. A long search on the web for a copy of the marvellously entitled *Look, Stranger!* would be well worth it. (In the US the book was called *On This Island*, from another part of the title poem's first line.) Safely in hand, the light but weighty volume reminds us that a few individual poems are where a reputation starts from. Actually there are other Auden slim volumes that yield even richer rewards, but only *Look, Stranger!* has poem No. IX (in a fit of pseudo-simplicity, the rebel angel was avoiding verbal titles in that period), and only poem No. IX starts with the mind-bending line 'The earth turns over, our side feels the cold . . .'. When I first read that, I didn't precisely fall out of my chair, but the chair moved about three feet sideways across the linoleum, propelled by my spasm of delighted awe. How did he do that? He did it again late in the book, with the last three lines of the almost equally excitingly entitled poem No. XXX: 'And all sway forward on the dangerous flood / Of history, that never sleeps or dies, / And, held one moment, burns the hand.' It seemed so effortless. And so it was, but only for him.

Richard Wilbur, *Poems 1943–1956*

If I had to pick the greatest separate book of American poetry since Robert Frost, Richard Wilbur's *Poems 1943–1956* (published only in Great Britain, by Faber) would have to be the one, even though it contains elements from three of his separate books, *The Beautiful Changes, Ceremony* and *Things of this World*; even though his *Collected Poems 1943–2004*, arranged in reverse so as to track his career from his later days back to the start, is in itself a mighty book; and even though his initial example was so infectious that at least one of the very best Wilbur poems was written by someone else. (Anthony Hecht's wonderful poem about Japan would never, I am sure, have been the meticulous miracle that it is if Wilbur hadn't set the standard for a filigree stanza.) The truth about Wilbur is that his post-war impact was so big it had to be largely ignored if the race of poets was to survive. Robert Lowell's first volume *Lord Weary's Castle* is easier to take, even when you open it at 'A Quaker Graveyard in Nantucket'. Anyone who doubts this contention should open Wilbur's book at 'A Baroque Wall-Fountain in the Villa Sciarra' and note once again the elegant swagger with which a GI could come home from Europe with a whole cultural heritage in his pocket. On the aspiring poets among his fellow Americans he had the impact of a rococo asteroid, burning up their air with his displays of cool fire. Anyone capable of appreciating his artistry was helpless not to emulate it, and emulation guaranteed mediocrity. Wilbur's brand of conscious artistry could be sustained only by his instinct for a phrase, the impulse 'that flings / The dancer kneeling on nothing into the wings.' Perfect. Some said just perfect, but they said it in helpless envy. The most corrosive enemy of his reputation, though, was the silence of critics to whom his clarity left nothing they could add.

Philip Larkin, *The Whitsun Weddings* (1964)

Philip Larkin is the most extreme case of a great modern poet who was threatened with a second death when his poems were edited into chronological order for a *Collected Poems* that forgot even the titles of the separate volumes published in his lifetime. Luckily the mistake has been corrected since, and a compendium which restores the original groupings is now available: but it was a close-run thing, because the design of each slim volume was critical to its overall effect. Of the three mature volumes, the second one, *The Whitsun Weddings*, would be my pick for a favourite, although in fact I was introduced to him through the first, *The Less Deceived*, and for years kept it with me, convinced that nothing could come near it. But the true proof of Larkin's supreme art was that he could go on so intensifying his achievement that he defeated the law of rising expectations. With a tonal range stretching effortlessly from colloquial punch to high-flying sonority, *The Whitsun Weddings* turned out to have everything, including a title poem whose last line about the arrow shower ('Sent out of sight, somewhere becoming rain') became a call sign for a generation. It even had the portents of death that mark the third volume, *High Windows*, and the volume beyond, the one never completed, that would have contained the blood-chillingly desolate 'Aubade'. There might not, at first blush, seem to be much joy in him; but he gets the whole truth of life's transience into unforgettably beautiful poetry, and it is hard to think of a greater source of joy than that.

Interlude

In my click-bait list of five favourite poetry books, all the poets are important but in my view none of them, not even Yeats, should be called revolutionary. That very adjective is an incongruous diversion into the tumult of politics, whereas poetry is written in pursuit of something more stable, even if not serene. As Richard Wilbur once argued (and his book of critical arguments, *Responses*, is an exemplary prose work about poetry) there might be the occasional revolution in poetry, but it will always be a palace revolution. If he had written that statement after the collapse of the Soviet Union, instead of before it, he might have added that when the stretch of history instigated by the Russian revolution had finally run its course, Mayakovsky, who had convinced himself that his poetry was a historic political instrument, finally stood revealed as having been important only in the history of his art. This should be importance enough, but even by that measure, the mission of the poet is to enrich literary history, not to change it. When the academic study of a poet begins to concentrate on his supposedly game-changing impact on the history of literature, it's time to watch out. All too often it will be a case of the publicity outstripping the event. After the Second World War, Ezra Pound was still alive, and already it was being taken as gospel, throughout the burgeoning international network of academe, that he was the incarnation of modern poetry. His posthumous reputation reinforced that status: the living thaumaturge became an eternal guru. For a while I tried to believe it myself, until I realized – too gradually, alas – that the key requirement of admiring him was to be insufficiently receptive to anyone else.

THE ARROW HAS NOT TWO POINTS

In recent times I have gone back to Pound's *Cantos* to find out if I was correct in so thoroughly getting over my initial enthusiasm for them, or it. (Whether *The Cantos* is, or are, a singular or a plural, is a question that I believe answers itself eventually, but only in the way that a heap of rubble gradually becomes part of the landscape.) Fifty years ago, when the mad old amateur fascist was still alive and fulminating, I fell for the *idea* of his panscopic grab bag the way that I was then apt to fall for the idea of love. As that sweet-if-weird moment in that sad-if-stilted passage in *The Pisan Cantos* has it: 'What thou lovest well remains, / The rest is dross.' I especially liked the sound of that at a time when my knowledge of eternity was nineteen years long.

When I fell out of love with *The Cantos* I fell all the way out, but one of my critical principles, such as they are, is to take account of the history of my critical opinions, on the further principle that they have never existed in some timeless zone apart from the man who held them, but have always been attached to him, like his hair, or, lately, like his baldness. There is a promising analogy there, somewhere: my hair yielded baldness as my enthusiasms yielded disenchantment. First the one thing, then the other, and the second thing clearly definable only in terms of the first.

But just as we can scrutinize the ageing remains of our bodies in the mirror and decide that these loose remnants would not even be here to be looked at if we had not been strong and healthy when we were young, so we can look back to when we were wrong, and decide whether we were as wrong as all that. Youth and health have their virtues even in envious retrospect, and perhaps some of our early and ridiculous appreciations were pure and nourishing. Maybe, that is, we later overcorrected, like one of those terrible old men who write articles against the sexual laxity of youth when they are no longer capable of pursuing their notorious careers as indiscriminate lechers. Maybe we overdid the disillusionment.

In the case of *The Cantos*, I don't think I did. I think I can nowadays go right through the long text of that doomed project and show that although it has some arresting passages, they are not quite as arresting as their author meant them to be, and indeed claimed them to be by the way he chose their diction and set them into position. I hasten to admit that for my younger self the claims seemed valid, and that I could not have been more arrested if I had been caught breaking into a liquor store. Back there in the late fifties, in the cafeteria of Manning House, the Women's Union building at Sydney University where the male aesthetes were generously allowed to hang out between lunch and dinner, I used to sit alone at a table fortified with a revetment of books containing, or dealing with, or else directly relevant to, *The Cantos*.

My basic *Cantos* collection was the impressively fat Faber and Faber 1954 edition that held everything previously published from Canto I to Canto LXXXIV, including the sequence that had been separately published as *The Pisan Cantos*. (Somehow the Roman numerals seemed historically significant in themselves: as, clearly, they had to Pound, even while what he was fond of referring to as the Fascist Era was still running. When the Era was over he called it 'the Dream'.) Visible from afar in its strident yellow wrapper, that thick, black-clad book – black as a shirt, now I come to think of it – was the Faber edition. A well-off but wildly original architecture student called Douglas Gordon outranked me because he had brought the New Directions edition back from a trip to the US, and in those twilight days of the old Empire a US edition of anything seemed more outlandish, more international. Gordon, always ready to prove that he could quote even the non-lyrical stretches of *The Cantos* at length, died cruelly young a few years later: I don't suggest that the two facts were related. Gordon was nuts all right – nobody who had seen him in the university revue playing Richard III in Australia's first public example of a black leather posing pouch could doubt that – but he was probably born that way. I've just remembered that it was Gordon who got me started on Pound, like a drug pusher with a genuinely religious connection to the product. He had caught me reading Eliot and he had said: 'The *Quartets*, eh? It's OK, but he's a minor poet. The *major* poet is Pound.' Next day I was reading Pound for the first time.

I also had the 1957 fascicle, exotically entitled *Section: Rock-Drill*, with the super-exotic subtitle '85–95 *de los cantares*'. (The foreign language, whichever one it was, seemed particularly resonant at a time when I could read scarcely a word in any language but English: a lesson, there, in the dangerous enticement of unfamiliarity.) For once devoid of roman numerals, a third collection, *Thrones: Cantos 96–109*, had only recently been published. Along with all these *Cantos* books, and the always attendant collection of Pound's shorter poems, *Personae*, was my treasured copy of his big book of essays, *Make It New*; and, of course, the inevitable copy of Hugh Kenner's commentary, *The Poetry of Ezra Pound*. The books were stacked up around the edge of the table. In the middle of this redoubt, my notebook was open to receive the jewels as I unloaded them from the main text. I can't remember ever having been more excited in my life, but even at the time I spotted a difference between what I was up to and the way I had first read 'Rhapsody on a Windy Night'. When I was reading Eliot, I had forgotten my participation in the event of reading. Posturing inside my gun pit of Poundiana, I was in no danger of forgetting myself. In my capacity as literary editor of the student newspaper *honi soit*, I accepted and printed long, sententious articles about Pound that I myself had written and submitted.

Finally I decided that I had been having myself on, as we say in Australia. On the ship to England I was reading late Yeats and early Auden, and my opinion of Pound was deflating fast. In London I insanely wasted the last of my eating money on a beat-up first edition of Pound's early prose scrapbook, *Pavannes and Divagations*, extracted from a dust pile in a Chancery Lane second-hand bookshop, but I already knew that the thrill of his poetry was irreversibly gone, and for a subsequent half-century I held the opinion that the would-be sublime bits of his central extravaganza were undone by the solemn insistence with which they claimed their own worth. All too often, in conversation, I scornfully quoted that supposedly many-layered line from *The Pisan Cantos*, 'the ant's a centaur in his dragon world', pointed out that not even an ant who had studied Dante would be able to attach any meaning to it, and wound up my case with the quick assurance that all the other putatively memorable bits in *The Cantos* (' "In the gloom the gold / Gathers the light against it." ' etc.) had never repaid the investment necessary to memorize them in the first place.

I was wrong about that. A lot of the 'good' stuff in *The Cantos* really is worth the sweat of digging it out, even if you conclude that rather less sweat went into dreaming it up than Pound was wont to claim. But you can say that he was asking for the impossible in ever wanting the thing to be taken as a unity. At one point, late in his life, he even admitted this, saying that he 'could not make it cohere'. The failure was implicit in the language of the admission. In a unified work of art, the coherent vision must be at least partly present at the launching point: the work can't be expected to produce the whole of its own impulse. But really nobody since Hugh Kenner in his heyday, when he was the arch example of the brilliant critic with greater communication skills than his nominal subject (if you wanted to know what Ezra Pound, James Joyce, T. S. Eliot, Wyndham Lewis, and William Carlos Williams were *really* on about, you waited until Kenner had spoken), has seriously believed that *The Cantos* is, or are, all of a piece. In the UK, Clive Wilmer has lately been given whole pages in the *TLS* to continue with the old-style defence of *The Cantos*, but even Wilmer would concede that a lot depends on the consciously lyrical bits – what the Victorians would have called 'the beauties' – actually being beautiful. I wouldn't want to sail in and say they aren't. Certainly they still try. The typical deliberately gorgeous passage in *The Cantos* is working harder to be aesthetically loaded than a room decorated by Whistler, and time has added to the effect in just the same way. Something so perfectly in period acquires the pathos of freeze-dried evanescence.

To take a much praised example, the opening stretch of Canto

XVII – a rhapsodic Arcadian evocation which will be more or less reprised many times throughout the magnum opus – is clearly meant to be nothing except lovely, but it is everything except specific:

> With the first pale-clear of the heaven
> And the cities set in their hills,
> And the goddess of the fair knees
> Moving there, with the oak-woods behind her.

And more ('And the water green clear, and blue clear') in the same vein, or seam: more then, and much more of more or less the same thing later, again and again. At irregular intervals, usually after a long excursus on economics and/or the pervasive evil of the international conspiracy of usurers, the vision returns, but the hope that it will snap into focus next time is never fulfilled. Instead, there is yet another rearrangement of standard components: the effect is at its most persuasive in the long lyrical sweep of Canto XLVII, but the props look well-worn even there, and elsewhere you are all too often reminded of how the Soviet press, as the Chinese press still does today, used to set up the leader's clichés in ready-made slugs of type so that his latest speech could be reported in jig time. Palaces, terraces, marble columns, clouds, green sea, rocks, sea under the rocks, rocks under the sea, columns above the clouds, and so on for ever.

What Pound did instead of specificity was to toy with a kit of parts, each of them producing not much more than a blurred suggestion of neoclassical architecture with its edges outlined in neon, like a Vorticist version of a painting by Alma-Tadema. Pound *said* he was specific – as his criticism reveals, bringing the thing out in all its thingness is practically the key item among his poetic desiderata – but he said so more than he did so. If it weren't for its quirky syntactical mounting, would the 'first pale-clear of the heaven' be any more than a stock phrase for the break of day? Aren't 'the cities set in their hills' just cities in the hills? And does saying 'still' and 'stillness' over and over really make things seem still?

in the stillness,
The light now, not of the sun.

'Not of the sun' is meant to be interesting because the light *is* from the sun, and our appreciation of the light has been purposely displaced from its source. But how interesting is the displacement? Elsewhere in the work, but along the same lines, as it were, we get 'And the palazzo, baseless, hangs there in the dawn / With low mist over the tide-mark; / . . . / And the sea with tin flash in the sun-dazzle' (Canto XXI). From a passage like that the 'tin flash' tends to stay with you, because it is less abstract than the imagery around it, but it rather emphasizes that the imagery around it is standard issue, even if you believe that 'baseless' might be a nifty pun. (Personally I think it's tin-eared: people who construe Pound's relentless jokiness as proof of unusual sensitivity to tone often have trouble accepting that he could be deaf to his own bum notes, but it could be doing him a favour to concede that he sometimes was.)

Cumulatively, in the course of decades, it emerges that Pound's measures for architectural monumentality, and its relation to landscape, were all archaic, like one of those Japanese temples that are rebuilt once a decade but are always the same. Some twentieth-century artists in various fields showed up in *The Cantos* (Brâncuşi, Gaudier-Brzeska, George Antheil, T. S. Eliot, E. E. Cummings) but it was always numbingly apparent that the built world of modern times meant nothing to him poetically. He could respond to an old palace but not to a new skyscraper (Manhattan was of more interest to Whitman than it ever was to Pound), and the Wright brothers might as well never have bothered.

In Canto XLVI there are a catchy few lines about snow and rain:

Snow fell. Or rain fell stolid, a wall of lines
So that you could see where the air stopped open
and where the rain fell beside it
Or the snow fell beside it.

Some actual perception has gone into that, but it's not often that he makes the effort. By the time one of the work's generally accepted great lines arrives – in Canto LXXIV, first of the Pisan sequence – its strategy and components are familiar: 'To build the city of Dioce, whose terraces are the colour of stars.' But unless we are looking through a telescope, what colour are stars? Doesn't the line just mean that the terraces are as *bright* as the stars? And why would it be a good thing for terraces to be that bright, except in Las Vegas? Further into the work, up into its last published phase, *Drafts and Fragments of Cantos* CX–CXVII (after mysteriously disappearing during the *Thrones* sequence, the Roman numerals had just as mysteriously returned), the spasmodic reflex action of his strategies suggests that they had always been mechanical, even in their heyday. Feeble gestures like 'as of mountain lakes in the dawn,' sounding like the last flourishes in an old manner, can't help reinforcing one's suspicion that there had always been a manner, and not much more. A few hundred gleaming specks in the pan: not a lot of pay dirt after sluicing a whole hillside.

Pound would have called all these little fragments 'particulars'. The deliberately non-mellifluous rhythm (supposedly all the more inexorable because rarely iambic) is meant to sweep them all along in the cumulative dynamism of an impressive congeries – a word much favoured by Pound and Poundians. ('Juxtaposition' was another – a fancy way of claiming weight for the practice of bringing incongruous objects together and waiting for a compound meaning to emerge: the hope and faith of every crackpot who creates elaborate wall charts with fragments of evidence joined together by string.) But you eventually realize that if even the bigger assemblages of bits and pieces were not being carried forward in the sluggish flood, they would look, separately, pretty much like flotsam and jetsam, not to say junk.

Despite the emphasis he had put on the isolated perception since his first phase as an Imagist, Pound in *The Cantos* isn't really very good at being evocatively singular about things seen, and mainly it is because the things seen are seen generically. In the gloom, gold does indeed gather the light against it, but so does Indian costume

jewellery. The unshakeable particulars are in fact amorphous, and his
best technique for firming things up is to produce a tangle, like the
one brought into being at the end of the same canto with the solemnly
isolated clinching line 'Sunset like the grasshopper flying.'

But isn't that just what a sunset isn't like? Brought up in the South
Pacific, I've seen some quick sunsets in my time, but they were all left
standing by even the most moribund grasshopper. Or is the reference not to speed at all, but just to evanescence? And why are we left
asking?

The answer, I think, is that his main way to leave you wondering
is to leave you puzzled. Even the statements most obviously aimed at
creating an impression of limpidity (a loudly trumpeted limpidity, if
such a thing were possible) raise the question of whether very much
is going on at all. A typical moment of stentorian tranquillity is 'and
with hay-fields under sun-swath.' It means, when you peel back the
appliquéd anachronism of the vocabulary, that the hayfields are in the
sunlight. It is important to register how commonly he uses this trick
of defiant obviousness, because the avowedly compressed moments,
his proclaimed quiddities, are a deliberate escalation of it, and we had
better be sure that what is supposedly being intensified actually exists:

> The sun is in archer's shoulder
> in crow's head at sunrise.

This comes in Canto LII, in a passage marked with his favourite tag –
flatteringly delivered to the reader as if one Renaissance prince were
advising another – about the necessity of calling things by their right
names, lest misrule ensue. (In various English forms and in other
languages, including Chinese, this incontestable exhortation recurs
throughout the work, decade after decade, with never a concession
that some of Pound's heroes, notably Mussolini, misruled whether
they called things by their right names or not, and were often enough
numbered among their own victims, a pretty convincing indication
of wisdom's absence, one would have thought.) But I can't see how the
sun being in the archer's shoulder, or even in the crow's head, or in

both, tells us much more than the contention that the ant's a centaur in its dragon world.

Robert Conquest was the first critic ever to dare question the centaur status of Pound's Pisan ant, but in the early sixties it was still too soon for Conquest to shake even the Soviet Union's reputation, let alone Pound's. Nor did Randall Jarrell, who could appreciate the best of Pound but used that as the exact measure for finding *The Cantos* a mess, ever manage to put a big enough dent in the masterwork's reputation to hamper the academic attention that gathered against it like light against pyrites. The less precise Pound was, in fact, the more he invited explication. But if we don't know, and can't know, what one of Pound's more arcane pronouncements means to us, we are left with the obligation to be impressed that it means a lot to him. It's just a bad gag when he assures us that 'ZinKwa observed that gold is inedible.' ZinKwa, or someone like him, crops up frequently, straight out of an episode of *Kung Fu* and always making an observation that nobody in his right mind would ever try to rebut. A proclivity for Confucius-say-style, potted wisdom was high among Pound's worst habits, almost on a level with his admiration for the monetary theories of the Social Credit pundit Major Douglas. The two kinds of verbal tic were particularly deadly when connected, like a scorpion's double tail. In Canto LXXVIII there is a passage meant to get Pound's economic theories into a nutshell:

> taxes are no longer necessary
> in the old way if it (money) be based on work
> done
> inside a system and measured and gauged to
> human
> requirements
> inside the nation or system

Or, indeed, inside the space station of *Battlestar Galactica*. Every economic system features money based on work done inside a system and gauged to human requirements. The question is about whether it is based well or badly. But no amount of exhortation and incantatory repetition can make a guide to conduct out of hot air. In *Section: Rock-Drill*, Pound's faith that a sufficiently gnomic utterance will yield an unswerving truth reaches absurdity with such lines as 'The arrow has not two points.' Well, it certainly shouldn't have one at each end. Usually these cracker mottoes are adduced as translations of Chinese characters floating on the page in isolation. For too much of his life, Pound was convinced that his grasp of Chinese was improving proportionately with the length of time he would spend gazing at the form of a character. But reading Chinese involves a lot more than looking at the pictures, just as understanding an economic system involves a lot more than analysing the metallic composition of its currency. Pound was convinced that he could assess whole countries, periods, empires, and eras by whether and how much their gold and silver coins were debased. Even as late as Canto 103 of *Thrones* he can be heard saying, 'Monetary literacy, sans which a loss of freedom is consequent.'

He was always convinced that he possessed monetary literacy. With better qualifications both by heredity and on paper, the same conviction was later to be shared by Bunker Hunt, who tried to corner the market in silver, and found out the hard way that money is a lot more than chunks of precious metal. But it was certainly true that Pound never possessed much literacy about the loss of freedom, even his own. *The Pisan Cantos* are correctly regarded as the height of the work, the best it ever got, and even the admirers of his epic historical sweep would admit that they are because they contain the most of his personal story, at a time in his life when not even he could dodge the obvious about what had happened to a world which had been ravaged by some of his theories having become actual.

Yet *The Pisan Cantos*, the strongest examples of his favoured form, are surely at their weakest when they presume to deal with his personal despair. There is the total and crippling failure to realize that his own personal despair doesn't rank very high against the personal despair of many others whose fate he never cared about, and who were not, like him, fed, looked after, and given reasonably humane treatment when they fell into the hands of their enemies. (To be fair, it should be noted that much later, in his last years, he was ready to admit that anti-Semitism had been the ruin of his mind.) There is also his incomprehension of 'the Dream' he had been mixed up in. A line like 'Not getting it about the radio' is shorthand for his contention that the diatribes he broadcast on behalf of Fascist Italy had been wilfully misunderstood by his own countrymen. The facts, alas, proved that his accusers had found no difficulty in 'getting it about the radio'; that he had been locked up for a good reason; and that he was very lucky to be still alive. It was mightily impertinent of him to suggest that to condemn him for his broadcasts was a denial of freedom. Since his broadcasts had not only proclaimed the irrelevance of democratic freedom, but had also suggested the desirability of its being denied to the politically helpless, this stuff has to be called the ravings of a crackpot in order to save him from the consequences of calling it a reasoned argument.

Though we might question the putative greatness of a poet who can't get much out of his own spiritual disaster beyond a display of self-pity occasionally energized by spite, there could have been an excuse for his solipsism. He was undoubtedly miserable, and misery is not relative. The conditions he was kept under were calculated to make him realize that he was not in a hotel: he can be excused for feeling lousy. But to excuse him for being vague is harder. After all, the poems in *Personae* had boasted of their precision, and he had supposedly left the smaller forms of those poems behind, and got into the limitless form of *the* poem, *The Cantos*, mainly in order to be precise on larger scale. In the Pisan sequence there is an admission that something has gone wrong: but what has gone wrong, he would have us believe, has gone wrong with the world, not with his view of it. Perhaps because so narrowly personalized, his recorded anguish is curiously unspecific in the detail: the abiding fault of the whole work is, in its best part, brought to a head along with all its virtues:

> When the mind swings by a grass-blade
> an ant's forefoot shall save you

But if the ants hadn't got into his pants, he would still have been done in by the bees in his bonnet, and one of them was his unquenchable conviction that every image was an epic in embryo. To the end of his life, he went on believing that if he could just define every aspect of existence clearly enough, it would all add up. Not all that far in the future, his central belief would be echoed all over the Internet, and really *The Cantos* is, or are – or perhaps was or were – a nut-job blog before the fact. But there were considerable poets who were inspired by him directly – Bunting, Logue – and there is no modern poet who has entirely escaped his influence, if only through the salience with which he raised the question of whether there can be any worthwhile poetry beyond the poem. And I, for one, owe him for that first blaze of his enthusiastic example. Reading his absurdly confident critical prose, I could scarcely catch my breath when he talked about poetry as if it were the most exciting thing in the world, which indeed it is.

Interlude

One of the many dangers posed by the academic study of poetry is that the student might be encouraged to worship giants. And indeed if the history of poetry were like the field of study we usually call history, Ezra Pound would loom like Bismarck. But a collection of big names would give us only a skeletal account of what has happened to poetry in modern times. There were things the lesser names could do that the greater names couldn't. If you were looking for a major poem about the anxious political and cultural texture of the late 1930s, for example, a batch of Pound's *Cantos* would tell you drastically less than Louis MacNeice's *Autumn Journal*. For one thing, MacNeice had the flexibility of technique to make a plain narrative into a medium for every shade of both the factual and the lyrical. For another, he was sane: storms of enthusiasm were confined to his love life, and in his social views there were no radical fashions that he fell for. At his creative best – which came both early and late in his career, but not, alas, quite so much in the middle of it – he was the necessary counterweight for W. H. Auden. Unfortunately Auden was the more newsworthy, and in the long run MacNeice's reputation always had to be fought for by his admirers, and could never be taken for granted. I never forgot how I had been spellbound by his early poems, several of which I learned by heart; and in my later years I have made a point of mentioning his name to the young. Some of the Irish poets of my generation also admired him as a recent ancestor, but for them, because he was born in Belfast but lived in England, there were often complex questions of nationalism and loyalty. My own affection was unencumbered. So when the National Literacy Trust organization Reading for Life asked me to introduce him in a few words, my only task was to arouse curiosity. With a poet so inventive, you can do that with a few quoted phrases: a powerful hint that the energy of a poem saturates its every component.

MEETING MACNEICE

As is only proper, we go on forever hearing about W. H. Auden. But we never hear enough about his friend Louis MacNeice, although there were things MacNeice could do that even the prodigiously facile Auden could not. One of them was *Autumn Journal*, my favourite long poem of the 1930s, an intoxicating cocktail of classical metres, conversational rhythms and reportorial detail. There is no long poem like it for its concentration of the pre-war atmosphere. But there are short poems that give the same flavour of threatened tranquillity, and most of those, too, are by MacNeice. The pick of the bunch is 'Meeting Point', which the poet included in the 1936–1938 section of his *Collected Poems 1925–1948*. (It's the 'collected' to have, if you can find it second-hand: the later, posthumously edited one weighs like a tombstone.)

'Meeting Point' is the poem that every young man should learn to recite by heart if he wants to pull classy girls, and every classy girl should have on the tip of her tongue when she bumps into a scruffy poetic type that she feels the urge to civilize. 'Time was away and somewhere else' runs the refrain. The two lovers are alone together in a public place. It's a coffee shop, expensive enough to have a waiter, but fortunately he does not show up to interrupt them. ('The waiter did not come, the clock / Forgot them and the radio waltz / Came out like water from a rock.') By the power of their combined imaginations, the little table in between them becomes all the world. ('The camels crossed the miles of sand / That stretched around the cups and plates . . .')

The camels remind you of Auden's reindeer in 'The Fall of Rome', but MacNeice's vision of the faraway animals comes from his close-up on the human beings in their prosaic local setting. Compounding achingly self-conscious gentility and torrential lyricism, he has precisely tapped into the perennial British conviction (stand by for *Brief Encounter*) that heterosexual love between adults should reach its emotional apotheosis at a public meeting point where the most intense thoughts must stay unspoken, with the world crowding around to stifle the passion. Trevor and Celia, though, are nowhere beside these two. There was never a more burningly focused romance, so vast a drama with so few props. ('There were two glasses and two chairs / And two people with the one pulse . . .') Almost fifty years have gone by since I first read the poem, and it still thrills me to bits. If you can find a copy of that excellent Penguin anthology *Poetry of the Thirties*, edited by Robin Skelton, you can see what the poem looks like alongside some of its competition. There is some terrific stuff there, but 'Meeting Point' still reaches out: a *Brief Encounter* without Rachmaninov, but with its own, tenaciously lingering music.

Interlude

In MacNeice's poem 'Meeting Point', the two tables and two chairs are reportage, but the camels that cross the miles of sand are an image. The image could be usefully posited as the key component of any lyric poem if only there were not so many successful lyric poems that have no images at all. But usually they do. Rarely, however, does the first image of a poem shift the reader into a layer of enriched oxygen quite as thoroughly as Gerard Manly Hopkins manages with the thrush's eggs in the first few lines of 'Spring' – a straightforward poem for him, although for the reader who is just making a start with him it is likely to have a revolutionary impact. The revolution might not always be welcome, however. In the case of Hopkins it has to be admitted that such a thing as an informed dissent might occasionally be possible. One of the most justly praised among the British poets today thinks that Hopkins is mainly noise, and early in my life I was startled to find that A. D. Hope, the dominant figure in Australian poetry at the time, and wide-ranging in his appreciations, said that while he enjoyed most of Hopkins, he thought that the 'academic rage' for Hopkins had gone too far, and that Hopkins had tried to elevate constipation to the role of a poetic muse. On top of his critical views on the subject, Hope wrote a parody of Hopkins that expressed outright hatred. So Hope had mixed feelings at best, and perhaps any readers of Hopkins can forgive themselves for feeling the same. But to have no feelings at all would be simply a mistake. As always, the proof is in the way the phrases stick. In the case of Hopkins they stick like burning phosphorous: there are flashes of fire that can only be his.

LITTLE LOW HEAVENS

Any poem that does not just slide past us like all those thousands of others usually has an ignition point for our attention. To take the most startling possible example, think of 'Spring', by Gerard Manley Hopkins. Everyone knows the first line because everyone knows the poem. 'Nothing is so beautiful as Spring' is a line that hundreds of poets could have written, and was probably designed to sound that way: designed, that is, to be merely unexceptionable, or even flat. Only two lines further on, however, we get 'Thrush's eggs look little low heavens' and we are electrified. I can confidently say 'we' because nobody capable of reading poetry at all could read those few words and not feel the wattage. Eventually we see that the complete poem is fitting, in its every part, for its task of living up to the standards of thought and perception set by that single flash of illumination.

But we wouldn't even be checking up if we had not been put on the alert by a lightning strike of an idea that goes beyond thought and perception and into the area of metaphorical transformation that a poem demands. A poem can do without satisfying that demand, but it had better have plenty of other qualities to make up for the omission, even if the omission is deliberate, and really I wonder if there can be *any* successful poem, even the one disguised as an unadorned prose argument, which is not dependent on this ability to project you into a reality so drastically rearranged that it makes your hair fizz even when it looks exactly like itself.

It's possible that Shakespeare spoiled us. It was Shakespeare who made such dazzlements a seeming requirement, and indeed Hopkins's picture of eggs like little low heavens might well be attributed to Shakespeare by any practical criticism class going in cold, even if its brighter members have read enough of him to know that he hardly ever actually says that things 'look' like something when he says that they look like something. Considering the readiness with which Shakespeare's metaphorical pinpoints come back to memory ('the morn, in russet mantle clad' etc.), there is a temptation to identify the metaphorical pinpoint as the building block of his poetry and consequently of anybody else's who came after him. In my weak moments as a critic I envy the nuclear physicists of old, and would dearly like to have a few building blocks to work with: some hulking protons and electrons you could get between with a chisel. But the criticism of a poem, to the very limited extent that it is like science at all, is much more like particle physics, in which new and smaller entities keep on proliferating the bigger that the accelerators and colliders get. Yes, there is often at least one pinpoint metaphorical moment in any poem, but there are some successful poems without any moments at all, and there are also, bewilderingly, moments that disintegrate their poem of residence instead of encouraging it to form a unity.

Previously I mentioned the Amy Clampitt poem with the exquisite few lines about the cheetah whose coat, when she ran, turned from a petalled garden into a sandstorm. Nobody who has ever read that poem can possibly have forgotten the moment. But I bet that almost everybody has forgotten the poem. In the other direction, there is the moment that seems to stop a poem growing at all. A good instance of that would be the line that turned up in one of Philip Larkin's composition books after his death: 'Dead leaves desert in thousands.' He wrote a poem, called 'Autumn', to go around it, but he never published the poem, perhaps because that one strong line made all the others sound weak. Such an example certainly knocks on the head any assumption that a metaphorical breakthrough is necessarily a source of life. It could be a death blow. The ignition point for attention is not necessarily the ignition point for invention.

•

As it happens, most of Shakespeare's metaphorical creativity, his Olympian playfulness, is in the poetry of the plays, and not in the poems; and especially not in the sonnets, which tend to get their most arresting effects from syntactical structure ('Had, having, and in quest to have, extreme') and in some cases, from start to finish, consist, or seem to consist, of nothing except argument that can be paraphrased into prose. Yet in English literature the Shakespeare sonnets are at the apex of what I think has to be called the poem, rather than poetry. A Shakespeare sonnet is the essence and exemplar of the poem as the separable, stand-alone thing. Even when a Shakespeare sonnet is part of a sequence, it is there for itself. It will be said that the whole corpus of the sonnets is a sequence, and there will always be room for interpreters to say what the story of that sequence is. My own favourite interpretation is that of Auden, whose long essay about the sonnets first appeared as the introduction to a Signet pocketbook that I once carried with me everywhere. Qualified scholars would nowadays no doubt decry Auden's opinions on the subject, let alone mine, but he had two advantages as an interpreter. First, he was gay, and second, he was a great poetic technician.

The first qualification surely helped him to grapple with the multiple sexual orientations of what was going on in the apparently stable creation before his eyes. But powerful as that qualification was, it was trumped by the second. There was almost nothing Auden couldn't do in the writing of a poem, and he was thus, in the reading of Shakespeare's most intricately wrought achievements, well qualified to assess what Shakespeare was up to at the level of technical performance. During the Second World War, the British and the Americans carefully studied captured enemy aircraft. The engineers learned a lot by taking them to pieces, but finally the judgements that mattered came from the test pilots. Auden was a test pilot, and we must try to take the same attitude, measuring the thing as a mechanism by the way it performs. Sonnet 129, for example, the perfectly self-contained poem that begins with the line 'Th' expense of spirit in a waste of shame', consists almost entirely of syntactical tricks worked to compress and energize plain prose statement. The foreign student would need to be told that the 'waste' is a desert and not merely a prodigality of expenditure, but otherwise, apart from the similes about hunting and the poisoned bait, there is nothing metaphorical in the whole fourteen lines. Anyone who tries to get the poem by heart from moment to moment will find that most of the moments are based on verbal echoes, correspondences, and oppositions ('to make the taker mad; / Mad in pursuit'). If one has ever built a sonnet oneself, however unremarkable or clumsy the result, the experience must be a help in assessing the prodigious flexibility of Shakespeare's craft within a set form, and thus in broaching the subject of whether a poem's structure might be not just a source of astonishment in itself, but an example of metaphorical transformation in which an argument is so cleanly articulated that it transcends the real by modelling the balance of its interior forces, as the surface of a DVD generates halos by being, apparently, so clean and true. That would get us into an area a long way from the thirties, when most poets – and their critics along with them – started taking it for granted that a straight statement could only be banal.

Geoffrey Grigson, the most irascible of London's young literary arbiters in that era, hated the assumption that was supposed to be its mark: the assumption that no plain statement could be poetically interesting. In thrall to Auden, he nevertheless had no hankerings for the wilfully meaningless, and when the art deco modernism of that decade gave way to the surrealism of the next, he was ready with a pressure hose of cold water. In his hard-to-find but treasurable *Private Art: A Poetry Notebook*, Grigson repeatedly insists that only a poet could have useful critical opinions about poetry. Much as I always liked his approach, I also always thought that he was overdoing it. Though Grigson was an excellent editor and an unrivalled anthologist, his own poetry, nervously echoing Auden's oratorical verve, was never distinctive enough to establish his credentials for such an ex cathedra confidence. Grigson was able to reach the correct estimation of most of the 'apocalyptic' poets of the forties – i.e. that they were writing junk – without analysing anything except their hopelessly arbitrary diction, and anyway there are always critics who are not poets but whose opinions we find fully adequate to the level of what they are examining.

Frank Kermode has consistently been a fine instance, especially in his later phase, when he has had less time to waste tolerating the theorists, and when he has allowed the weight of his accumulated experience as a reader to push him to the point where he can argue, about the later Shakespeare, that the metaphors probably seemed impenetrably mixed even to listeners at the time they were first spoken. That judgement is as good as any by a poet, although we have to remember that Kermode himself *was* a poet when young, and might even have gone on being one if he had not lost his composition book on his way home from the war. Usually you find that a critic who talks sense about poetry gave it a try early on. But it would be foolish to rule out the possibility that somebody incapable of writing a single convincing line could still say something pertinent about someone else's poem as a whole. Just because Dr Leavis, for example, who never wrote a poem, rarely said anything interesting about one either, does not prove a case. But with all that considered, and in all fairness, it still seems legitimate to contend that for once, in a way, it's a case of those who can, teach.

•

Must we, however, resurrect Samuel Johnson's reputation as a poet just so that we can give him more weight as a critic? Let's hope not. Argued in verse, Johnson's moral points are worth noting, but not remembering: he put them better in prose. Beside Goldsmith, Johnson is in the same area, and yet he is nowhere. Johnson not only didn't write *The Deserted Village*, he couldn't have. He had the technique – when Goldsmith asked him to contribute a few lines to the poem, he was able to do so – but Goldsmith's socially sensitive vision was not one that Johnson could share at the creative level. To that extent, the great man was limited. And yet the craft of Johnson's couplets gave him the knowledge to spot a serious recurring flaw in Pope. The real strength of Johnson's *Lives of the Poets* is in his kitchen criticism. It was the term that the Elizabethans once used for the analysis of poetic technique: when to invert the foot, how to get a spondee by dropping a trochee into an iamb's slot, and things like that. Kitchen criticism is a term that should be revived, because its unlovely first word might have the merit of persuading the fastidious to make themselves scarce until they can accept that there is an initial level of manufacture at which the potatoes have to be peeled. Johnson had a feel for the practical in the making of verses. He had constructed enough couplets of his own to see that the form, when used in a narrative, must continually present the problem of the same pair of rhyme-sounds cropping up too early.

English is so rhyme-poor that the same few pairs are always trying to get back in. Keeping them out is part of the ingenuity. Johnson knew that Pope could be wonderfully ingenious in loading and balancing the interior of a line, or pair of lines, or even four of them. But Johnson was right to say that Pope was too often not diligent enough at reading back to see how long ago he had used the same terminal sound as in the pair of rhymes he was currently putting together, and that the effect of inadvertent repetition undermined the intended air of inexhaustible virtuosity. Johnson's strictures on this point have the large implication that Pope was better in the brief passage than in the grand sweep, and any critic today who wants to write about the meaning of the word 'form' when it comes to Pope could profitably start from where Johnson left off. (He might even find a hard-news reason for contending that the 'Essay on Man' is badly argued: its author chose a bad form to argue in.) It would not have been impossible for a non-poet to have noticed what Johnson noticed about Pope, but it would have been far less likely.

•

Christopher Reid's recently published selection of the letters of Ted Hughes shows that Hughes was well aware of how his wife Sylvia Plath, in her last phase, was working miracles. I remember the time well. In London during the same cold winter of her death, I was reading over and over a batch of her poems in the *London Magazine*. One of them was 'Cut', the poem that bleeds from a sliced thumb. (Since 1965 it has been one of the most immediately thrilling things in her key book *Ariel*.) Without trying to, I memorized several moments from that poem, most conspicuously the lines that start with the 'Kamikaze man'. I was already wondering why Hughes himself was showing signs of no longer finding such specific vividness desirable in his own poetry. I thought, and still think, that his early poems were his best, and that the very best was the one about the jaguar in the zoo, especially in its last line, 'Over the cage floor the horizons come.' If he could do that once, why didn't he do it again? (The admiring reader is always potentially censorious, because the enjoyment is so childish: do it *again*.) And here was Plath, getting into that same wizardly area of concrete perception generating the purely poetic. For many years I prided myself on the fact that I didn't have to read the cut thumb poem to remember everything that went on in it.

Recently I read the actual text again and found that I had remembered too much. I had remembered something that wasn't there. In my memory, the kamikaze man had worn a 'Gray gauze Ku Klux Klan / Babushka'. But Plath never included the word 'gray'. That word had leaked in from my own memory, where gauze tends to be gray because when I was very young I was always cutting myself up somehow, getting the wounds bandaged, and wearing the bandages until they were dirty. The same sort of personal memory association has given Plath what amounts to the punchline of the poem: its vocative penultimate line, a two-word sentence addressing the bloody wound: 'Dirty girl.' How brilliant, and how it tempts us to believe that this is the atomic stuff of poetry, fit material for the catastrophic expansion of a career into a supernova of publicity.

But what about all the poets since her death – and especially the women poets – who have delved into their traumas to dig up the same sort of stuff, and yet have produced poems more boring than somebody telling you their dream? The answer is not just in what Plath said, but in the suave swing with which she said it. The lines about the kamikaze man, terrible in their content, coast blissfully along like cool jazz: you can practically see Milt Jackson's hammers bouncing on the silver leaves of the vibraphone. In Australia, Gwen Harwood (whom I didn't find out about until later) shared Plath's gift for placing a phrase on the music like Blossom Dearie singing in a cocktail bar. Hardly anybody can do it. When you think of the few poets who can, and of how what a jazz musician would call their 'feel' unites them, surely you are getting close to another kind of building block that is set apart from the semantic even if never getting beyond it – the building block constituted by the propulsion of a line.

There is an elementary way of propelling a line of iambic pentameter which almost anyone can do. (How would we know, without further evidence, that 'Nothing is so beautiful as Spring' even with the novelty of its truncated first foot, hadn't been written by Mrs Hemans, as famous in her day as Sylvia Plath, but no more dangerously exciting than a pile of clean napkins?) Kitchen criticism tells us that non-elementary ways, or variations, were being looked for well before Shakespeare was born. Throughout the history of English poetry, the tightly packed line that *tells* you it is tightly packed has been a way of sharpening up the basic pentameter. It is even there in Chaucer, and by the time of Shakespeare's sonnets it is already getting near the limit. The penultimate line of our already adduced Sonnet 129 is a supreme example: 'All this the world well knows; yet none knows well'. Reversing the two words 'well knows' so as to wind the spring at the end of the line gives a reserve of energy to launch the last line like a crossbow bolt: 'To shun the heaven that leads men to this hell.' But even standing on its own, the penultimate line is arresting for its effect of being packed with energy.

Part of that effect comes from the way the iambs are morphed into spondees as the conversational accents are played off against the meter. In everyday speech, the word 'well' would get at least as much emphasis as 'knows'. In the meter, the stress gives it less. The combination gives both words equal weight. The same thing happens at the end of the line, so that the three words 'none knows well' seem to be stressed equally, in a monotone on a falling cadence. Put it all together and the effect is far from being tum-ti-tum. (The iambic pentameter is always being called tum-ti-tum by people who couldn't write even the tum-ti-tum version if their lives depended on it.) The effect of the packed line is to reinforce expectation by defeating it. The elaboration on the underlying structure spells out the structure: spells it out by outplaying it.

All depends, however, on the reader's knowing what to expect. George Herbert, in his showpiece poem 'Providence', could depend on his readers being able to place the conversational phrasing of 'want of heed' against the strict iambic meter when he asked 'Should creatures want, for want of heed, their due?' Shelley could depend on the reader's awareness that he was playing passion against law when he wrote 'Stay yet awhile! Speak to me once again.' The expectation is still there underneath. Far into the twentieth century, poets in English could still depend on the reader's knowing that there was a simple rhythm under the complex one and that the simple was what made the complex possible. Empson's poems almost entirely depended on the reader's knowing that. ('Stars how much further from me fill my night.') Empson further stoked the packed line, to such a pressure that an effect which had begun before Shakespeare came to be called Empsonian. In Geoffrey Hill's sonnet 'The Eve of St Mark' there is a line which I am sure deliberately echoes Empson ('Along the mantelpiece veined lustres trill'), and which I suspect is trying to hitch a ride on the Empsonian wagon that collected the echoes of packed sonorities – especially in religious poetry – from a five- or six-hundred-year tradition of poets writing stanzas that could not easily be set as songs or hymns: the by-product of a trade-union demarcation dispute half a millennium long.

But once again, the trick demands that the underlying frame should not be broken. When Samuel Johnson called Donne's numbers 'rough', he meant that Donne was not keeping count while he worked his distortions. Quite often, Johnson was right. Donne's jawbreakers, often coming at the knotty point of a conceit, are always fascinating, but they are still jawbreakers. Poets write jawbreakers when, usually through enthusiasm, they lose touch with the meter they are presuming to supersede. Johnson disapproved of enthusiasm. What even he could never anticipate, however, was a condition in which hardly any reader knew the difference between a procedure varied and a procedure violated. We are in that condition now.

•

A critic today, I think, should be able to see that Tony Harrison, famous for composing in couplets, mangles them almost as often as he gets them right. (By academics who can't count even on their fingers, the wreckage is called vigour, spontaneity, bold re-energizing of a convention, etc.) The same critic should be able to see – it is the same perception, redirected – that Peter Redgrove, say, maintains an unswerving strictness under his seeming freedoms. These three lines from his poem 'Travelogue' are based on an elementary iambic pentameter with nothing but lexical brilliance to disguise it:

> La Place de Jeunesse is portcullised shut,
> dust rests on skiing tanned shop-window dummies,
> board pavements echo, you can't get a drink.

Since I myself try not to write anything that can't be read aloud, I would have covered the possibility that 'board' could be heard the wrong way, but in all other respects I found those lines, when I first read them, as naturally sayable as if they were handwritten in the Tower of London by Sir Walter Raleigh, wrapped in his muddied velvet cloak, and warming his hands at the blaze of his own vocabulary. I don't believe, however, that smoothness of recitative in itself is enough to make poetry, let alone a poem. Early on, Conrad Aiken had a reputation nudging that of T. S. Eliot as a poet who could narrate in iambic meter. Today Aiken looks empty, and he should have looked that way at the time. His torrential mellifluousness fooled almost everybody, and eventually it fooled the Oxford University Press (American branch) into publishing a complete *Collected Poems* more than eight hundred pages long. On page 457 appears a poem called 'Sea Holly' which has its charm, and on page 797 'The Lady in Pink Pyjamas' would be almost not bad if only a) some of its bravura could be removed and b) he had never written anything else in his life.

I mention Aiken because there is an upside to the fact that the beginning reader in poetry no longer knows much about meter. All the dull poetry that was ever praised for its technique is effectively no longer in existence. Churned out by hundreds of poets, published in thousands of volumes, there was a whole stretch of correctly genteel English poetry composed in the British Empire from the late Victorian era onward until the Georgians were invaded by modernism. It was fully matched by an American equivalent that was far less influenced by Whitman than we might retrospectively wish. All of it – comprising millions of lines impeccably turned – is gone as if it had never been. A student who took John Drinkwater down from the shelf now would scarcely even recognize that he was nothing. Once, he was famous: and not just as the author of a quite good play about Abraham Lincoln. He was a famous poet.

So the idea that a poem can be made poetic by its structure alone is open to question, at the very least. I would still like to contend, however, that any poem which comes to exist without having first been built might be destined for the same pit of oblivion that all the well-wrought dross went into. Such a fate seems especially likely when the poem without form has nothing else to grab your attention either: no little low heavens, no gauze babushkas, nothing to see or even hear. Today's deliberately empty poetry can get a reputation for a time: there will always be a residency for J. H. Prynne. But it will never be as interesting as the question of how it got there. Some would hold Charles Olson personally responsible, but I fear – fear because of the size and volume of the scuffle I might get into – that the culprit was William Carlos Williams. When he realized, correctly, that everything was absent from Whitman's poetry except arresting observations, Williams, instead of asking himself how he could put back what was missing, asked himself how he could get rid of the arresting observations. The result was a red wheelbarrow: no doubt intensely significant, but a long way short of those little low heavens.

Interlude

To speak of the poetic moment, and then of the rhythmic frame-work in which it is contained, brings us naturally to the rhythmic progress from moment to moment, and hence to the question of how, in any poem that strikes us as being integrated, the effects seem joined up by an inexorable progression. From that progression, any poem that impresses us with its integrity is likely to gain an extra poetic charge, sometimes to the point of convincing us that the way it goes is the secret of what it is. In the course of a lifetime there might be several times that a reader comes across a poem that can't be fully explained but can't be left alone either. For me, two examples would be 'Gone to Report', by Brian Howard, and 'War of Nerves' by Frederic Prokosch. Both poets were well-known literary names in the 1940s, and both of them are forgotten now, but each of them wrote a poem whose driving force of argument I still can't get out of my head even though I have spent half a century wondering about what the argument actually is. (I leave it to the reader to track those poems down. The search will be part of the puzzle: Raiders of the Lost Text!) The Australian poet Francis Webb wrote several strangely beautiful poems whose authoritative coherence refuses to be reduced to ordinary comprehensibility: but Webb was a mental patient. At times in modern poetic history the temptation to let go of rationality has risen to the status of a command, just as, in the history of modern painting, it became compulsory to let go of the figurative. To ignore the results would be wilful obtuseness, yet surely, if only to secure a brief respite from the barely intelligible, it is forgivable to favour those poets who show signs of knowing what they are saying. From them we might get, occasionally if not always, the poem that gains extra vitality from the way it has been made complete. Stephen Edgar's 'Man on the Moon' is just such a poem: clear from moment to moment, and clear in the way that one moment leads to the next, it accumulates so much clarity that you need dark glasses to look at it.

ON A SECOND READING

On a second reading of a poem that has wowed us, we might grow even more interested, but we start to sober up. For my own part, initial admiration for a single poem often tempts me into a vocabulary I would rather avoid. The Australian poet Stephen Edgar's poem 'Man on the Moon' can be found in his collection *Other Summers*, or – more quickly, and for free – in the selection devoted to his work in the Guest Poets section of my website, clivejames.com. With a single reservation, I think it is a perfect poem, although 'perfect' is an adjective I would rather not be caught using. The word just doesn't convey enough meaning to cover, or even approach, the integrity of the manufacture. I knew that already on a first reading. But on a second reading, I begin to know how I knew it:

> Hardly a feature in the evening sky
> As yet – near the horizon the cold glow
> Of rose and mauve which, as you look on high,
> Deepens to Giotto's dream of indigo.

Giotto is dreaming of indigo because he couldn't get enough of it: in his time it was a pigment worth its weight in gold. Edgar is always good on facts like that. I could write a commentary picking up on such points, but it wouldn't say why the poem is perfect, or almost so. The obvious conclusion is that I don't need to say that. But I want to, because a task has been fudged if I don't. There are plenty of poems full of solid moments, but the moments don't hang together even by gravity. So why, in this case, do they cohere?

> Hardly a star as yet. And then that frail
> Sliver of moon like a thin peel of soap
> Gouged by a nail, or the paring of a nail:
> Slender enough repository of hope.

We can already see the moments cohering. The indigo sky of the first stanza has supplied the background for the moon, which has become two different things, one growing out of another: the soap paring and the separated crescent of a fingernail, possibly the same fingernail that scratched the soap, but probably not, or he would have said so. These specific but metaphorical details provide the warrant for a general but more abstract statement about hope. Out on its own, the abstract concept of hope could be the town where Bill Clinton was born, or a mantra in a speech by Barack Obama. We don't know what the poet's hope is about yet, but here it looks planted securely on firm ground, because of the store of specific noticing that has already been built up:

> There was no lack of hope when thirty-five
> Full years ago they sent up the *Apollo* –
> Two thirds of all the years I've been alive.
> They let us out of school, so we could follow
>
> The broadcast of that memorable scene,
> Crouching in Mr. Langshaw's tiny flat,
> The whole class huddled round the TV screen.
> There's not much chance, then, of forgetting that.

Now we see where hope was going: all the way to the moon. The *Apollo* mission landed there in 1969. Add a 'full' thirty-five years to this and we can calculate that the poem was written in 2004 or perhaps the year after. Increase thirty-five years by a third and we find that the poet is about fifty-three years old at the time of writing. And he was about seventeen at the time of the landing. So he was in high school, with Mr Langshaw for a teacher: a dedicated teacher, living alone in tight circumstances, here made tighter by the presence of the whole class. The number of boys in the class is the only statistic we can't work out, but it must have been a substantial number or the word 'whole' would not have been used for effect.

Because these two stanzas form one unit, the first bridging syntactically into the next, we can see that the pace has picked up. The first two stanzas of the poem made one statement at a time, but they were just the overture. This is the opera. Or at any rate the operetta: there is an air of lightness to it, mainly conveyed by 'that memorable scene', which is a knowing allusion to a time-honoured line of poetry (from Marvell's 'An Horatian Ode upon Cromwell's Return from Ireland'), and is obviously put there on the assumption that we also know it, or can at least guess that the heroic elevation of an archaic-sounding phrase is deliberately being used to say that this, too, is history. Those who remember the story of Marvell's poem will be glad to realize that this time nobody is getting executed. In Marvell's poem, it is Charles I, and not Cromwell, who bravely faces death, and the diction is a token of the poet's generous scope of understanding. But to borrow the phrase is also a way for this later poet, Stephen Edgar, to say that literature now must make room for the machines. Readers who go further into his work, as they surely must, will find that Edgar is unusually sensitive to science and technology. They increase his vocabulary, which is lyrically precise over a greater range of human activity than anyone else's I can think of, with the possible exception of his senior compatriot Les Murray. More of a city boy than Murray, Edgar has fewer words for evoking life on the land. But for all other realms he has whole dictionaries in his head:

> And for the first time ever I think now,
> As though it were a memory, that you
> Were in the world then and alive, and how
> Down time's long labyrinthine avenue
>
> Eventually you'd bring yourself to me
> With no excessive haste and none too soon –
> As memorable in my history
> As that small step for man on to the moon.

And this, suddenly and unexpectedly, is another realm, the realm of personal emotion. One of Edgar's favourite strategies is to set up an area of public property, as it were, before bringing in the personal relationship: a way of spreading inward from the world. The effect, especially acute in this case, is to dramatize his isolation. But as yet we don't know that the isolation will mean loneliness. Perhaps he and 'you' are still together. The portents, however, are ominous. For one thing, she is probably younger than he. She was in the world then, but the wording suggests that she might not have been so for very long. She was on her way to him, down a 'long labyrinthine avenue' that sounds as if it has passed through the mind of Philip Larkin. Edgar is fond – sometimes too fond – of echoing Larkin, but he is usually, as here, careful to echo only the cadences, not the wording. Larkin often used a monosyllabic adjective before a polysyllabic one, with no separating comma. The sonorous glissando of the device was useful to give the pathos of passing time. But Edgar undercuts the evocation of inevitability by giving the loved one an air of caprice. She brings herself (good of her) with no excessive haste (what kept her?) and none too soon (finally she deigns to turn up).

On a fine point of technique, rather than a larger point of tactics, the way that the poet, in the penultimate line quoted, gives 'memorable' and 'history' their full syllabic value recalls Auden, and in the final line of the octet we can hear Empson, as we can always hear him when trochees are laid over an iambic pattern to give a spondaic tread. Since Edgar obviously weighs his words with care, it is safe to assume that he knows Neil Armstrong blew the script. Armstrong should have said 'one small step for a man'. When he fluffed it and said 'one small step for man', he ensured that 'man' and 'mankind' would mean the same thing and that the sentence would be deprived of its intended contrast. But Edgar seems to be saying that even the giant step for mankind is small – small enough, at any rate, to be matched by the moment in his own history when he and the loved one met:

How pitiful and inveterate the way
We view the paths by which our lives descended
From the far past down to the present day
And fancy those contingencies intended,

A secret destiny planned in advance
Where what is done is as it must be done
For us alone. When really it's all chance
And the special one might have been anyone.

Here again, a whole argument is bridged over two stanzas, and this time with only a single terminal comma, so that the effect of a lot being said at once is reinforced by the technical fact of compressed syntax. The word 'inveterate' gets a hypermetric emphasis, making it sound important enough for us to figure out exactly what it means here, or to look it up if we've never seen it. (If we do look it up, we find that the current meanings of something long established and settled by habit are underpinned by a historic meaning of something hostile – an undertone which soon turns out to be appropriate.) In the last line of the stanza we have to deduce, in the absence of the poet's spoken emphasis, that the word 'intended' is an adjective qualifying the noun 'contingencies'. That's one of the tasks fulfilled by the comma: to tell us that the contingencies aren't about to intend anything, but are, themselves, intended. The other task of the comma is to set up a development in which the contingencies amount to a destiny, which turns out to be the wrong idea. 'Where what is done is as it must be done' has a playful musicality, but the play is sad, because it isn't true: determinism is an illusion. Chance rules, and when the repetition in the line is matched by the repetition in the last line, the game is over. The poem, however, isn't. Casting our eyes down we see that there is more of it to come, although not much more. It's going to have to cover a lot of distance in a short time if it is to bring these themes together:

The paths that I imagined to have come
Together and for good have simply crossed
And carried on. And that delirium
We found is cold and sober now and lost.

This time the argument is confined to one stanza and has the effect of
a summary. We know that there is more of the poem to come, but it
could conceivably end here. The separate trajectories of the mission
and the moon successfully met each other according to plan, and
the Apollo Lunar Module came down in the right spot. The separate
trajectories of the poet and the loved one met each other as well, but
each of them kept going. Ecstasy (called 'delirium' in retrospect, as if
it had been a fever) didn't hold them together, and the return of so-
briety revealed that it couldn't have. What was 'lost' was a big chance,
but a chance was all it was. The under-punctuation is an indicator,
telling us that he's had time to work this conclusion out, and that it
can therefore be set down economically, as a given. The whole story
can be seen in the turn of the second line into the third. The phrase
'And carried on' comes out of the turn with a reinforced inevitability.
(In the heyday of practical criticism, such an effect would have been
called 'enactment', but when it was eventually realized that almost any
technical feature could be called enactment, the term thankfully went
into abeyance.) The idea that if their two paths crossed they might
stick together was a wrong guess on his part. Was it the wrong wish?
Well, separation seems to have been her decision, so perhaps she was
the wrong woman. Maybe delirium wasn't what she wanted. We are
left free to speculate about all those things as the poem spreads out-
wards again, and makes an end:

The crescent moon, to quote myself, lies back,
A radiotelescope propped to receive
The signals of the circling zodiac.
I send my thoughts up, wishing to believe

This is only the first stanza of a conclusion that spreads over two stanzas, but let's break into the flow and see how it works. My own first judgement was that an otherwise unstoppable advance had interrupted itself. On a second reading, I still think so. When I mentioned that I had only one reservation about the poem, the phrase 'to quote myself' was it. He isn't quoting any other part of the poem, so what is he quoting? Investigation reveals that he is quoting another of his poems: 'Nocturne', the second part of a two-part sequence called 'Day Work', which was collected in his previous volume, *Lost in the Foreground*. A poet need not necessarily be asking too much when he asks us to read one of his poems in the light of others in the same volume, or even in other volumes. In the later Yeats, to take a prominent instance, there are plenty of individual poems making that demand. But when a poem has successfully spent most of its time convincing us that it stands alone, it seems worse than a pity when it doesn't. It seems like self-injury: a bad tattoo. It was the poem itself that made us wish it to be independent, so it has revised its own demand.

Edgar's poem can have this flaw and still remain intact. (Presumably the crack in the golden bowl did not stop it holding fruit.) But it's definitely a blip in the self-contained air of infallibility. The perfect has momentarily become less-than-perfect, with the sole advantage that one is forcibly persuaded that the word 'perfect' might mean something. (If it means 'stand-alone', 'independent' and 'self-contained', then those are already better words.) But the argument continues despite the backfire. The motor hasn't stopped running. It powers the radio telescope of the moon, which is listening to the stars, appearing here in their old-style, pre-scientific form. What does he wish to believe about the possible destination of his thoughts after they are beamed up to the soap paring, or nail paring, that has now become a parabolic dish? (This poet doesn't mix his metaphors: he morphs them.) The answer is in the two-part coda's second stanza, which is the last stanza of the poem:

That they might strike the moon and be transferred
To where you are and find or join your own.
Don't smile. I know the notion is absurd,
And everything I think, I think alone.

He wants their two trajectories, his and hers, to join again. But we
have seen that they haven't, and now we are told that they won't,
because when he addresses her, she isn't there, except in his head.
This is a drama for one person, and it's over. He has been talking to
himself all along.

•

When reacting to a poem, the word 'perfect' is inadequate for the same
reason that the word 'wow' would be. But it isn't inadequate because
it says nothing. It is inadequate because it is trying to say everything.
On a second reading, we begin to deduce that our first reading was
complex, even if it seemed simple. Scores of judgements were going
on, too quickly for us to catch but adding up to a conviction – first
formed early in the piece and then becoming more and more detailed
– that this object's mass of material is held together by a binding force.
Such a binding force seems to operate within all successful works of
art in any medium, like a singularity in space that takes us in with it,
so that we can't pay attention to anything else, and least of all to all
the other works of art that might be just as powerful. We get to pay
attention to them only when we recover.

But recover from what? A spell? Here again, all the natural first
words are suspect. I could say why I picked this less-than-perfect,
but almost perfect, poem by Stephen Edgar out of all the scores of
perfect poems by him, and out of all the hundreds of perfect poems
by other people. I could say I picked it out because it haunts me. If
haunting is what ghosts are good at, hanging around to rattle the pots
and rearrange the furniture when you least expect it, then 'haunt' is
the right verb. But it's a verb that I would rather not use. I think Edgar
is a fine poetic craftsman. But in that sentence there are two other
words I would rather not use either. The word 'craftsman' always

sounds like a doomed attempt to give an artist the same credibility as a master carpenter, and 'fine' smacks of self-consciously upmarket (i.e. effectively downmarket) American advertising, as in 'fine dining', 'fine linens', and 'fine wine'. Well, yes, of course the poet is a fine crafts-man, and of course his poem haunts you with its perfection. All these superannuated words we should take for granted when talking about any poem that is properly realized. Actually to put them back into print is like diving on a wreck, with no yield of treasure except scrap metal.

Yet we need the ideas, if not the vocabulary, if we are to begin talk-ing about why and how the poem in question is a made object, and not a foundling. Every bit of it might well be a *trouvaille* – how phrases are assembled and lucky strikes are struck is an even deeper question – but all the bits are put together by someone who either knows exactly what he's doing or else can control the process by which he doesn't, quite. You could say that the poet, right from the start and without interruption, transmits an air of authority, but I doubt that the phrase counts for much more than all those other words I've been trying to avoid. (Even the author of a jingle on a birthday card has an air of authority if you like the sentiment.) The thing to grasp is that the fine words and phrases are standing in for a complex reaction. They serve as tokens for a complete discussion of an intricate process that doesn't just happen subsequently, on a second reading, but happens initially, on the first reading. Most of the analysis that I have supplied above almost certainly happened the first time that I read the poem, but this time I have written it out.

So much can happen, and in such a short space, only because we bring our own history to the poem, even as it brings the poet's history to us. Contained within the first reaction are all the mechanisms we have built up through reading poems since we were young: reading them and deciding they were good. (We might have learned even more from the poems that we decided were bad, but we could do that only by having first learned to recognize the good.) This mental store that the reader brings into play on a first reading is, I believe, the missing subject in most of what we call criticism. The missing subject needs to be illuminated if we are fruitfully to pursue all the other subjects that crop up as we speak further. Without that first thing, all the subsequent things might be full of information, but they will lack point. It makes little sense, for example, to say that a poem fits into the general run of a poet's work if we don't first find ourselves saying why it stands out even from that. We can say later that it blends in, but it had better be blending in only in the sense that it stands out like a lot of the poet's other poems. A poem doesn't, or shouldn't, express the author's 'poetry', and it's a bad sign when we contend that it does. It was a fateful turning point for the career of Ted Hughes when his later poems were discovered to be 'Hughesian', i.e. characteristic instead of unique. The idea that a poet should be praised for producing sequences of poems, and even whole books of poems, that give us nothing but a set of exercises in his own established manner, is ruinous for criticism, and is often the sign of a ruined poet. The great mass of later Lowell is weak when tested by the intensity of early Lowell. Read 'A Quaker Graveyard in Nantucket' again – or merely recall the bits of it that you have in your memory – and then try to find anything as strong in the bean silo of *History*. It takes a critic who has never appreciated the strength of Lowell's early poems to think that the later work is a development rather than a decline.

In the sum of a poet's achievement, it isn't enough that the same tone recurs, and often it's a sign of deterioration when it does. Edgar, always precise about shades of colour at each end of the day, is a modern master of what I would like to call the daylight nocturne, but I would expect to arouse suspicion if I praised one of his poems for having no other characteristics. As it happens, almost every poem he publishes is impossible to reduce to a kit of favourite effects. The argument and its illustrations always serve each other inseparably: they can be discussed separately, but they flow back together straight away. So everything I can say about him follows from his capacity to produce the unified thing. From that initial point, the discussion can widen. We can say that Edgar suffers from the peculiar Australian critical climate in which it is widely and honestly believed that a rhymed poem in regular stanzas must be inhibiting to a sense of expression that would otherwise flow more freely. The elementary truth that there are levels of imagination that a poet won't reach unless formal restrictions force him to has been largely supplanted, in Australia, by a more sophisticated (though far less intelligent) conviction that freedom of expression is more likely to be attained through letting the structure follow the impulse.

In that climate, Stephen Edgar's name is not yet properly valued even in Australia. To believe that it one day will be, you have to believe that something so good is bound to prevail. But that might not happen. Australia (and here we enter into sociology and politics) has a small literary market anyway, and for poetry it is minuscule, so prizes and grants count. Though his position has somewhat improved lately, Edgar has been awarded remarkably few of either: partly because, I fear, the committees are stacked with poets who couldn't write in a set form to save their lives, and with critics and academics who believe that the whole idea of a set form is obsolete. It would be nice to think that this tendency could be reversed by the example of a single poet. But of course it can't. All one can do is argue for the importance of his work, and that argument must start with the certainty of our first judgement, made on a first reading: a judgement which is not yet concerned with advocacy. On a second reading we can, and must, begin to propose a restoration of the balance. There is a place for free forms: they no longer have to justify themselves. There should be a place for regular forms too, but they now have to justify themselves every time. One of Edgar's dictionaries is a classical dictionary. He can read the ancient languages, and might have written poems with no properties except those from the far past. But his work participates in a new classicism, fit to incorporate the modern world, in which it deserves a high place. Almost any of his poems will tell us that, on a first reading. The second reading tells us why we should try to tell everyone else.

Interlude

The poem which strikes us as enjoying perfect success all on its own, and does not just rank as a typical item in its author's inventory, has the status of treasure, and someone will always have the urge to collect the treasures into a treasure house, like the cave on Captain Kidd's island, or the Kaiserliche Schatzkammer in Vienna. The most common form of treasure house is the anthology. The student can be confidently advised not to overlook anthologies whenever they show up on the shelves of second-hand bookshops. The further back in time from which the poems in an anthology emanate, the more likely is that era to be represented fairly. Closer to now, the question of permissions looms. Sometimes there are poets – Edith Sitwell was one such – who don't want to be anthologized, regarding their total achievement as too grand to be appreciable by the fragment. But more often it is a question of the price. Luckily, in Britain, the increasingly vast, web-based and world-girdling sound museum called the Poetry Archive counts as an anthology that every poet wants to be in, while any publisher is glad to count the publicity as sufficient payment. The Poetry Archive is one of the many initiatives for which we should thank the generosity and imagination of Andrew Motion, who in his role as Poet Laureate took a larger view of his task than merely to pay homage to the Royal Family. He turned all the best poets of his time into a royal family, and got them to speak into the microphone. The results quickly accumulated into a treasure house. One of its most glittering features is the series of guided tours to favourite poems. When I was asked to conduct one of these tours I at first thought it was impossible to convey the full measure of appreciative enthusiasm in a single paragraph. Then I remembered that it's exactly what we do in life: when we want to switch people on to a specific poet, we don't deliver a complete lecture, we try to hook them with a sentence.

POETRY ARCHIVE TOUR

'Mayflies' by Richard Wilbur

After he came back to the US from the fighting in Europe, Richard Wilbur set a standard for post-war American lyric poetry which nobody else could quite match. Some had the sense of form, some the originality of imagery, but he had both. His stanza forms, many of them invented by himself, can be analysed forever, but his details can be enjoyed instantly. In the little poem 'Mayflies' there is a moment I love, when the tiny creatures, rising and descending in the air, are called 'the fine pistons of some bright machine'. How did he think of that?

'The Whitsun Weddings' by Philip Larkin

Otherwise hard to criticize in his poetic greatness, Philip Larkin was sometimes called a dull reciter of his own poetry, but in fact he was good at that too. His unexciting looks were matched by an unexciting voice, but unlike almost all professional actors he knew how to observe his line endings, and never made the mistake of trying to put extra emotion into lines that already had, packed within them, all the emotion they could take. He must have known that 'The Whitsun Weddings' was a great poem, but he read it out with deliberate matter-of-factness, reminding us that it largely is a matter of fact. As the everyday details succeed each other, the story is built up which comes to its magnificent climax in the final image of the arrow shower – one of great poetic moments of modern times, a coup on a level with Shakespeare, and, when read out by its author, all the more effective for being merely said, and not declaimed.

'A Subaltern's Love Song' by John Betjeman

In this recording, it is only appropriate that Betjeman, on being asked to recite 'Joan Hunter Dunn', has to search for it in his book, unable to find it because it isn't called that. The heroine of the poem, the most dominating of the poet's long line of strapping sports girls, became so famous she stepped out of the shrine he had built for her and took on a new, permanent life. Betjeman's poems got into the national consciousness like nobody else's, and they did so at every level of class: it wasn't just the gentry who relished his music. Some of the critics hated it because they thought poetry should sound harder to come by, but if they had known more about poetic technique they would have seen Betjeman to be the dedicated craftsman that Philip Larkin so much, and so rightly, admired.

'Jerusalem' by James Fenton

As a reciter of his own work, James Fenton has the precious double gift of speaking with unaffected naturalness while retaining all the rigorous construction of his verse forms. The exemplary counterpoint comes in especially handy when he recites 'Jerusalem', which is composed of verbal fragments, and would easily seem to fall apart if his voice failed to match the control of tone that holds it together. Many of the phrases come out of those areas of contemporary experience that unsettle us all by threatening to bring us into the firing line. 'Who packed your bag?' Fenton, who has actually seen the firing line from close up, is very generous in supposing that his readers might be as concerned as he is about a world in conflict, and his poetry in general can be said to arouse the disturbing possibility that history will give us a poetry more interesting than serenity.

'The Red Sea' by Stephen Edgar

Stephen Edgar is the Australian poet who most convincingly, and most rewardingly, continues and enriches the line of the orderly lyric that was established after the Second World War by Richard Wilbur and Anthony Hecht, but Edgar has a range of pinpoint registration exceeding even theirs, mainly because he doesn't hesitate to avail himself of a scientific vocabulary. In 'The Red Sea', the poem is into its second stanza before we realize the yachts are toys, and there is a new revelation at least once per stanza until, in the end, the threat of the real world arrives in the form of Macbeth's bloodlust. The vast scale of argument packed into small melodic stanzas is typical, as is the quiet voice, which reminds us that only a carefully schooled detachment could possibly see so much.

'Machines' by Michael Donaghy

The late Michael Donaghy was a renowned reader of his own work. He had his poems by heart and recited them without a hint of histrionics, relying always on the natural music of the colloquial American voice. As a consequence there was an often striking contrast between the ease of the delivery and the intricacy of the construction. 'Machines' is an artefact at least as well built as either the harpsichord or the bicycle celebrated in the narrative, the two miracles of construction being brought together in marriage in the final lines, which are understated in the writing, and even more so when he reads them aloud. As his fine critical writings continually emphasize, Donaghy was a great believer in the formal element, but he always left room for the reader to discover it.

Interlude

When talking about Michael Donaghy's poem 'Machines' I made the large assumption that a poem's form can be appreciated while the work is being recited. My own view is that if the recital is careful enough, it can; but the contrary view is easier to hold, because bits of the poem, unless we already know the poem well, will snag the attention and divert the concentration. Such diversions, indeed, can be called a key requirement. What is a poem whose single moments do not arrest you? It sounds as if it might be pabulum. Nevertheless, no matter how brilliant the fragment, we are not likely to attribute poetic virtue to its author until we get some structural evidence that he or she is not writing prose. Usually, for evidence, we need a stanza; and it has always been my own conviction that you need the ability to build a stanza if you are to get into the game. A stack of stanzas would be better; but failing that, one stanza is the necessary minimum. By that measure, the author of the scurrilous 'Ballad of Eskimo Nell' was a poet but Jack London was not. They both wrote poems about the deadly rigours of the frozen North, but Jack London, though he longed for success as a poet, never wrote a stanza that anyone wanted to remember: his whole gift was for prose. Thus, poor guy, he was condemned to fame and wealth: a fate that most poets avoid.

THE NECESSARY MINIMUM

At a time when almost everyone writes poetry but scarcely anyone can write a poem, it is hard not to wish for a return to some less accommodating era, when the status of 'poet' was not so easily aspired to, and the only hankering was to get something said in a memorable form. Alas, we would have to go a long way back. Samuel Daniel (1562–1619) certainly wanted to be thought of as a poet – it was his career, even when he was working for nobles as a gentleman servant – and there must have been critics who wanted to deny him the title, or they would not have attacked him for too often revising his work, and he would not have defended himself thus:

> And howsoever be it, well or ill
> What I have done, it is mine owne, I may
> Do whatsoever therewithal I will.
>   I may pull downe, raise, and reedifie.
> It is the building of my life, the fee
> Of Nature, all th'inheritance that I
> Shal leave to those which must come after me . . .
>   – from 'To the Reader'

The battle was fought out more than four hundred years ago, and Daniel won it. Unless we are scholars of the period, we might have small knowledge of his work in general, but this one stanza is quite likely to have got through to us. It is often quoted as an example of how there were poets much less important than Shakespeare who nevertheless felt that they, too, might be writing immortal lines to time, and were ready to drub any popinjay who dared to suggest that they weren't. But clearly the stanza did not get through to us just because of the story it tells or the position it takes. It got through by the way it moves. Within its tight form, it is a playground of easy freedom: not a syllable out of place, and yet it catches your ear with its conversational rhythm at every point.

It would be tempting to say that any poet, in any era, needs to be able to construct at least one stanza like that or he will never even join the contest. Daniel's technique was so meticulous that it can teach us how words were pronounced in his time. The opening line of one of the sonnets in which he complains about harsh treatment from his vainly adored Delia runs 'Fair is my love, and cruel as she's fair.' Thus we can tell that the word 'cruel' was probably pronounced with a full two syllables, or there would be a syllable missing from the line. (If he had written 'she is' instead of 'she's' we would have known that he scanned 'cruel' as one syllable, and perhaps even pronounced it that way too, as we do now.) Unfortunately Daniel seldom wrote an entire poem – not even his beautifully entitled 'Care-charmer Sleep' – in which every line was as vivid as that. But he did compose that one stanza, and we only have to read it once before we are drawn in to see how it is held together, and to start asking why we put up with so much unapologetic awkwardness from poets now. Limping numbers from poets writing in free verse are presumably meant, but limping numbers from poets who are avowedly *trying* to write in set forms must be mere clumsiness. The perpetrators might say that they are getting back to the vitality of an initial state, in which Donne demonstrated the vigour that roughness could give before the false ideal of smoothness arrived. But Daniel was already writing before Donne, and we have at least one stanza to prove that lack of vigour was not his problem. All too often his lines lacked semantic pressure, but they always moved with a precise energy, and he could put them together into an assemblage that danced.

Perhaps to ask for a whole stanza is asking too much, and just a few lines will work the trick. The drawback there, however, is that the few lines tend to break free not just from the poem, but from the poet's name. Very few readers of poetry now, however wide their knowledge, would be able to give a name to the poet who wrote this:

> At moments when the tide goes out,
> The stones, still wet and ringing with
> The drained-off retrogressive sea,
> Lie fresh like fish on market stalls
> And, speckled, shine. Some seem to float
> In crevices where wavelets froth
> Forgotten by the watery
> Departure towards the moon.

As a thought experiment, I see myself presented with this fragment in a practical criticism class of the kind that I took in Cambridge in the mid-sixties. Even with the benefit of the knowledge that I have acquired since, I might still be at a loss to name its author, partly because it could have had so many authors. Almost certainly it stems from a period when free-form modernism was already being reacted against: all the scrupulous tension of modernist diction is in it, but there is also a conscious heightening, as of a return to well-made elegance, so we are probably, at the very earliest, somewhere in the years after 1945, when the American formalists were already operating and Britain's phalanx of Movement poets were on their way up. The line 'The drained-off retrogressive sea' might have been turned by Philip Larkin, who was fond of coupling his adjectives into a train. The fresh fish on the market stalls might have come from 'The Avenue Bearing the Initial of Christ into the New World', the long poem in which Galway Kinnell took out the patent on fish imagery. Except that Elizabeth Bishop took out a rival patent when she, too, got into the seafood business. Could it be her? With my supervisor looking at his watch and pressing for an answer, I would have to say that the watery departure towards the moon sounds like Richard Wilbur writing just after the end of the Second World War, or perhaps James Merrill a bit later, or perhaps Stephen Edgar writing last year, or perhaps . . . But the flock of names, mere shorthand for a flock of tones, would only mean that I had found a single voice unidentifiable. And indeed the poet's name is probably still unidentifiable when I reveal it: Dunstan Thompson.

I would have liked to say that Thompson (1918–1975) is the missing man from the post-Second World War poetic story, but the sad truth is that he has gone missing for a reason. Born and raised in America, he had an enviably cosmopolitan education that culminated at Harvard, from which he went into the army. During the war, his poetic career started off brilliantly with his collection *Poems* (Simon and Schuster, 1943) and continued after the war with *Lament for the Sleepwalker* (Dodd, Mead and Company, 1947). These were big-time publishing houses and he won big-time recognition, his name often included in the magic list of voices built to last. Stephen Spender gave Thompson a papal imprimatur, thereby, perhaps, signalling that there might be a fertile context waiting for Thompson across the Atlantic. When Thompson's second book came out he had already resettled in England, and there he began the long business – difficult, for one so prominently placed in several of the 'war poets' anthologies – of ensuring that he would be forgotten. There was quite a lot to forget, and how exactly he managed to translate prominence into oblivion raises some unsettling questions. He wrote one poem, 'Largo', whose qualities should have been remembered, even though it runs to some length and not all of it is in tight focus. Here is a sample stanza:

> All friends are false but you are true: the paradox
> Is perfect tense in present time, whose parallel
> Extends to meeting point; where, more than friends, we fell
> Together on the other side of love, where clocks
>> And mirrors were reversed to show
>> Ourselves as only we could know;
>> Where all the doors had secret locks
> With double keys; and where the sliding panel, well
> Concealed, gave us our exit through the palace wall.

> There we have come and gone: twin kings, who roam at will
> Behind the court, behind the backs
> Of consort queens, behind the racks
> On which their favorites lie who told them what to do.
> For every cupid with a garland round the throne still lacks
> The look I give to you.

This majestic form, one of his own devising, is continued through all ten stanzas of the poem, with a scarcely faltering interplay between the hexameters, tetrameters, and trimeters – everything except pentameters, in fact. Anywhere in the poem's wide panorama, the half rhymes are handled with an infallibly musical tact: the modular balancing of 'well', 'wall', and 'will' in the quoted stanza is only a single instance of a multiple enchantment. You would say that a man who could build such an exquisite machine could do anything, technically. But even though bringing all this mastery to bear, he couldn't do anything definite with the subject matter. From what thin biographical evidence exists, it is possible to conclude that Thompson was one of those gay male poets trapped between the urge to speak and the love that dare not speak its name. Auden escaped the trap by scarcely dropping a hint until the safety whistle blew decades later. But Thompson wanted to spill the beans, not just about Damon and Pythias and Richard II and A. E. Housman – whether named or merely alluded to, they all crop up during the poem – but about himself and his lover, evidently a fellow serviceman. Unfortunately he could spill only a few beans at once. There were limits to what he could say, and the result is a flurry of tangential suggestions, a cloud of innuendo. 'Largo' was a clear case – the only clear thing about it – of a poem written before its time, and by the time its time had come, the poem was gone. Oscar Williams, the best anthologist of the post-war years on either side of the Atlantic, published it in his invaluable *A Little Treasury of Modern Poetry*, but I have never seen it anywhere else. I would like to call the poem magnificent. But it gives only flashes of the total effect it might have had, and there lay the problem that dogged Thompson's poetry for the rest of his career, and eventually buried him.

In England after the war, Thompson went on writing poems, most of which were collected posthumously in *Poems 1950–1974*. The book has an impressive physical appearance, rather along the lines of a Faber collection of the shorter poems of Auden or MacNeice. But the publishing house was an off-trail outfit called Paradigm Press, who can't have printed many copies. During decades of haunting second-hand bookshops all over the world, I only ever saw a single copy, and that was in Cambridge in 2006. I picked it up, wondering who he was, read the lines about the seashore quoted above, and took it home to read it through.

Fragments of high quality were everywhere, but a completely integrated poem was hard to find. 'Seascape with Edwardian Figures' came nearest, but even that one tailed off: when the tide departed towards the moon, the poem went with it. There was a long poem, 'Valley of the Kings', about Egyptian tombs. Freighted with his curious learning, it could have rivalled the stately march of 'Largo', but its points of intensity were scattered, like the momentarily illuminated wall paintings in the tombs themselves, and nothing held them together except the darkness between them. Flaring moments slid away into shadow:

> This painted food will feed
> Only imperishable people. Stars which glow
> Like real stars lose
> Their seeming lustre when you need
> Them to disclose the way. From what? I do not know.

I talk about 'Valley of the Kings' in the past tense because it is no longer alive, and the same applies, alas, to the whole of his later achievement. There is just too little of Samuel Daniel's 'It is mine owne' and too much of Dunstan Thompson's 'I do not know'. Throughout the book, Thompson's talent – in the complex sense that involves perception, precision, and musicality – is everywhere, but that's just the trouble. It's everywhere without being anywhere. The lesson, I think, is that a talent might be the necessary minimum, but it will not be sufficient if it can't produce a poem, or at least a stanza, assured enough to come down through time and make us ask, 'Who wrote *that?*'

James Merrill (1926–1995), another gay American poet who came to prominence a little later, wrote a poem about his upbringing, 'The Broken Home', that would have ensured his survival even if his every other manuscript had gone up in smoke. The poem doesn't bring his sexuality into focus – other poems did – but it does illuminate his early life. This single passage about his father would have been enough to prove that a masterful voice had arrived:

> Each thirteenth year he married. When he died
> There were already several chilled wives
> In sable orbit – rings, cars, permanent waves.
> We'd felt him warming up for a green bride.
>
> He could afford it. He was 'in his prime'
> At three score ten. But money was not time.

I quote the passage because it was the first thing I read of Merrill's that made me realize I would have to read everything else. When I began to, I soon realized that the assurance of his early formal patterns provided the warrant for following him when his patterns became more complicated and finally ceased to be patterns at all. In the twentieth century, this was a not uncommon progression among revolutionary spirits in all the arts. Picasso had conspicuously mastered every aspect of draughtsmanship and painting that had ever been applied to the recognizable before he moved on into the less recognizable, and the best reason for trying to follow what he was up to was that he had proved he could actually do what he was no longer doing. Stravinsky composed melodies you could hum and whistle – I can still do my version of the major themes from *Petrushka* unless somebody stops me – before he moved on to composing what could only be listened to, and the best reason for listening hard was your memory of the authority he had displayed when the listening was easy. In poetry, Eliot went on proving that he was a master of tight forms even as he became famous for works that apparently had no form at all, and that was the best reason for supposing that those works still depended on a highly schooled formal sense. So there was nothing new about Merrill's progression from poems with apprehensible boundaries to poems whose lack of boundaries was part of their subject. It was in the tradition of modernism. But it depended on an assurance that made paying attention compulsory. This compulsory quality was what Dunstan Thompson lacked even in his brightest moments. Thompson didn't have Merrill's vast financial resources – which enabled Merrill to do pretty much what he liked all his life, including, commendably, helping other poets when they were short of cash – but Thompson did have nearly all of Merrill's technical resources. Exploiting those, he might have built an impregnable position for himself, but you can't help feeling that he didn't really want to. His relocation from America to England need not necessarily have been fatal. Earlier in the century it had worked triumphantly for Pound and Eliot, and the only reason that Lowell made a hash of it later on was that his intermittent psychic disturbance had become almost continuous, and had weakened his strategic judgement to the point where he failed to recognize that he wasn't getting beyond the discipline of his wonderfully self-contained early poems, but was neutralizing that discipline in the name of an illusory scope. And it wasn't as if Lowell lacked a welcome in London. (If anything, he was too welcome: the locals would print anything he gave them.) The possibilities of working on both sides of the pond were rich, as was proved in the next generation by Michael Donaghy, who was born in New York in 1954 and died in London at the age of only fifty.

At the time of writing, Donaghy's complete works are being published in Britain by Picador in two neatly matched volumes: *Collected Poems*, which contains all four of the collections published in his lifetime plus a sheaf of previously unpublished poems uniformly excellent, and *The Shape of the Dance*, which amounts to his collected prose. I was asked to write the introduction for the prose volume and was glad to do so, because I think Donaghy was an important critic, even a necessary one. But the reasons to think so would be crucially fewer if he had not been so authoritative as a poet. Within the first few lines of any poem he writes, he has made paying attention compulsory. There are simply dozens, even scores, of poems by which this fact could be easily demonstrated, but let's make it harder for ourselves, by choosing a poem where the reader has to dig a bit to figure out what is going on. That we feel compelled to dig is, I think, a further illustration of the quality of command that we are talking about. The poem 'Shibboleth' was the title poem of the first collection he published in 1988. Here is the poem entire:

> One didn't know the name of Tarzan's monkey.
> Another couldn't strip the cellophane
> From a GI's pack of cigarettes.
> By such minutiae were the infiltrators detected.

> By the second week of battle
> We'd become obsessed with trivia.
> At a sentry point, at midnight, in the rain,
> An ignorance of baseball could be lethal.

> The morning of the first snowfall, I was shaving,
> Staring into a mirror nailed to a tree,
> Intoning the Christian names of the Andrews Sisters.
> 'Maxine, Laverne, Patty.'

For anyone of my generation it is obvious that this poem is about the Battle of the Bulge in 1944, when a special SS unit formed by Otto Skorzeny penetrated the American lines with a view to creating havoc. The SS men – most of them *Volksdeutsche* who had been brought up in America – wore American uniforms, carried captured American weapons, spoke perfect English, and could be identified only by what they didn't know, because they had spent the last few years in Germany. One could make an objection based on just that point: none of the suspects would have shown an 'ignorance of baseball' in general. They just would have been ignorant about the latest scores. (And two of the Andrews Sisters have their names misspelled: 'Maxine' was really 'Maxene' and 'Laverne' was really 'LaVerne'.) But Donaghy has a far wider audience in mind than just my contemporaries. For his own contemporaries, the whole episode might not be in their frame of reference; and he has done very little to clue them in. They have to figure it out. The reference to 'GI's', to the Andrews Sisters, or perhaps to Tarzan's friend Cheetah, would probably be a starting point to help them identify which war it was. Finally they will get it right, and thus find out that the shaving narrator can't be Donaghy, who, at the time, was ten years short of being born. He has put his narrator into a war that could be any American war in which infiltrators have to be detected according to their knowledge of American culture. It's a *Battlestar Galactica* scenario, with the Germans as the Cylons. The new generation, who are just coming to poetry now, might have that as their first thought. Donaghy future-proofed the poem by cutting back on its context. He often did that; or, rather, does that – let's put him in the present, where he belongs.

The typical Donaghy poem isn't typical. Each poem has its own form and, remarkably, its own voice. Underlying this protean range of creative expression there is a critical attitude, which is probably best summed up in a single essay contained in *The Shape of the Dance*. The essay is called 'American Revolutions' and it sums up his life-long – lifelong in so short a life – determination to make sense out of the twentieth-century conflict between formal and free verse. As a musician by avocation, Donaghy had no trust in the idea of perfectly unfettered, untrained expression. He agreed with Stravinsky that limitations were the departure point for inspiration. Donaghy believed that a living poem could emerge only from an idea in 'negotiation' (the key word in his critical vocabulary) with an imposed formal requirement, even if it was self-imposed, and might be rendered invisible in the course of the negotiation. The split between form and freedom, in his view, had begun with the difference between Walt Whitman and Emily Dickinson. He favoured formality, to the extent of hailing Richard Wilbur as the supreme phrasemaker. But he could also see that freedom had been fruitful. He was ready to welcome vital language wherever it came from, even if it came from the uninstructed. (This readiness made him the ideal teacher of creative writing, even though he was suspicious of the very idea: there is a whole new cluster of young poets in London now who show the benefits of his example.) Form and freedom: in all my reading about modern poetry – as opposed to my reading *of* modern poetry – I have not seen anything to equal Donaghy's treatment of this crucial matter for its extent, depth, and fundamental tolerance. As an underlying attitude for justifying the adventures of his own poetry, it could not have been better. But there is something underlying even the attitude, and for that I can't think of a better word than confidence.

Confidence is the attribute that can't be taught. It can be damaged by circumstance, and encouraged when it falters, but the poet has to have it. Samuel Daniel, whose courtly music played at the start of this disquisition, was confident enough to make a career out of his calling. When Thomas Campion questioned the need for rhyme in English poetry, Daniel set him straight. When Daniel's critics upbraided him for too much revising, he told them to get lost. If Gerard Manley Hopkins, a greater poet who was all calling and no career, had come back from the future and accused him of being one of the founders of the deadly Parnassian measures whose default mode was an easy smoothness, Daniel would have known how to defend himself. He believed in his profession. The same could be said for James Merrill, whose financial support for other poets – one of them was Elizabeth Bishop – was motivated by his personal experience of the consuming nature of the art he practised. The same could be said of Robert Lowell, who was right in never questioning his mission to speak, even though, at those times when sanity was subtracted from his awesome mental equipment, he so often spoke to his own detriment. The name we have to leave off the list, alas, is Dunstan Thompson. Auden once said that there are poets who have everything except the desire to step forward. Thompson stepped forward in the beginning, but later he stepped back, and fell into the oubliette. Possibly there is such a thing as being so concerned with the self that one loses sight of the poet's privileged duty, which is to be concerned with everything, in the hope of producing something – a poem, a stanza, even a single line – that will live on its own, in its own time.

Interlude

Though a stanza might be the desirable measure by which we remember poets who write in stanzas, a more usual measure for remembering the greatest of all poets is the piece of a verse paragraph. Shakespeare, in our memories, exists as phrases, lines and groups of lines, and just as often by the group of lines as by the phrase. Unless we are actors who must learn a part, no other playwright, not even Marlowe, gets into our memories more than a phrase or two at a time; but anything by Shakespeare that we recall is always on its way to being a speech; and, as Camille Paglia points out in her book *Break, Blow, Burn*, those compulsively memorable pieces from a Shakespeare play count as poems. Indeed they aspire to that condition. But they also aspire to being the human voice overheard, and they are always hurrying past the listener's ears. Some of the first listeners were professional copyists, sitting in the auditorium and writing down in haste what the actor had just said. The result, for the printed editions, was a plentiful infection with distortion, error and ambiguity. In the epigraph of this book, there is a good case for spelling 'lightning' as 'lightening'. Which word was the word the writer meant is a matter for scholarship; a humanist activity which in the case of Shakespeare is almost as endless as it is with Dante, and just as indispensable. Some tutors believe that the Arden edition should be the first text of any Shakespeare play that the student reads. From my own experience, I would call that the right idea, but misplaced. Footnotes can be a forest, and there is such a thing as reaching a first acquaintance with Shakespeare without doing very much at all of moving the eye-line down from the text to the notes crowding the bottom of the page. The distraction is least likely when there are no notes at all, as with the old Selfridge's

complete Shakespeare, with a preface by Sir Henry Irving, that I
carried with me on my travels until long after it fell to pieces. But
eventually you will need the benefits of scholarship and commentary,
or else bruise your understanding from too much flying blind. There
have always been learned poets who, fancying themselves as scholars
of Shakespeare, think that they can provide a more pure and practical analysis than the critics and professors. But usually they have
overrated their intuitive powers. Not even Empson was clever enough
to supersede the scholarly heritage, which was largely academic; and
it will always be advisable for the beginning enthusiast, once he has
finished mocking the academic world, to make his peace with it, and
learn something. One of the many attractive features of the Shakespearean criticism written by John Berryman was that he was best
pleased with himself when he sounded most like a scholar. There was
not much he was humble about, but he was humble about that.

A DEEPER CONSIDERATION

Had he not been a poet, John Berryman would have been a Shakespearean scholar, and well qualified for the task, even though his drinking habit was as ungovernable as his beard. In addition to his vast knowledge of the field, Berryman had unusually sensitive instrumentation for measuring the intensity of language. As a critic, if not always as a poet, he was especially good when deciding whether a fine phrase had a deep thought behind it, or was just showing itself off. And he was very convincing when he argued that Shakespeare had the same priorities.

According to Berryman, the older and better Shakespeare got, the more he was concerned that the verse should spring from what we might call a deeper consideration. Berryman pushed this line to the point of feeling able to say that if a stretch of verse in one of the plays seemed sufficiently preoccupied with the question of how the words needed thought to spring from, then Shakespeare might well have written that passage later in his career, even if it was inserted in a play dating from earlier on. Berryman said as much about the interchange between the king and Bertram in *All's Well That Ends Well*. The interchange – which is really a paean to Bertram's father, addressed to the son by a king who doesn't mind holding his interlocutor captive while he explores the subject so as to pin down every nuance – is not a passage which does very much for the plot of the play into which it has been introduced. It is more like a little play all on its own.

Coleridge once said that Polonius, in *Hamlet*, is the embodiment of a reputation for wisdom no longer possessed. The king in *All's Well* really is wise, but he has Polonius's habit of worrying at a point while his interlocutor, usually much younger, sneaks impatient glances at the nearest sundial. But Shakespeare, this time, isn't making a joke of it. The king is on to something that interests the playwright as a matter of professional conviction. We could quote from the scene for as long as it lasts, and indeed one short bit is reasonably well known, although nothing like as well known as most of the Shakespearean 'old man's wisdom' quotations that we carry around in our heads if we have lived long enough. The king says:

> Since I nor wax nor honey can bring home,
> I quickly were dissolved from my hive,
> To give some labourers room.

Instruct the actor (if necessary at gunpoint) to hit the hidden extra stress in the word 'dissolvèd', so that the second line, which must be expressed as a wish, becomes as rhythmically forceful a pentameter as the first, and you've got one of those little show-stopping moments that should happen every few minutes as the night goes on. Unless they are badly spoken, they don't really stop the show, of course: but they do lift the listener's heart, to make him forget time as the fragments of deeper consideration join up throughout the evening.

There is a lot more in the interchange, however, than that fine idea. The king has been considering wisdom, and the speaking of wisdom. And he wants to tell Bertram that his, Bertram's, father was the embodiment of how that should be done. To make sure that Bertram gets the message, the king wields his monarchical privilege of repeatedly telling Bertram what he, Bertram, must know already, and even takes the liberty of quoting one of Bertram's father's speeches: something that Bertram could probably have done better, except that he – and this is the armature of the scene's dynamics – is too young to feel yet what the king has come, through time, to know is true.

> 'Let me not live,' quoth he,
> 'After my flame lacks oil, to be the snuff
> Of younger spirits, whose apprehensive senses

> All but new things disdain; whose judgements are
> Mere fathers of their garments; whose constancies
> Expire before their fashions.'

These lines about a judgement being had only so it can be snazzily dressed up to fit the fashion have a nice symmetry with the more famous passage, in the same play, where old Lafeu warns young Bertram against the showmanship of the fop Parolles: 'there can be no kernel in this light nut; the soul of this man is his clothes.' You could easily quote it as verse, but Lafeu, as it happens, is expressing himself in prose: the kind of toughly, densely argued prose that Hamlet uses when he gets down to bedrock.

There is a notion of bedrock throughout Shakespeare's work almost to the end: a notion that the essential meaning, the deeper consideration, has to be protected against all transient distortions, including the poet's own gift for . . . what? Well, the answer is in the opponent's name: Parolles. Words. Words are the bewitching enemy, the beautiful seducer.

The threat posed by the spectacular expression that outruns its substance was a long-running theme in Shakespeare, and is surely one of the preoccupations that now make him seem so modern. Though he seems modern in every age – modern all over again – he seems especially modern in ours, when we look at him from the angle of analytical philosophy, a school of thought which has, at its tutorial centre, a concern for scrupulosity of language: the scrupulosity that was incarnated by Wittgenstein, and as much in his likes as his dislikes. Wittgenstein's admiration for Mörike depended on the poet's determination that the word should not exceed the thing. We should be slow to read back from the grim philosopher agonizing over a conceptual nuance for weeks on end in his cold digs to the fluent playwright composing a whole different version of Act V on Monday night before the new play opened on Tuesday, but it still seems legitimate to propose that Shakespeare was concerned enough by the capacity of his own facility to fly off by itself, and thus to want it anchored to something solid.

It might seem madness to suppose that Shakespeare shared the same conviction about the seductive power of words as Wittgenstein, but it should be possible at least to entertain the notion that Shakespeare could not have created his most evocative enchantments without a notion of limit and precision; and all precision, in language, eventually depends on a disciplined adherence to thought. The process of composition might produce a new thought – always one of the best reasons for composing in verse at all – but the new thought, too, has to test out, meeting a standard of quality if not of contiguity. Although the combination of thoughts might fiercely resist being reduced to a prose equivalent – think of almost any striking stanza by, say, John Crowe Ransom – it must be something more than a vague suggestion towards the indefinable. (If Mallarmé seems to do that, it is because he is treating the indefinable as his subject.) When, in later Shakespeare, we have trouble anchoring an image to a thought, it's at least worth considering that the thought has gone awry – that the deeper consideration is not fully formed – before deciding that we have been granted an insight into the inexplicable. But we would not even conceive of such a possibility if we did not have, as a measure, everything that Shakespeare had already done. It's his store of dazzling clarities that warns us against the assumption that there might be a further profundity in the obscure.

•

Shakespeare in his last years was still young, even by the standards of the time. We tend to think of men of genius, in the long age before modern medicine, as struggling to make it past the age of fifty, but the tendency takes a battering when it runs into the case of, say, Titian, still painting at the age of ninety. It seems fair to say, however, that the later Shakespeare was getting on, and fair also to look on his later work as a field of study that might help illuminate all that happened earlier. Perhaps there are developments occurring that we don't quite grasp because we ourselves aren't old enough. As my own dotage approaches, heralded by instances of forgetfulness that I would list here if I could only remember them, I fall further and further out of love with the common idea that lyrical talent, like the talent for original mathematics, burns out early. I would like to think that a lifetime of experience gives me more to say, and that any early exuberance which I can no longer summon was partly the product of an emptier head. Give me maturity or give me death.

Mature to a fault even when he was young, Samuel Menashe has spent a long lifetime avoiding publicity. It was a measure of his self-effacement that the Poetry Foundation felt compelled to give him, in 2004, its Neglected Masters Award. The neglected master's most recent and perhaps climactic collection, *New and Selected Poems*, which contains ten more poems than his 2005 Library of America compilation, was published in America in 2008, but I am ashamed to say that I never noticed it until it was re-published in Britain later on by Bloodaxe Books. Since his name has always been slightly less obscure in Britain than in America – after the Second World War he was taken up in London by the poet Kathleen Raine – I was intermittently aware of him, but from this book I can get his full force, which is no noisier than a bug hitting your windscreen, except that it comes right through the glass. Take the poem called 'Beachhead':

> The tide ebbs
> From a helmet
> Wet sand embeds

That's the whole poem, and there is a whole war in it. Like Richard Wilbur and Anthony Hecht, Menashe was a soldier in the last campaigns of the war in Europe. He was at the Battle of the Bulge, in which thirty German divisions were stopped only at the price of nineteen thousand dead GIs. Menashe must have seen terrible things, but none of them is evoked directly in his poetry. It is remarkable, and instructive, how little either Wilbur or Hecht wrote directly about what they had seen, but even more remarkable was that Menashe – rather like J. D. Salinger, who also saw it all from close up – wrote even less. Yet he wrote about the helmet in the sand, and somehow his wealth of sad experience is in that single tiny haiku-like construction.

It makes his war a nation's war. The deeper consideration is that he was one among many, and, unlike too many, he lived to speak. That he speaks so concisely is a condition of his testament: consecration and concentration are the same thing. This is a world away from the expression of the self. This is bedrock.

All Menashe's poems give the sense of having been constructed out of the basic stuff of memory, a hard substratum where what once happened has been so deeply pondered that all individual feeling has been squeezed out and only universal feeling is left. The process gives us a hint that the act of construction might be part of the necessary pressure: if the thing was not so carefully built, the final compacting of the idea could not have been attained. There could be no version of a Menashe poem that was free from the restrictions of technique, because without the technique the train of thought would not be there. Even when he writes without obvious rhyme, he has weighed the balance of every syllable; when he uses near rhymes, the modulations are exquisite; and a solid rhyme never comes pat, but is always hallowed by its own necessity.

In a poem by Menashe, an awful lot goes on in a short space, and it might seem like cherrystone scrimshaw at first. But so does a little poem by Emily Dickinson, until you look harder. Menashe is in her tradition, packing sound together to shed light. Compared to 'Beachhead', his poem 'Cargo' is gigantic, but it is still only ten short lines. Here is the whole thing:

> Old wounds leave good hollows
> Where one who goes can hold
> Himself in ghostly embraces
> Of former powers and graces
> Whose domain no strife mars –
> I am made whole by my scars
> For whatever now displaces
> Follows all that once was
> And without loss stows
> Me into my own spaces

For all we know, one of his scars is the memory of the Fifth Panzer Army heading towards him through a snowstorm. But what we can be sure of is that he had a lot to get over. When he finally went home to New York, he disappeared into a fifth-floor walk-up whose lack of luxury has to be seen to be believed. The Bloodaxe edition has an accompanying DVD that shows him in situ, reading his poems aloud. His voice is wonderfully rich, but everything around him spells poverty. Obviously this monk-like self-denial is part of his dedication, although you might say that he sacrificed his purity when he let a camera through the door. One is very glad, however, that his privacy was invaded, because the message of dignity in old age, after a long life of uncomplaining commitment, is one that all young poets should hear. That, and the message that there has to be bedrock beneath meaning even if the bedrock is no longer visible. Kandinsky's abstract painting grew from the precisely drawn outlines of the church and the town square.

•

When proposing, as an ideal, the art of getting a lot said in a small space, one should in fairness keep room in the mind for the counter-argument by which some poets who get a little said in a long space are still saying something unique. (Think of Christopher Smart's *Jubilate Agno*, whose demented sprawl contains far more lyricism than his lyrics.) As critics get older, they very easily succumb to the notion that there is no more room in the pantheon. But there is always more room in the pantheon, because the pantheon is not a burial chamber for people who have said things, it is an echo chamber for things that have been said. I was in the middle of concocting some pontifical statements about Shakespeare's powers of compression when a long chain of memory led me back through Ovid (whose *Metamorphoses* Shakespeare knew by heart) to Ovid's title *The Art of Love*, and from that to the niggling recollection that Kenneth Koch had written a longish poem of the same name, and that I had once thought enough of it to make a mental note that I should read it again one day.

Nowadays, dogged by the knowledge that 'one day' had better

be soon, I try to follow up these mental notes if I recall them. So I searched out Koch's *Selected Poems* of 1991 and soon found myself enjoying a passage of his 'The Art of Love' against my will – almost always the best way to enjoy anything. I like things kept short, and Koch, even in a comparatively short (for him) work like 'The Art of Love', spread himself around as if his readers had all the time in the world. The poem is a kind of how-to handbook, telling prospective lovers what to do in a variety of circumstances:

> What to do when one lover is in a second-floor apartment,
> the other in the first-floor one;
> Openings in the ceiling, and how to make them; how to answer
> the question
> 'What are you doing up there on the ceiling?' if someone
> accidentally comes home.

Whitman is somewhere behind the technique, or at any rate behind the conscious lack of it, but there is a *Tom and Jerry* cartoon behind the mental picture, and really the vividness of the image settles the question: without the casual looseness of the construction, the gag wouldn't work. As for whether the gag is poetic: well, how is it not? Is lovemaking ever a dignified posture, even for Leda and the swan? It's quite easy to imagine our learned quarrel continuing indefinitely, but the longer it does continue, the more it becomes certain that Koch was only one of the names among the many American informal poets who achieved effects in a conversational tone which a formal structure would probably not have allowed.

My favourite post-war Americans might be strict formalists like Wilbur and Hecht, but my appreciation of them – and of semi-formalists like Lowell and Bishop – would be weaker, I think, if I did not recognize that there were things done by ragbag technicians, or even dedicated anti-technicians, which nevertheless achieved the most concentrated possible version of an effect. Michael Donaghy was quite right to say that Ginsberg's *Howl* was the result of hard re-working. But the work went into making the lines sound as if they had never been worked at even once, and the aim, surely, was to sound as if he was just saying it, without really having written it. It's the 'just saying' that the reader with book learning finds hard to accept. He should accept it, because the rewards have to be acknowledged.

In James Wright's poem 'Lying in a Hammock at William Duffy's Farm in Pine Island, Minnesota' we have the perfect placement of the final sentence, borrowed from Rimbaud, 'I have wasted my life.' We love it when Gregory Corso cries out 'I want penguin dust.' Few of these effects would have been brought into being by the pressure of a form. It's more likely that they were brought into being by the pressure of avoiding a form. (The urge goes deep, and a long way back: Ben Jonson cursed Petrarch for his Procrustean urge to shape everything into a sonnet.) One's chief objection, when reading such poets, should come about as a result of noting the successes; and then noting that they are few and far between. If Koch could have put more of his best moments beside each other he would be a much brighter light now.

Whether formal or informal, the post-war Americans were blessed with a vast reservoir of colloquial language to draw upon. (Once, in conversation, the British critic Al Alvarez – who promoted the American heavyweights to the detriment of his own countrymen, much to the annoyance of Philip Larkin – trumped my contrary argument by saying, truly, that the Americans by now had the advantage in the spoken language: 'Their gags are better.') The verbal bounty was already apparent before the Second World War, in the scripts of the screwball comedies, but the war gave it a tremendous boost. It makes some sense to contend that the informal poets deliberately broke the dam of form so as to release the flood within, but it makes at least as much sense to say that the flood did the job all by itself. The free-form idioms got into everything. Before the war, S. J. Perelman wrote whole prose poems that consisted of nothing except showbiz jargon, restaurant menus, and billboards. After the war, the poets could pull the gold dust out of the air.

Considering this fact, it is remarkable how John Ashbery, by now revered as the supreme American post-war poet, decided not to avail himself of the abundance. In his poem 'Pyrography' he wrote 'This is America calling' but in most of his later work the calling is not notably American, or anyway not the American of everyday flip talk. Early on, he made full use of it: most notably in 'Daffy Duck In Hollywood' which I think is one of the great modern American poems. (I would mention it less often if more critics and scholars would hail its qualities: but they seem to like him better when he says nothing that doesn't need them to explain it.) The poem's riches are too sumptuous to list: the brand names and cheap objects pile up like a satirical paragraph from H. L. Mencken ('a mint-condition can / Of Rumford's Baking Powder, a celluloid earring, Speedy / Gonzales') and resonant lines of dialogue are seemingly designed to be used against the poet by a puzzled customer ('If his / Achievement is only to end up less boring than the others, / What's keeping us here?').

But nothing I have tried in any of Ashbery's collections since the Daffy Duck poem was written has captured me in the same way. It is a bit like my failure to engage with the later Wallace Stevens, a failure made all the more uncomfortable for me by the fact that I was so transfixed by one of the early poems from *Harmonium* ('The Emperor of Ice-Cream') that I can still recite it from memory. Like the later works, it too is hard to figure out, but every part of it is a flaring image; whereas later on, I find, and especially in the long poems, all the components link together in a blur, smooth but bland: mere words, an extended flourish by Parolles, using his hat like Osric. I still haven't given up on the mature Stevens, even though he seems to me to have matured in reverse, but I would be grateful for a revelation, in which all the later work became, if not clear, at least vital. Nobody should mind incomprehensibility as long as incomprehensibility is not the aim. Rimbaud didn't set out, when he wrote *Le Bateau Ivre*, to be the subject of a thousand theses. He just had a lot to put in the one place. I would like to think that the same is true of the later Ashbery, and that I have so far merely failed to concentrate properly. Certainly the Daffy Duck poem, which I love so much, has bits in it that I can't figure out. But they thrill me even as they puzzle me. There is a passage that starts:

> How will it all end? That geranium glow
> Over Anaheim's had the riot act read to it by the
> Etna-size firecracker.

The rhapsody goes on unbroken for a full ten lines and I still can't understand it. But I think the world of its movement and imagery, and if I can't find those things in his later decades, it is always possible that I haven't looked hard enough. I doubt, however, if I will ever now find him getting down to bedrock. For some reason he decided that such an aim wasn't interesting enough. Shakespeare thought it was, but perhaps he did such a good job of proving it he scared everyone else off.

And there is no doubt that poetry can spring from the way a bedrock statement is rearranged to show that the lyricism, rather than in the thought, is in the arrangement, as when Anne Sexton says of the pheasant:

> He drags a beige feather that he removed,
> one time, from an old lady's hat.
> We laugh and we touch.
> I promise you love. Time will not take away that.

By putting 'that' at the end, she puts emphasis on it, as Seamus Heaney puts the emphasis on 'it' when he writes 'I'll dig with it.' The syntactical bravura is not just catchy, it has become part of the impulse. If we are looking for characteristics that define modernism, that would surely be one of them. The urge to make the syntax do tricks could emerge only after the long, founding age when the syntax was always a modest servant. But one of the paradoxes of Shakespeare, to get back to him, is that even his modesty was spectacular. In *Henry V*, the young king is proud of speaking 'plain soldier'. And indeed, talking to a few of his plain soldiers by firelight, he is trying to express himself as simply as he can when he warns against optimism:

> The man, that once did sell the lion's skin
> While the beast liv'd, was kill'd with hunting him.

So there they are, the thought and the words together, and even though, to the enchanted ear, the combination is as light as pumice, still it is bedrock, the deepest of all considerations, and as far as you can get from mere words.

Interlude

Until, in modern times, the brief fad for 'concrete poetry' proved that any poem which made a shape on the page was unlikely to accomplish much that George Herbert hadn't, the idea of concreteness still seemed attractive. Concrete language supposedly entailed a use of language more specific than abstract. The result, surely, would be closer to bedrock than any metaphysical argument could go. In actuality, there are good reasons for thinking that metaphysical poetry was more concrete than anything that happened for almost two centuries afterward, but in the long term the wish for a hard-edged diction always lingered as something to be desired. The desire grew intense in the twentieth century, and finally reached its full crystallization in the use of brand names. A language prevalent in newspapers and magazines, on the walls of buildings, and finally on a shining screen, could be relied on, it was thought, to register the tone of the age like nothing else. We already lived in a manufactured world. After poetry began using the names of the manufactured goods, industry was accepted into poetry, and might even, it was fondly hoped, have been civilized by the process. The use of brand names, however, if too emphatic, could easily look like a complicit submission to capitalism. It was less reprehensible to just place the product: a casual mention, as if the artefact was an occurrence in the natural world. By now we have been taught by the young and alert, who live and breathe these developments, that the movies are full of placed products: nothing with a name shows up by accident. There is even a reverse language, by which a corporation of sufficient power forbids the sight of its name without payment, even when its name is part of the landscape: hence the absence of Coca-Cola signs in the otherwise authentic sets of *Boardwalk Empire*. Things haven't reached that stage in poetry yet and probably never will, because the audience is too small, too poor and – let's be proud of it – too bright. All that has happened is that there has been an increase in the vocabulary of reality: the words and phrases that were in the language already have been augmented by the words and phrases dreamed up by advertising copywriters, some of them with every poetic gift except the ability to live on a pittance.

PRODUCT PLACEMENT IN MODERN POETRY

Early in the twentieth century, E. E. Cummings was as hot against materialist society as only a poet living on a trust fund can be. Along with his love lyrics that achieved notoriety by fragmenting all over the page like sexy grenades, he wrote poems that were meant to be satires. In his 1926 collection, *is 5*, the star among the would-be satirical poems was 'POEM, OR BEAUTY HURTS MR. VINAL'. (Always playing tricks with typography, Cummings might have put the title in capitals specifically so that later editors of anthologies, when they cited it accurately in the contents list, would look as if they had made a mistake.) In the poem's opening stanzas, capitalist America is mockingly addressed:

> take it from me kiddo
> believe me
> my country, 'tis of
>
> you, land of the Cluett
> Shirt Boston Garter and Spearmint
> Girl With The Wrigley Eyes (of you
> land of the Arrow Ide
> and Earl &
> Wilson
> Collars) of you i
> sing: land of Abraham Lincoln and Lydia E. Pinkham,
> land above all of Just Add Hot Water And Serve –
> from every B.V.D.
>
> let freedom ring

All those brand names were fresh contemporary references at the time. Any American reader would have spotted them with ease. Later on, it would have taken consultation with an old-timer or several trips to the library. Reading the poem for the first time in Australia in the late fifties, I committed the lines to memory without having a clue what the proper names referred to, except perhaps for Abraham Lincoln and Wrigley's Spearmint gum, which had been handed out by American troops all over the Pacific area with such liberality that it was a byword even in Japan. Nowadays we can all look up the names on a machine. The reader will come away from an hour of googling with a lot of information. In 1929, a few years after the poem was written, Cluett Peabody, makers of shirts, took over the Arrow brand, and in 1985 the remnants of Cluett Peabody were absorbed into the GTB (Gold Toe Brands) Holding Corp, which today still holds the licensing rights to the 'Sanforized' process of pre-shrinking fabric, originally devised by Sanford L. Cluett himself. In the advertising for Arrow shirts, the Arrow man, a predecessor of the Marlboro man but dressed up for an elegant evening out instead of being dressed down for the West, was a painted fantasy by the eminent commercial artist J. C. Leyendecker.

Though he didn't exist, the Arrow man drew up to 17,000 fan letters a day: a fact worth filing away if you are trying to convince yourself that there will never be enough American voters to put Sarah Palin in the White House. Securing an immortality some-what more certain than the one conferred by Cummings's poem, the Arrow man can also be encountered in chapter seven of *The Great Gatsby*. Ide collars were manufactured by George P. Ide & Co. and had nothing to do with today's Integrated Drive Electronics. Lydia E. Pinkham's highly successful herbal medicine might have owed some of its popularity among women to an impressive ethanol content. The standard treatment for acute menstrual pains at the time was to remove the ovaries, so getting slightly blotto was no doubt an attrac-tive alternative. The poem was a few years too early to record that the firm of Bradley, Voorhees & Day hired Johnny Weissmuller to be the face, as we would now say, of their product, BVD men's underwear, but their advertising already carried the slogan 'Next to Myself I Like BVD Best.' Since BVD was purchased in 1976 by Fruit of the Loom, and since, in 2002, Fruit of the Loom was in turn purchased by Berkshire Hathaway, the original acronym is currently under the control of none other than Warren Buffett, one of the richest men in the world. Buffett, judging from his parsimonious ways, probably wears the product under his business suit. But in a sense he would be wearing it even if he dressed more expensively, because BVD has entered the American version of the English language as a general term for any brand of men's underwear.

Today we are used to the idea that a free market economy, except when it collapses, goes on changing and growing inexorably, with a multifariousness that can be analysed only up to a point, and never fully described. No matter how dumb, every artist and intellectual has caught up with what Ferdinand Lassalle tried to tell Karl Marx: that capitalism was something far more complex and productive than he, Marx, could honestly reduce to a formula. Marx preferred to believe that capitalism was heading towards extinction. And indeed, in the twenties there was a crisis on the way, but it was still boom time when Cummings was writing satirical poems in Greenwich Village. The commercial world had a creative force of its own, to which the creative artists could not help responding, even when they despised it politically. Hart Crane scattered brand names throughout his long poem *The Bridge*. A monumental three-part novel much less read now that it once was, *U.S.A.* by John Dos Passos, is punctuated with free-form poetic rhapsodies full of industrial facts and names. Those passages are by far the liveliest parts of the book. Many of the names are unrecognizable now, but strangely they remain as enticing as when he first transcribed them. The same applies to the trademarks in Cummings's early poems.

There is a paradox here, which needs to be unpacked on the level of language, because by now there is no other level on which it exists. My own solution would be to say that the writers were taking on a fresh supply of vocabulary. As a sponge can't resist liquids, they were bound to respond to the linguistic bustle of the printed advertising and the radio hoopla. Theoretically they might have despised the land of Just Add Hot Water And Serve, but in practice they loved the slogans. Readymade cheap poetry, the scraps of advertising copy, properly mounted in a poem, could be made to look expensive, in just the way that Picasso could mount a scrap of newspaper in a collage and make it look as interesting as a pot carried by a slave girl on a Pompeian wall – ephemerality perpetuated.

Not all poets since that time of discovery have taken immediately detectable advantage of the fresh supply of language. Like all new tricks it soon looked old hat if pursued to excess, and Robert Frost, who can plausibly be put forward as the greatest modern poet of them all, never touched it: in his verse an axe was just an axe. Not even the achingly up-to-date W. H. Auden supplied brand names for 'The tigerish blazer and the dove-like shoe.' But many poets, and some of them among the most striking in their diction, have, at least part way, followed the same course in connecting now and always. It's one of the biggest differences I can see between the English language poetry of the modern era and the poetry of all the eras preceding. In pre-modern poetry, Shakespeare, who mentioned everything, would probably have name-checked products if he could, but there were few goods with the maker's name on them: though he would specify the street or town which had given origin to a certain cut of sleeve, Lady Macbeth at her most wild would never have been the face of Vivienne Westwood, even if Shakespeare had known that a louche female designer of that name had a studio under the castle eaves.

You do get the sense, however, that Milton, though he could stuff a verse paragraph full of classical furniture until it groaned, wouldn't have raided a supply of contemporary proper names, had such a thing existed. There was a conviction, which he inherited and concentrated, that too much concern with the evanescent blocked the way to the eternal. It wasn't remarkable, then, that Pope, a meticulous recorder of the knickknacks on a young lady's dressing table in *The Rape of the Lock*, named no name that might not have been remembered. Nor, moving on, is the same forbearance remarkable in Tennyson, whose infallibly musical ear would certainly have picked up on, say, an

Emes & Barnard sterling silver mustard pot if he had thought such a reference advisable. Hopkins, who could see everything, seems not to have seen an advertisement in a newspaper. Hardy, in his poem about the *Titanic*, never mentioned the ship's name, though you might have thought that it sounded classical enough. But then suddenly, only a little further into the twentieth century, poets in the English language were pulling words off billboards the way that late nineteenth-century French painters had put billboards in their paintings, and probably for the same reasons.

There had been a philosophical shift: if not in philosophy, then in the arts. It had finally been recognized that the artificially generated language of here and now could be continuous with the everlasting. It didn't *guarantee* the everlasting, and even today so keen-eyed a poet as Seamus Heaney will tell you everything about a plough except the name of its manufacturer: but a reference system in the temporal present was no longer held to be the enemy of a poem's bid for long life. For poetry, the modernizing process had begun in France, and well before the painters made the same change visible. Victor Hugo began the breaking down of the standard poeticized diction that the French call *poncif*, and the brilliantly original Tristan Corbière, for whom Paris was one enormous *brocante* full of used objects crying out to be mentioned, led the whole of his short life while Renoir was still getting into his stride, and Monet was still editing the landscapes in front of his eyes so that smokestacks were magically eliminated. In all histories of modern literature, it's a standard theme that modern poetry in English really got started when Pound and Eliot picked up on such Frenchmen as Laforgue, but really the influence was already operating in the fin-de-siècle English poet Ernest Dowson, in whose poems the protagonists were drowsy with absinthe.

Dowson, however, never quoted the name on the label of the bottle. That came later, and after it did come it never went away. In Eliot's poems there weren't just sawdust restaurants with oyster shells, there were ABC restaurants with weeping multitudes. Eliot didn't care that the ABC restaurants might not be there one day. As things have turned out, the name ABC for restaurants has proved hard to kill – you can visit one in Buenos Aires – but the original chain of restaurants that Eliot was talking about is long gone. He wasn't betting on their durability, though. He was betting on a sure thing: the way they sounded. The noise the set of initials made was as important to him as the picture it evoked. New words made for new phrases, and did so with an abundance unseen since Elizabethan times. We need to bear this in mind when getting deeply involved in academic discussions about whether the modern poets reintegrated the sensibility that had become dissociated since the metaphysical poets – a key notion of Eliot the critic. Listen hard enough to Eliot the poet, and you can hear something more fundamental than a soldering iron reconnecting loose wires in the apparatus of sense: you can hear an incoming surge of fresh linguistic forms.

Even those poets who did not refer directly to the manufactured names of the commercial world referred to the world of manufactured things. Poetry took in more and more of what was already there, instead of leaving it out in order to remain uncontaminated by evanescence. If the expansion was incremental, it still happened awfully fast. In the poetry of Pound, the revolutionary who now looks merely transitional because he was so far outstripped by what he started, skyscrapers were never mentioned. Yet Pound was still in his manic prime when Auden, in September 1939, took it for granted that he could use skyscrapers for decor:

> Where blind skyscrapers use
> Their full height to proclaim
> The strength of Collective Man.

Actually, as Nazi Germany and the Soviet Union were both already demonstrating elsewhere, Collective Man had more daunting ways of proving his strength than to erect the Chrysler building, but even if the thought was superficial (a weakness that the later, self-punishing version of Auden would have admitted) the phrasing sounded all the more classical for being so contemporary: a seeming anomaly that we will have to deal with eventually. For now, enough to say that

Wordsworth and Coleridge had wished to reopen poetry to common speech, and might even have done so, to some of it: but modern poetry did so to all of it, including the common names for all the trappings of energy, illumination, entertainment, and transport. (Tennyson travelled frequently by train but he never mentioned trains in a poem, except perhaps for a single, notably unobservant reference in 'Locksley Hall': perhaps the thought of the puffing locomotive that took him to see the Queen might have disturbed the landscape of the *Idylls of the King*.) And this must have been at least partly due to the surrounding centripetal pressure of commercial language, which was just as busily inventive as poetry was, and more energetic for being better paid: for being the product of competition in a stricter sense than any art.

It also had the advantage of being so undeviatingly utilitarian in its aims that it was begging to be hijacked, as an aesthetic duty. Of all the poets of the thirties, John Betjeman pulled the most daring heist. Auden, MacNeice, and Spender were either praised or blamed as Pylon Poets, but they themselves never said who made the pylon. Betjeman unblushingly said who made everything. It was the biggest difference between him and his pre-modern predecessor. Both of them wrote performance pieces meant to be recited by an amateur standing beside the piano after dinner, but Kipling, though in his poems about India he carefully specified the colonial equipment of the sahibs, seldom mentioned the London shops where they bought their kit. Kipling's Empire was full of British exports ('In the name of the Empress, the Overland Mail!') but with the conspicuous exceptions of Pears' soap and Pears' shaving sticks he rarely cited a brand name for effect. Betjeman never stopped. He wrote whole stanzas full of trademarks, and there were lines that differed from advertising slogans only in having a more finely judged lilt. Even when evoking the immediate past, he brought to the task the cataloguing eye and ear of the present.

> Scent of Tutti-Frutti-Sen-Sen
> And cheroots upon the floor.

Sen-Sen was an Edwardian breath-freshener, so by citing the name he was harking back to a time when no poet would have cited it. After the Second World War, Betjeman was often disparaged as a social throwback, and today, although his prominence is no longer seriously questioned, there is still a remarkable list of important anthologies which do not include any of his work. But at the time his fellow craftsmen knew that he was at least as up to date as they were. Geoffrey Grigson might have turned down Betjeman's poems for *New Verse*, but Eliot wanted them for the *Criterion*. There would have been no doubt of Betjeman's originality if he had taken Faber's offer when it came. With Eliot in command of the editorial board, Faber already had the power of an establishment institution specifically equipped for deciding which new poets were modern enough to last. But as Alexandra Harris outlines in her excellent book *Romantic Moderns* – and if only all cultural analysts had her style, scope, and concision – Betjeman stuck with the more fustian house of John Murray because, as a cultural conservationist dedicated to the preservation of a vanishing England, he didn't want his books to look modern at all. He didn't want a front cover showing nothing but a typeface: he wanted little drawings of herbaceous festoons and time-honoured architectural doodahs, like illustrations from Ruskin. He did, however, from within the neat boxes of his four-square stanzas, *sound* more modern than anybody. And later on Philip Larkin picked up on it. Larkin admired Betjeman so much for his intelligibility and poise that today whole platoons of busy scholars tend not to notice how the admiration was also reflected in a deep technical homage. Larkin might be indebted to Yeats and Hardy, but to Betjeman he is enslaved. The obeisance can be traced through the use of proper names. Betjeman's longing for beautiful women was translated, when he failed to attain them, into the sensual pleasure of naming their accoutrements: in his wartime poem 'Invasion Exercise on the Poultry Farm', the mouth he yearns to kiss is still, today, otherwise occupied:

Marty rolls a Craven A around her ruby lips.

A reader from outside the British Empire might have needed telling that Craven A was a brand of cigarette, but Betjeman was working on the assumption that the Empire was still a big enough audience for an act which was, on at least one level, vaudeville: he came on, made a topical reference, and paused for the laugh of recognition. Larkin borrowed Betjeman's gaze in order to read the seaside billboard that featured the beautiful girl who will not survive the seasons and the graffiti artists:

> Come to Sunny Prestatyn
> Laughed the girl on the poster,
> Kneeling up on the sand
> In tautened white satin.

Her threatened image is pure and tragic Larkin, but Betjeman's merriment bubbles underneath. Verve travels.

It could be said that verve is the only thing that does travel. Perhaps we need a more expensive word for it. The word 'rhythm' is overworked for something so hard to pin down, but at least it gives you the idea that vocabulary is not enough. The fresh words must lead to a phrase, and the phrase must have impetus, which must help to propel the line, and so on. Otherwise nothing is being built except a lexicon. In twentieth-century America, especially after the Second World War opened up the old world to young hopefuls armed with the GI Bill, there were lexically gifted American poets who could join the United States (the country whose beauty hurt Mr. Vinal) to a greater, more Europeanized sophistication. In brute fact, the European glossy magazines – French *Vogue* was the prime example – were already under the control of American capital, but it remained true that Americans were still in search of cultural validation. L. E. Sissman, whose name first came to prominence in the sixties, was an expert at bringing to a poetic narrative the lustre of high-end products then deemed exclusive. Here he is in a plush hotel, about to receive his dinner companion, a dizzying young fashion plate called Honor, whom we might imagine as a

a version of Holly Golightly with her own money, or Paris Hilton
with taste:

> The maitre d'
> Steers for my table, bringing, in his train,
> Honor in Pucci, Guccis, and Sassoon
> Hair-do, a little younger-looking than
> I saw her last at twenty.
>   – from 'Pursuit of Honor, 1946'

Blah blah blah, and bling bling bling. Even then, none of the exclusive
stuff excluded anybody who could afford the tab, and it's all terribly
familiar to us now; but it was quite exciting at the time. Just not
quite exciting enough. In prose, social notation through the listing
of products had been taken a long way by John O'Hara, and J. D.
Salinger had already pushed it to its limit. (The limit is reached when
anybody can successfully parody the style except the author himself.) In poetry, Sissman was already mining the depths even while
he was getting famous for it. There is a big hint here that vocabulary
isn't enough: there has to be a phrase, and quite commonly to be too
fascinated with words is a bad preparation for the forming of phrases.
When not banging away with a stack of names out of showcase
magazines, Sissman could use words from other sources – restaurant
menus were a favourite – which told you all too well that he had no
real notion of connecting with his readers, except, perhaps, for the
purpose of leaving them with the nagging sense that they should get
out more:

> Aboard, they dine off Chincoteagues, Dover
> Sole (hock), endive, rare *entrecôte* (claret),
> And baked Alaska.
>   – from 'New York: A Summer Funeral'

Not only does it sound indigestible, the sound is indigestible. Sissman
had all kinds of gifts – including the rare one of cramming a socially

complex narrative into a small space – but he lacked the crucial one that makes you remember a poem. He could place a word so that it stopped you cold, wondering why you were bothering to read him at all. Since his vocabulary was so desperately modern – modern beyond now, more modern than tomorrow – we are forced to deduce that the crucial gift has something to do with establishing an impetus which draws the reader in, and along.

The most spectacular American poet at the moment for his use of blue-chip commercial properties is Frederick Seidel. One of those poets who get discovered late in life, he made things hard for himself by neglecting to write separately memorable poems. Instead he wrote, and still writes, poetry: poetry notable chiefly for its rich incidence of branded products so relentlessly top of the range that you and I could never reach them with all our credit cards combined. Now of advanced years, Seidel makes it clear that the writer behind the work still shares the same expensive tastes as the persona within it: like Malcolm Forbes in his dotage, Seidel goes everywhere by motorcycle, but the motorcycles in Seidel's case are masterpieces by Ducati, built like jewellery and described that way.

Eerily unruffled by the raging slipstream, his suits, when he arrives at his appointment with some young countess who leaves Sissman's Honor looking like a waitress, are from a firm of Italian tailors you won't have heard of. The same goes for his shoes: John Lobb of London produces work boots compared with the things on Seidel's feet. None of this, alas, sounds very far from product placement: for all the undoubted vigour of his urge to register the minutiae of the privileged life – like Cummings he started off with the support of money from home – there is a stickily over-made-up heaviness to the pictures he paints, rather like the sumptuous yet depressing visual odour that assails you when you flick through an issue of *Vanity Fair* in search of the articles among the glamour spreads: and somehow the articles, supposedly factual, seem less so in a context where not even Kate Winslet or Anne Hathaway is deemed quite perfect enough, and needs to have her waist trimmed and her legs lengthened. Photoshopping and airbrushing reduce things to an essence, but it is the essence of falsity.

The overload of high-society notation in Seidel's verse, however, would be less onerous if he could more often develop his phrases into lines. Despite his unfortunate propensity for kiddie rhymes, he can do phrases that pull you in like an Inuit fisherman whose hook is suddenly taken by a killer whale, but only very seldom do you find complete lines forming, and hardly ever does one line generate another, as it once did in an early poem called 'Morphine':

> What hasn't happened isn't everything
> Until in middle age it starts to be.

Seidel, if he had wanted to, could have done that in every poem; have made whole poems instead of piles of glittering fragments; and have never needed to regret being 'late for a fitting at Caraceni', whose *bottega* – but of course you knew – is situated in Milan. Reading Seidel now, in my own old age, it saddens me that I have spent my long life dressing like a student: like a slob, in fact. I should have put more art into the everyday. Seidel would have given us the makers of Auden's tigerish blazer and dove-like shoe. But he was never impressed enough that Auden didn't. Auden didn't need to give us the names, because he could give us the rhythm. In his greatest single short poem after the Second World War, 'The Fall of Rome', Auden carved one line after another that was as contemporary as a Boeing Stratocruiser yet as classical as the tomb of Augustus. The poem concluded with one of his most beautiful quatrains:

> Altogether elsewhere, vast
> Herds of reindeer move across
> Miles and miles of golden moss,
> Silently and very fast.

He didn't even say where the reindeer were: they were just elsewhere. The rhythm welded the now and the then together. Evocation needs more than notation: it needs impetus. You can't Just Add Hot Water And Serve. Looking back with as much penetration as I can now achieve with tired eyes, I think I must have guessed that already, during those days in Sydney when I walked around reciting E. E. Cummings to an audience of trees, traffic, and puzzled pedestrians. I didn't just go for the bric-a-brac satires and the crazily lush love lyrics, I went for lines that verged on nonsense. 'To eat flowers and not be afraid.' Not good advice in Australia, which has flowers you should be very afraid of indeed. But whatever he was talking about, even if it was nothing, his phonetic force drove whole poems into my head like golden nails. Fifty years later I'm still trying to figure out just how the propulsive energy that drives a line of poetry joins up with the binding energy that holds a poem together.

Interlude

Held together, if at all, by not much more than kiddie-rhymes, the poems of Frederick Seidel, though often fascinating from point to point, are mainly not poems at all, but instalments of a bulkier thing that we might call his poetry. I would call it a larger thing except that there is really nothing larger in the taxonomy of poetry than the poem. Though Seidel obviously doesn't think so, the ideal ought to be the separate artefact that the reader can take home. Seidel has a right to dissent from that ideal. After all, Wordsworth did. Wordsworth wrote 'Composed Upon Westminster Bridge', which we can all memorize in its entirety, but he also wrote the 'Immortality Ode', which we couldn't memorize in its entirety even if we tried. I personally know a poet who did memorize it, when he was young, but later on he forgot almost all of it except the bits that you and I remember too. Those memorable bits are surely the nub of the matter. It's about them that our judgements are made: we rate a poet by the brightness of a glimpse. It might be thought at first that the Odes of Keats make a nonsense of that idea. At one time or another I knew each of them by heart. But now, with age, I can risk confessing that I readily remember only the moments that excited my attention in the first place. If I want to join those moments up, I have to look at the text. The moments, it need hardly be said, beg for such treatment. When I first realized that the title of F. Scott Fitzgerald's novel *Tender Is the Night* was drawn from the 'Ode to a Nightingale', I went back to the text and learned everything else that gave a context to the phrases and lines I had remembered. In another Keatsian Ode, the 'Ode on Melancholy', the same thing happened because of the tenaciously memorable phonetic force of a single idea: 'Then glut thy sorrow on the salt-sand wave.' The three stresses for the three syllables of 'salt-sand wave' worked like drumbeats around the tempo. And so on with the other Odes, with all of which I have always been familiar. But I am always forgetting them as well as remembering. This might have something to do with a protective mechanism, a mental machine to ward off the inhibiting effect of having a head full of too much perfect poetry by other people. Leaving aside the question of whether it might not be even worse to remember too little, it still might be best to accept that you won't get much of your own done if your memory is overstocked, and it might therefore be desirable to maintain your store of remembered poetry in the form of fragments, a set of potentialities, splinters from a surface that imply a form. Memorizing a poem is a form of hero worship, to which there has to be a limit. Maria Sharapova, to help perfect her service action, watched videos of Pete Sampras over and over. But not forever. Eventually she had to try it for herself.

TECHNIQUE'S MARGINAL CENTRALITY

At the court of the Shogun Iyenari, it was a tense moment. Hokusai, already well established as a prodigiously gifted artist, was competing with a conventional brush-stroke painter in a face-off judged by the shogun personally. Hokusai painted a blue curve on a big piece of paper, chased a chicken across it whose feet had been dipped in red paint, and explained the result to the shogun: it was a landscape showing the Tatsuta River with floating red maple leaves. Hokusai won the competition. The story is well known but the reaction of the conventional brush-stroke artist was not recorded. It's quite likely that he thought Hokusai had done not much more than register an idea, or, as we would say today, a concept. A loser's view, perhaps; though not without substance. If Hokusai had spent his career dipping chickens in red paint, he would have been Yoko Ono. But Hokusai did a lot more, and the same applies to every artist we respect, in any field: sometimes they delight us with absurdly simple things, but we expect them to back it up with plenty of evidence that they can do complicated things as well. And anyway, on close examination the absurdly simple thing might turn out to be achieved not entirely without technique. Late in his career Picasso would take ten seconds to turn a bicycle saddle and a pair of handlebars into a bull's head and expect to charge you a fortune for it, but when he was sixteen he could paint a cardinal's full-length portrait that looked better than anything ever signed by Velázquez. You can't tell, just from looking at the bull's head, that it was assembled by a hand commanding infinities of know-how, but you would have been able to tell, from looking at Hokusai's prize-winning picture, that a lot of assurance lay behind the sweep of blue paint, and that he had professionally observed floating red maple leaves long enough to know that the prints of a chicken's red-painted feet would resemble them, as long as the chicken could be induced to move briskly and not just hang about making puddles.

When we switch this test apparatus to poetry, we arrive quickly at a clear division between poets who are hoping to achieve something by keeping technical considerations out of it, and other poets who want to keep technique out of it because they don't have any. R. F. Langley, one of the school of poets around Jeremy Prynne, died in 2011. As an adept of that school, he had put many dedicated years into perfecting the kind of poem whose integrity depends on its avoiding any hint of superficial attraction. Part of one of his poems was quoted in tribute by the *Guardian* obituarist, himself an affiliate of the Prynne cenacle. It was instantly apparent that the poet had succeeded in all his aims:

> We leave unachieved in the
> summer dusk. There are no
> maps of moonlight. We find
> peace in the room and don't
> ask what won't be answered.

Impeccably bland, resolutely combed for any hint of the conventionally poetic, its lack of melody exactly matched by its lack of rhythm, Langley's poem had shaken off all trace of the technical heritage, leaving only the question of whether to be thus unencumbered is a guarantee of novelty. Hard not to think of how far modern poetry has come since T. S. Eliot continually improved his technical command in order to make his effects by leaving it unemphasized, a vastly different approach to the question:

> They are rattling breakfast plates in basement kitchens,
> And along the trampled edges of the street
> I am aware of the damp souls of housemaids
> Sprouting despondently at area gates.
> > – from 'Morning at the Window'

To write a stanza like that, with no end-rhymes but with a subtle inter-play of interior echoes, the poet, we tend to assume, needed to be able to write the rhymed stanzas of 'Sweeney Among the Nightingales', and then sit on the knowledge. At the time it was written, even the most absolute of enthusiasts for modern poetry would have hesitated to point out the truth – that the stanza was held together by its rhyth-mic drive – unless he further pointed out that it was also held together by the sophisticated assiduity with which it didn't rhyme. In other words, the whole of English poetry's technical heritage was present in Eliot's work, and never more so than when it seemed free in form. But since that time, there has been a big shift in belief, and we are living with the consequences now. Ezra Pound might have insisted that only a genius should excuse himself from traditional measures, but he soon decided that he himself was a genius, and several generations of his spiritual descendants either felt the same about themselves or – much more likely – took the new liberties more and more for granted as time went on. The moderns not only conquered the fields of art, they conquered the fields in which art is thought about. The idea that form can be perfectly free has had so great a victory, every-where in the English-speaking world, that the belief in its hidden technical support no longer holds up. Or rather, and more simply, the idea of technique has changed. It is no longer pinned to forms. If few territories go quite so far as Australia, where it is generally held to be unlikely that a poem can be formally structured and still be modern, nevertheless the general assumption that beginning poets had to put in their time with technical training, like musicians learning their scales, is everywhere regarded as out of date. This near-consensus is wrong, in my view, but you can see why it prevails. And it does have one big advantage. Though a poet who can't count stresses and syllables might write mediocre poetry, there is a certain kind of bad poetry that he won't write.

Every editor in the world knows what kind of bad poetry I am talking about. It arrives by the sheaf, by the bundle, by the bale. The poet, usually young, but sometimes in his old age, has discovered his power to rhyme, and what he thinks is rhythm. The editor, in his turn, discovers over and over that the more a poet's creativity might be lacking, the more his productivity will be torrential. The trouble with a really awful poem is not that its author lacks technique, but that his technique is fully expressed: whatever he can do, he does, especially if he has got past the early, drunken stages of finding rhymes and has entered the determined stage of making lists. Whole careers have been ruined by virtuoso exuberance, as when a tenor who can sing a clean top C spends all day singing nothing else, and leaves his chest voice in rags.

In the first half of the twentieth century, there was an accomplished poet in just that condition. He was the Australian émigré man of letters W. J. Turner. Having based himself in London, he had built up an enviable reputation as an expert on music: he was a valued friend of the great pianist Artur Schnabel, and his book about Mozart, still read today, was held to be in a class with the monograph by Alfred Einstein. But Turner was also a prolific Georgian poet, and in his prolificacy lay his ticket to oblivion. His work might have survived being wildly over-praised by Yeats, but it could not survive its own fluency. He had a certain success with a poem about the Aztecs. Studded with catchy pre-Colombian names, it was the sort of thing that could be recited after dinner in a drawing room. (On YouTube he can be seen reciting the poem himself, in an over-enunciated voice weirdly suggesting ectoplasm and planchette.) But in masses of other poems he overdid the catchiness, and everything in the poem was so attention-getting there was no way to recall it: the purposeless glitter was packed tight like a second-hand furniture dealer's storeroom full of chandeliers:

> In a sea Cytherean
> Billows are rolling, rolling, rolling
> Over stillness molybdenean
> Hung with the scrolling
> Abyss-plants whose fingers Chaldean
> Rock slumber under foam-froth where lumber . . .

Threatening always to give birth to Edith Sitwell like Venus in a sea-shell, even in its heyday such billowing foam-froth counted as high spirits at best, and in the long term a whole tradition was doomed by wordplay: you can hear why, a few decades down the line, the danger of making so much vapid noise should have driven the Prynne people to a Trappist vow of making no noise at all.

But on at least one occasion Turner wrote differently, and it was probably because he was in the grip of a real emotion. It was a case of the *visione amorosa*, in that especially painful version when the ageing man finds himself suddenly longing for the unattainable young woman. His title, 'Hymn to Her Unknown', betrays all his usual deafness (Hymn to Her Unknown What?), but the text itself, from the first line to the last, is fully judged, with no sign of automatism. He starts by setting the scene of a memory:

> In despair at not being able to rival the creations of God
> I thought on her
> Whom I saw on the twenty-fourth of August nineteen thirty-
>   four
> Having tea in the fifth story of Swan and Edgar's
> In Piccadilly Circus.

From then on, throughout the barely fifty lines of his tiny epic, his sole apparent trick is to go on raising the level of the diction, from the biblical through the heroic to the ecstatic. The unapparent tricks are many – he really did know how to balance a line – but they are all camouflaged in support of this main strategy, which he sensibly doesn't vary until the last stanza, when a few rhymes are allowed in as evidence of the effort it has taken to keep them out. The young lady is married, she has her child with her, and clearly, though she knows the poet is watching her, nothing he could do would alter her life as she might alter his if she so chose. Such is the powerful combination of her beauty and moral character that he can't describe her adequately, even with his language at full stretch:

What is the use of being a poet?
Is it not a farce to call an artist a creator,
Who can create nothing, not even re-present what his eyes
    have seen?

But of course in calling her indescribable he has described her, and
has defined a moment that we will all grow better at recognizing as
we grow older. The poet will be born again, and so will the young
woman that he adores. It is a stunning poem to have been almost
entirely forgotten. One of the questions the poem raises, however, is
whether Turner really had to learn all that tricky stuff he did elsewhere just to increase the effect of leaving it out here. With T. S. Eliot
the results of his formal work are so sharp that we can take it for
granted that the acquired skill helped to make his informal work
even sharper, although really we are betting on a case of correlation
as causation. But by now we have seen so many successful informal
poems that we must contemplate the possibility that there is such a
thing as an informal technique, in which it is no longer necessary
to count stresses or master any regular stanza. Most poets now will
never feel called upon to make a poem *look* organized. Those who do
feel the call often produce results so clumsy that we are tempted to
conclude that the thing can't be done without practice. But this again
might be an unwarranted assumption: maybe those particular poets
just haven't got the knack. This concession would leave room for the
further possibility that some poets do have the knack but it hasn't
shown up because they haven't felt called upon to exploit it.

Here we are perilously close to the pestiferous Lucy, the *Peanuts*
character who thought she could play the piano like her little friend
Schroeder if she just knew which keys to press down. Unfortunately
for any dreams of critical simplicity, such a fantasy is not empty. There
are some who are ignorant yet can perform prodigies, educating themselves with frightening speed as they go. Nobody devoid of a proper
musical education is ever going to saw away in a scratch orchestra and
produce a theme from Bach. Performance skill is too great a factor.
But in poetry, the performance skills for organizing chains of words

into forms seem often to be lying around piecemeal in the linguistic attainments of tyros who have never learned to count a stress. In a phrase that we tend to avoid because it doesn't sound precise enough, they have a feel for it.

In the Guggenheim Museum on Fifth Avenue you can see a nightclub scene by Picasso that proves he mastered the whole heritage of the Impressionist painters in about a month. The important thing here is not to belittle an intrinsically complex process just because it betrays less overt effort than we think appropriate. Take one of the smallest and apparently most elementary of the standard poetic forms, the couplet. For the poet, the heroic couplet is a wickedly difficult frame in which to narrate. This being known to be true, a whole critical mythology has built up about what Dryden did to develop the trick that Pope perfected. But really, as a form, the couplet was perfected long before. Not even Herrick was the first to do it, although he was perhaps the best:

> Come, my Corinna, come; and, coming, mark
> How each field turns a street, each street a park.

When Pope, in *The Rape of the Lock*, turned couplets as light and neat as that, he got famous for it. Nobody remembers Herrick for seeing the possibilities because he never exploited them. His favoured form, even in the most frivolous lyric, was an argued paragraph rather than a ladder of couplets: in that respect he was strangely like the much more serious, much more holy George Herbert, who would invent some shapely little edifice of words in order to fit the structure of a thought, and then move on. For Herbert, the thought was the poetic substance. Unlike Donne, he wasn't distracted even by imagery. Herbert could do images, but they had to fit the argument. This purity of purpose makes Herbert the most metaphysical of all the poets we give that name. The name has been prominent since the first appearance of Grierson's anthology in 1921, and famous since Eliot sought amongst metaphysical poetry the hard antidote for flummery. But what Eliot learned best from Herbert, what we all learn, is how to argue; or rather, we learn that the argument is the action. The contemporary American poet Daniel Brown writes as if he were taking classes from Herbert once a week. Throughout his slim but weighty collection *Taking the Occasion*, Brown proves that for him the reasoning is in command of the imagery and not vice versa. Since practically the whole of the modern movement in poetry, as we have come to recognize it, was based on the notion that imagery ruled, Brown's priorities would seem wilfully archaic if not for the functionality of his neatness, which reminds us that his hero Herbert, thinking as he went, necessarily operated in the here and now.

Reasoning is as contemporary an activity as you can get. In his poem 'On Being Asked by Our Receptionist If I Liked the Flowers', Brown makes capital out of explaining, for himself and us, the mental process by which the vase of lilies she was referring to had been condemned by her existence to the status of 'A splendor I'd have seen for sure, / If less employed in seeing her.' Herbert would have approved of how the image arose from the idea, and of the compactness of the wrapping: a couplet hard at work through making itself look easy.

Contrary to more than a hundred years of steadily accumulating scholarly opinion, Pope never made the couplet look easy, even at his most frolicsome. His social poems fit into a plaster and glass pavilion as though part of the furniture, but they are under a greater strain than their surroundings: an internal strain. Heroic couplets are closed, and the closure exerts pressure even when nothing much is being conveyed except atmosphere. When a reasoned argument is being conveyed, the pressure can split the pipes. It was recognized even at the time that the vaunted logical progression of 'Essay on Man' was a succession of limps and stumbles in mechanical shoes. By his very diligence, Pope proved that his favoured form's self-contained refinement was a clumsy vehicle for argument. Except when expressible in an individual aperçu, thought is seldom self-contained. Probably for that reason, the mature Shakespeare usually confined his use of the couplet to clinching a scene. The couplet stops the action. Pope never took the hint.

Just before the First World War, George Saintsbury, in his little book *The Peace of the Augustans*, found the right language for disliking 'Essay on Man' and also went deeper to spot something inflexible about the heroic couplet in itself: Pope's rigorously observed caesura, the central pause of the line, formed a 'crease down the page'. But really the heroic couplet had already been practically, if not critically, undone in the day of its domination, by poets who wished to keep the rhyme of the couplet but not its self-containment. Charles Churchill is not much thought of now, but his popularity at the time depended on his knack for making the couplet spring along instead of hanging about. Instead of being buttoned up at the end of the second line, the syntax of a so-called 'romance' couplet ran on into the couplet that came next. Samuel Johnson, rigorously formal author of 'The Vanity of Human Wishes', would have been horrified at the thought of letting a couplet do that; and Oliver Goldsmith, whose accomplishments as a poet Johnson rightly revered, wrote his masterpiece *The Deserted Village* without slipping out of the heroic frame even once. (At the author's invitation, Johnson even contributed a few couplets to Gold-smith's poem, and they fit right in: you can hardly see the join.)

But the new possibilities provided by the romance couplet were now there, and in the nineteenth century Browning made authoritative use of them to create the proudly demented narrative fluency deployed by the narrator of 'My Last Duchess'. Unimpeded by enforced caesura or end-stopped second line, the Duke's suavely heightened conversational virtuosity, as if emanating from the carefully trimmed beard of Vincent Price by firelight, doubles the impact when we realize that he is as nutty as a fruitcake. He killed her. Stop him before he kills again.

It is an open question which form of the couplet demands the more technique, heroic or romance. All we can be sure of is that each version demands plenty. Perhaps the romance couplet always demanded most, as it headed towards the freedom we enjoy now, in which we persuade ourselves that freedom from all predictability equals the perfectly expressive. Whether they stop and start or flow forward in a paragraph, couplets require their author to put his syllables and stresses in all the right places. Rhyming is the easy part of the job, and even that turns out to be devilishly hard after the initial spasm of euphoria. A first-timer is likely to go back to his opening night's work and despair of life, let alone of his poetic hopes. But here as always we must be careful not to underestimate the speed of assimilation that can be induced by the urgency of an idea. After the Second World War there was a show-stopping example of instantaneously acquired mastery when Vladimir Nabokov published *Pale Fire*, a work which revolves around a thousand-line poem composed in couplets. A tour de force of fake history and pseudo-scholarship, the book would have been daunting enough had the poem been clumsy. But it was perfect.

Perfect, or nearly so. A professional might have niggled that in line 497 ('In the wet starlight and on the wet ground') the second 'the', which ought to be stressed but can't be, dictates a needlessly attention-getting departure from strict rhythm; but otherwise scarcely a foot had been wrongly placed. The sweetly flowing tide of romance couplets even had fully formed heroic couplets occasionally decorating them, like candles floating on the water:

> The little scissors I am holding are
> A dazzling synthesis of sun and star.

There could be no objecting to that. Here was the occasion for the astonished reader to remember that Nabokov was a neophyte poet only in English. In Russian he had been an expert, and all the Russian expert poets are expert technicians, because Pushkin, the supreme technician, sets the historic pace. Nevertheless, Nabokov had pulled this marvel out of his hat the first time, a rabbit as big as a freight train. How was it possible?

The only answer is that he did it because he wanted to. He had had an idea about a prominent American poet being stalked by a conceited scholar who was really a wacko European monarch on the run, and for the screwball plot to work he needed a poem: so he wrote one. The urge had preceded the accomplishment, as it always must. If Nabokov had been writing a treatise on English prosody, it would not have led him to write the poem in *Pale Fire*. Technique is a subservient impulse. One of the ways we know this to be true is the mess that ensues when fashion makes it a dominant one, and artists in all fields start shoving stuff in just because they can do it. Critics become more useful when they learn to appreciate that the creative urge leading to a work of art may be a complex, irreducible compound of the impulse to get something new said and the impulse to get a new technique into action. But the second component should always attend upon the first, even when, as so often happens with a poem, a technical possibility is the first thing to hit the page. The possibility won't go far unless the constructive urgency takes over. The point is proved, rather than otherwise, by the poets who gush technique but hardly ever write a poem.

Turner's 'Hymn' was, and is, a unicorn raised among a herd of horses. Since the poem is impossible to find even on Google, I am very conscious at this point that I should get ahead with my long-cherished project to edit an anthology of one-off poems, by poets who wrote only one hit among their many duds, or never wrote anything except the hit. I have several titles for the book – 'They Never Had a Chance' and 'Poems of the Doomed' are two of them – but publishers want names, and names are usually what such poets don't have, even the productive ones, buried while they breathed under the tumulus of their own output.

It can take a long time for a poet to build a name, but once the name is built it affects everything, like gravity. In 2008 Elizabeth Bishop's copy of *Jude the Obscure*, in the Modern Library edition, came up for sale on the second-hand book market. The mere presence of her ownership signature on the flyleaf would already have put the price up, but putting the price through the roof was the presence in one of the endpapers of the draft for a poem. Never mind for the moment what such a rare occurrence says about the confluence of art and commerce. Let's just marvel at what it says about poetry and criticism. Here, we may be sure, is the clearest proof that we are dealing, down there at bedrock level, with an urge as strong as life, if no more simple. She was out somewhere without her notebook, and she had an idea. It couldn't wait, so she started writing it down on the only blank paper available. Any poet will read about this, scan his crowded bookshelves with a sad eye, remember the number of times he was caught by the same fever, and wonder if some book he once owned will ever be news because he scribbled in it. The chances are that it won't. But that's the chance that makes the whole deal more exciting than Grand Slam tennis. Unless you can get beyond yourself, you were never there.

Interlude

There is a dangerous half-truth that has always haunted the practice and the appreciation of the arts: too much technique will inhibit creativity. Despite constant evidence that too little technique will inhibit it worse, the idea never quite dies, because it is politically too attractive. Young women are usually less susceptible, but young men are often pleased to think that their creative activities would flourish best if they could spend more time getting up late in the morning and taking a longer nap during the afternoon. Hence the continuing popularity of Blake's emphasis on just letting art happen, without too much sweat. In Blake's case some of his lyrics are well enough crafted to prove that he had practice, but his general stance was to assert the value of spontaneity. In other fields than poetry, some of the energy of Mussorgsky's *Boris Godunov* is thought to have been drawn from the technical ignorance by which his orchestrations needed Rimsky Korsakov to finish them off, and some of the primitive appeal of Le Douanier Rousseau, who so impressed Picasso, is thought to have sprung from the fact that he didn't really know how to paint. These are wishful thoughts – indeed they are misinterpretations – but they are bound to thrive, because the know-how of any art form takes determination to acquire. Even though nobody can expect to master, without years of practice, a performing art such as playing the piano, there will still be the wish that music itself might be composed by an ignoramus. Back in the 1960s, a period which was a heyday for charlatanry, there was a brief vogue for the concept of a 'scratch orchestra', whereby a lot of people who knew nothing about music, but quite liked the idea of being musicians, would sit down together and hum on kazoos while they hit tin cans with sticks. It all went on for an unspecified time but the audience left almost immediately. Only the performers wanted to be there: a bad sign.

Scratch poetry is the kind of stuff that only its performers want to read. Nevertheless, despite conditions in which a limitless supply overwhelms an almost non-existent demand, the verbal waste paper piles up in drifts all over the world. For those who produce it, it answers a personal need. We must deduce that anything which stands out answers a need better than personal: it is something that has been put together so that it can exist by itself, and not just in reference to the person who signs it. Since there can be no putting together without technical assurance, technique will always be part of the poet's schooling. But the option of playing hookey is always available; and afterwards there is an excellent chance that a show of technique will be taken for the real thing. The absconder from the classroom should be advised, however, that approximate rhymes and arbitrary rhythms will not make the attempt at a set form seem more casual. The only way to hide the tensions of a set form is to perfect it.

A STRETCH OF VERSE

A stretch of verse can have quite a high yield of quotable moments but we still might not think of it as being in one piece, as something coherent and ready to be recited or even learned by heart. This rule of thumb can be brutally dismissive, but all too often it meets the facts. Nobody except a prisoner serving a life sentence learns Wordsworth's 'Immortality Ode' by heart. To think of it as the one thing, like any other poem you know and admire for itself, you would have to be sitting an examination. Yet it is well sprinkled with quotations. The distance between them gives us a measure of how long a stretch of verse can go on discouraging quotation without wrecking the poem in which it appears:

> The Rainbow comes and goes,
> And lovely is the Rose.

Occurring in the poem's second stanza, the line about the rainbow became famous enough to be raided, in the following century, for the title of a book by Lady Diana Cooper, *The Rainbow Comes and Goes*. Most people who bought the book would have known that it had a title from a poem, even if they didn't know that the poem was by Wordsworth. But nothing as catchy shows up in the next stanza or the next. 'Now, while the birds thus sing a joyous song' is so banal that it sounds Wordsworthian in the sense we have learned to dread, and 'Land and sea/ Give themselves up to jollity' is of interest only because he is saying the world is merry while he isn't. 'I hear, I hear, with joy I hear!' The tiptoed ecstasy would be pretty hard to bear if we didn't suspect that he was preparing us for the revelation of a contrary mood lurking underneath. The mood breaks through with a quotable couplet:

> Whither is fled the visionary gleam?
> Where is it now, the glory and the dream?

The Visionary Gleam has been borrowed for a book title on occasion, but to no very stunning effect. William Manchester did better with *The Glory and the Dream*, which he used as the title of his 'Narrative History of America'. He would not have lifted the motto if it had not already become proverbial. The moment got into the language and so did several other of the poem's moments, even if they were only a phrase long. The 'Immortality Ode' is the home of the phrase 'the vision splendid', and there is yet more splendour in the couplet that begins to sum up the poem near the end:

> Though nothing can bring back the hour
> Of splendour in the grass, of glory in the flower.

The key phrase, a truly delicious mouthful, was the title of Elia Kazan's big film of 1961, *Splendor in the Grass*; and it was thus, while watching Natalie Wood resisting the perils of sex with Warren Beatty, that I finally got interested in Wordsworth, after several years of being bored by him. In my experience, poetry often gets into the mind through a side entrance. When, as a student, I saw a production of *Long Day's Journey into Night* in Sydney in the late fifties, I went home with my head ringing to the cadences not of Eugene O'Neill's dramatic prose, but of Ernest Dowson's lyric poetry, which is quoted often throughout the play, but could never be quoted often enough to suit me. 'They are not long, the days of wine and roses', I told my bathroom mirror. Yes, it was Wordsworthian, but every phrase was begging to be said. Dowson liked to keep things short: short and tight.

The 'Immortality Ode' is laid out like an essay. It has an argument, which can be paraphrased. But it also has moments that can't, and as we read we find it hard to resist the conviction that those moments ought to be closer together. We tend to deduce that even a poem that is laid out like an essay is trying to be a short poem. It just might not have the wherewithal. This wish for the thing to be integrated by its intensity seems to be fundamental, although it might be wise to allow for the possibility that it has taken the whole of historic time for the wish to become so clear to us. Reading the *Aeneid*, you would like the whole thing to have the compact intensity of the Dido sequence. But that idea plainly never occurred to Dante, who worshipped Virgil; and still less could it have occurred to Virgil.

•

In 1813 Byron, still only twenty-five years old, wrote a letter to his protectress and surrogate mother Lady Melbourne which gives a strong hint of the kind of poet he would be when, in what we call his maturity – he was only in his thirties – he came to write his master-piece *Don Juan*. In the letter he quotes a fragment of social verse which includes the couplet

> A King who *can't* – a Prince of Wales who *don't* –
> Patriots who *shan't* – ministers who *won't* –

And then, straight afterward in the same letter, he tells her that she may read the couplet this way if she likes:

> A King who *cannot* – & a Prince who don't –
> Patriots who *would not* – ministers who won't –

If we count syllables we find the second version smoother than the first. The point here is that Byron himself counted the syllables: he filled in the gaps to make the lines more fluently speakable. In that sense, he was a technical perfectionist from the beginning. It's just sometimes hard to spot because he was so colloquial. In a letter to Henry Drury he mentioned 'the floodgates of Colloquy': fair evidence that he was attuned to the impetus of conversation. His best poetry is good talk based on knowledge, and even his finest poetic phrases are something he might have said. Certainly he might have written them in a letter, or in a journal. In the Alpine Journal of 1816 we find a glacier 'like a frozen hurricane'. Armed with this triple ability to observe something, remember it, and turn it to poetic account, he had every right, in a letter to Leigh Hunt, to deplore Wordsworth's tendency to make things up when he hadn't seen them.

•

When he started off as a poet, Seamus Heaney had the inestimable advantage of having been born and raised where hard work was done. The textures and odours of the farm and dairy were in his blood, and they got into his first poetry as a seemingly inexhaustible supply of imagery. Later on, Heaney gave a lot of credit to Patrick Kavanagh as an influence, but it seems likely that he had it by nature, and had it to burn. When he described a spade digging into the peat, you could see it and hear it. In the long day's work of churning butter, he could see the whole process with a specificity of memory that no literary description could have equalled, except perhaps his. Later on, as he got successful, his work was less impregnated with these memories, and some of us thought that he was running thin. If we were wise, we knew that it was only the difference between gold and beaten gold; and anyway, it wasn't necessarily true. Occasionally he would put in a moment to remind you that his best poems had always been beyond mere notation. He could still do the grand metaphor. In his poem 'Shore Woman' he is out fishing for mackerel at night in a low boat when he and his friend suddenly realize they have company:

> I saw the porpoises' thick backs
> Cartwheeling like the flywheels of the tide,
> Soapy and shining.

'Soapy and shining' counts as notation: he could have put it in a note-book, had the circumstances been conducive. But 'the flywheels of the tide' are metaphorical in the most transformative and connective sense of the word: they make the sea a giant engine. At such a time we have the right, indeed the obligation, to bring out the word 'vision'. These effects are open only to the visionary poet. And once again we have to ask ourselves whether we are wrong to wish them packed tighter together, with all connective matter compressed or excluded. Such an impulse was probably behind the advent of so-called 'Martian' poetry, which seemed like a terrific idea at the time: all climax and no build-up. In the seventies and eighties Martian poetry was the dominant poetic tone in Great Britain: exponents such as Craig Raine seemed to see anything as looking like something else. But after Martian poetry became a drug on the market it grew apparent that it might be better to have the narrator rowing out in his little boat to catch the mackerel, before the porpoises dramatically appear.

•

Keats lived for such a short span – ten years less even than Byron, who, we ought to remember, died tragically young – that it might strike us as absurd when scholars talk of his 'development'. But rereading Keats late in my life, I find more and more that everything that came before the dazzling batch of Odes is a development leading up to them: and then *The Fall of Hyperion*, written after them, still leads up to them. Though his first book, *Poems*, was a flop, there were always people who could tell he was promising: to anyone with a palate, the succulence of his phrasing was unmistakable. Yet even the longer poems that were meant to be masterpieces have a tentative air when put beside the short poems of his magic year 1819. To put it bluntly, we might conceivably study *Endymion* in order to read the Odes, but we wouldn't study the Odes in order to read *Endymion*. The smaller structure is the more integrated. In *Endymion* there are some seductive lines about a nightingale but they do not add up to the Ode on the same subject:

Thou wast not born for death, immortal Bird!

Barely out of my teens, I said it to the same bathroom mirror that had served me so well when I recited Dowson. 'They are not long, the weeping and the laughter.' Suddenly Dowson's death-knell poem seemed to embody a Keatsian sentiment, one of those fateful premonitions of which the Odes were so brim full, all the more poignant for being packed so tight. In the Odes, if the hero does any languishing, he can do it in a line: in *Endymion* or *The Fall of Hyperion* he goes on for a page.

We can't call this superiority of the short form a law because it isn't always true, and is sometimes conspicuously false. Important though Dante's lyric poems are, we study them in order to read the *Divine Comedy*, not the other way around. But the *Divine Comedy* is not only larger; when taken as a whole it is at least as compact as any of the minor poems. The *Divine Comedy* is a poem in epic form. It is said that there is always someone in Italy who can recite the whole thing from memory, but to believe this you have to take it for granted that someone, book in hand, spent many hours sitting with the reciter in order to check up. Nevertheless the urban legend is indicative of a quality. That it can be got by heart is one of the ways we tend to define a poem. When I arrived in London in the early sixties, Keats's 'Ode to a Nightingale', in a fair copy written in his own hand, was still on display in a glass case in his house. I got it almost by heart – 'almost' because it is very tricky to memorize – and can still recognize any phrase from it. It has always been raided for book titles but Scott Fitzgerald picked the plum: *Tender is the Night*. When my mind plays tricks, it assigns that phrase to the 'Ode on Melancholy': my favourite among the Odes, and indeed among all poems by anybody. And he was just a boy.

•

Ungaretti said that the touchstone of poetry was the hammered phrase within the singable scheme. Since he himself occasionally produced poems that were barely a phrase long, we might think that he turned an ideal into a fetish: but surely he was right about everybody else. Poets do their best to pick and mount a phrase so that it will generate music, both within itself and within the structure to which it contributes. Our objection to so much Victorian verse, and to what happened next, is that the phrases went clunk. When they rang clean, that particular small stretch of verse was often singled out later on, in the modern age, as an example of how poetry could defy its time. For just that reason, everyone still admired Tennyson. Eliot, to get his admiration within bounds, had to say that Tennyson had no brains.

Tennyson was a notable example of poetry getting into my mind by a side door. My science fiction phase lasted years and started early: I had SF books piled high long before I enrolled as a student at Sydney University. One of my favourites was John Wyndham's *The Kraken Wakes*, which quotes Tennyson's short poem 'The Kraken' as an epigraph. 'In roaring he shall rise and on the surface die.' I was entranced – it was good, solid, horror-show romanticism, worthy of being recited into the bathroom mirror – and therefore I was very ready to follow up on Tennyson when his *Idylls of the King* got a mention in first year English. I only just enjoyed it, and one of my teachers told me there was a reason: Tennyson's lengthy capital work was stretched far beyond its content, and to see how the same material could drive an epic I should read Malory. He was right. He had also set a teaching standard which I have ever since tried to follow: never discourage a student from reading something unless you can encourage them to read something better.

•

Philip Larkin once said that the influence of Yeats could be all-pervasive, getting into everything like the smell of garlic. Yet although we can recognize Yeats's influence on Larkin's monumental stanza forms (judged by the size and capacity of the stanza, 'The Whitsun Weddings' is a bigger poem than 'All Souls' Night') we don't often recognize the echo of Yeats's voice. The voice that got into early Larkin wasn't the voice of Yeats or even of Hardy, the poet he loved best. It was the voice of Auden:

> So you have been, despite parental ban
> That would not hear the old demand again;
> One who through rain to empty station ran.
>   – from 'So you have been, despite parental ban'

It's Larkin, but every construction in it is taken from Auden. One way or another, all the poets of the thirties and forties reacted to Auden, either by rejecting him or trying to absorb him. Even Empson, the most original poet of the thirties generation, was driven to parody; but really 'Just a Smack at Auden' is an act of homage.

> Waiting for the end, boys, waiting for the end.
> What is there to be or do?
> What's become of me or you?
> Are we kind or are we true?
> Sitting two and two, boys, waiting for the end.

In Larkin's generation, the most conspicuous victim of Auden's tone was Kingsley Amis. The case is especially fascinating because later on, when he had shaken Auden's influence off, Amis became so distinctive: a voice recognizable after a single stanza. But in his early work a single stanza was likely to be riddled with Audenesque effects:

> But love, once broken off, builds a response
> In the final turning pause that sees nothing
> Is left, and grieves though nothing happened here.

So close to Auden that it sounds as if it might be stolen, 'the final turning pause' is one of the many examples in early Amis of fine phrases that tried to cash in on Auden's knack for a resonant vagueness. Amis, who had a keen ear for a phrase, probably caught himself at it long before he quit, but he kept doing it because everybody else did. Auden's influence had been so immense that younger poets thought he had changed the weather.

•

It is always as if Auden has just arrived. He was the hero of the most conspicuous recent example of poetry getting in by a side entrance. The movie *Four Weddings and a Funeral*, which quotes

Auden's poem 'Funeral Blues', sent a lot of people away in search of more poetry by the same author. Faber made sure that their wish was satisfied. You could say that the film's popularity created an artificial market, but the poem would not have been in the movie if its writers had not been true Auden fans. Similarly, it was out of love for the poems that the creators of the musical *Cats* set about converting Eliot's *Old Possum's Book of Practical Cats* into a stage spectacle. My younger daughter, when I took her to see the show, was as happy as any human being I have ever seen. It was her second time, so she had already learned the words, and sang them silently along with the actors. Faber participated in the profits of the enterprise. Any publisher would like to do the same. It's comforting to say that poetry never makes any money but the chastening truth is that when it does it makes a mint, although seldom for the poet, who has already passed unto Parnassus, where the accommodation seldom reaches the standards of a Holiday Inn even on the higher slopes.

•

Milton trained himself from early on to clog any passage of his verse with learned references:

> Nymphs and Shepherds dance no more
> By sandy *Ladon's* Lillied banks;
> On old *Lycaeus* or *Cyllene* hoar.

By the time he reached the great poems, there seemed no stopping the mechanism by which he crammed into them their high quota of learned unreadability. Yet things could have been different. Near the end of *Paradise Regained*, at the eleventh hour, we find the line:

> Aim therefore at no less than all the world.

It is Satan, tempting Christ. Untouched by the italics that denote a classical reference, the line is perfectly speakable, even conversational.

Is there anyone among Milton's most diehard admirers who does not, coming across a line like that, wish that all of Milton were like that? Among poets I know who profess to admire Milton, I have never found even one who did not quote Shakespeare more often. But this is a dangerous theme. When T. S. Eliot professed to have acquired a respect for Milton to replace his earlier aversion, F. R. Leavis accused Eliot of treason. Leavis wanted Milton's reputation kept down. That was a long time ago, but the air is still smouldering in the corridors of English faculties all over the world. And I suppose Milton emerged unscathed from the battle. Certainly it is powerful evidence of his worth that Harold Bloom once proved to Charlie Rose that he could be given a starting point anywhere in *Paradise Lost* and go on to recite the rest of it. But was there somebody standing by with a copy of the book?

●

Dryden had a name for the happy phrase that came unbidden: he called it a hit. 'These hits of words a true poet often finds, as I may say, without seeking; but he knows their value when he finds them, and is infinitely pleased.' It is hard to think of Philip Larkin howling for joy except possibly at the sound of a clarinet solo by Pee Wee Russell, but he must have been infinitely pleased when the last lines of 'The Whitsun Weddings' occurred to him. That uniquely powerful little stretch of writing is all hits:

> There we were aimed. And as we raced across
> Bright knots of rail
> Past standing Pullmans, walls of blackened moss
> Came close, and it was nearly done, this frail
> Travelling coincidence; and what it held
> Stood ready to be loosed with all the power
> That being changed can give. We slowed again,
> And as the tightened brakes took hold, there swelled
> A sense of falling, like an arrow-shower
> Sent out of sight, somewhere becoming rain.

Of those three linked hits at the very end, the second one, 'sent out of sight', strikes me as the miracle among the miracles, because somehow it gets in the sense of the longbows being lifted and the strings let loose. At the start of the line, the phrase is perfectly placed. It's a fine example of a phrase finding its poem: the hammered phrase helping to generate the singable scheme.

Being in the right spot can make a phrase powerful even when it might seem frail heard on its own. Consider the placing of Louis MacNeice's lovely phrase 'the falling London rain'. It comes at the very end of his poem 'London Rain' and seems to concentrate all the phonetic force of the poem:

> My wishes now come homeward,
> Their gallopings in vain;
> Logic and lust are quiet,
> Once more it starts to rain.
> Falling asleep I listen
> To the falling London rain.

This is the least obvious version of the hit: when ordinary words become extraordinary because they are in the right spot. The most obvious version is when one or more of the words is doing strange work. When Auden saw the proofs of one of his poems he found that the printer had saddled him with 'and the ports have names for the sea' when what he had written was 'and the poets have names for the sea'. He decided to stick with the misprint because it was less predictable.

But the Auden hits that really stun us happen when a whole phrase gets transformed by its new use:

> The earth turns over, our side feels the cold.

By a mental mechanism that can only be guessed at, he saw the connection between the Earth turning and himself turning over in bed.

With the second phrase, 'our side feels the cold', guessing becomes entirely inadequate. Does he mean that our side of the bed is a simile for Europe torn by politics? Better for the reader to just enjoy the feeling of disorientation – or rather, of being oriented toward everywhere, a sliding universality. After the war Auden wrote a masterpiece of a lyric that was all hits from start to finish: 'The Fall of Rome'. Since there isn't a line in it that does not demand quotation, the poem is a cinch to learn. But few poems are packed as tight as that with memorable moments. Quite early in *Endymion* we come across

> Now while the silent workings of the dawn
> Were busiest.

The cadence is unforgettable, but there is nothing else like it for miles on either side. It's a hit. One can imagine a critical work of great length which would consist of nothing but hit moments extracted from poems from the beginning of time, with a paragraph attached to each quoted moment speculating on how it came into the poet's mind. An entertaining book, perhaps, and an enticing introduction to poetry: but as for the critical content, speculation is all that it would be. The truth is that Seamus Heaney had no clue where he got his picture of the porpoises as the flywheels of the tide: it was just something he could always do and the other boys couldn't.

•

Looking back through these pages, I catch myself in a posture about the 'Ode on Melancholy'. Like any other work of literature, it is my favourite only when I am reading it. One of the characteristics of a work of art is to drive all the other works of art temporarily out of your head. If comparisons come flooding in, it means that the work's air of authority is a sham. No such fears with the 'Ode on Melancholy', which, at the time I first went mad about it, I could recite from memory – well, almost. In the matter of memorization, length sets severe limits. Hence the absurdity in the final scene of the movie Truffaut made out of Ray Bradbury's supposedly prophetic dystopian novel *Fahrenheit 451*. People walk around in the forest reciting *Anna Karenina*, etc. A nice idea, but wishful thinking, even when applied to poems. In the old Soviet Union, where, for obvious reasons, there was a great emphasis on memorizing contemporary poems, the manuscript still counted. People remembered things only until they could get them safely written down.

Interlude

When Don Paterson asked me to write an introductory essay for Picador's projected collection of Michael Donaghy's critical writing, I saw immediately how such a piece might fit into a Poetry Notebook. So far I had several times touched upon the connection between poetry and the criticism of poetry, but I had not pursued the matter. When talking about Donaghy, the subject was unavoidable. He had put the adult part of his short lifetime into resolving just those two forces: to create, and to understand. His career also raised the topic of the relationship, in modern times, between Britain and America, as it was acted out in the literary haunts of London. Questions of national origin need not necessarily play a crucial part in the appreciation of a poem, but they often play a part in the history of how poetry gets written. Donaghy never lost his American voice, but there was an element in his critical prose that might not have been expected: definitely not from Deadwood, he was a deep believer in the formal element. Even when they sounded casual, his poems were dedicated to that conviction. His work was an example of the daunting thoroughness by which Americans, when they put their minds to it, can be better at making our stuff than we are, starting with moleskin trousers and elastic-sided boots. Daunted though we might be, however, we need to remember that this branch of American cultural imperialism is no more threatening than a dream come true. We wanted a world of the arts, and we got it. Donaghy enjoyed the cultural paradoxes that came with international territory. Even beyond his untimely death, his every paragraph is alive with delight, as critical prose ought to be.

THE DONAGHY NEGOTIATION

First published as the introduction to
Michael Donaghy, *The Shape of the Dance*, 2009

Michael Donaghy's death at fifty was a cruel blow but he had already done enough as a writer of poetry to establish himself firmly among recent poets who matter. His achievement as a writer about poetry, however, is still in the process of being assessed and absorbed. The first and best thing to say about his critical writing, I think, is that it was necessary, even when that fact was not yet generally realized. If we can see now why his views on poetry were so vital, it is because they help us to recognize what was missing. Nobody else in his generation had such a generous yet discriminating scope. It is still the kind of scope we need, but now we have his example. He called true poetry 'the alchemical pay-off', and his criticism shows how prose can be that too.

Born only two years before Allen Ginsberg's *Howl* was published in 1956, Donaghy grew up as an Irish Catholic in New York at a time when American poetry was supposedly breaking its last bonds with the transatlantic formal tradition. He was never automatically contemptuous of the results that accrued to this final freedom. He just doubted its validity as an historical movement. Whether by instinct or from his training as a musician – questions of underlying psychology preoccupied him all his short life – he was suspicious of the idea that freedom from all restriction could yield perfect creative liberty. (He always insisted that even *Howl* was not the Whitmanesque 'barbaric yawp' that Ginsberg claimed, but a carefully worked and reworked artefact.) At Chicago University, where Donaghy edited the *Chicago*

Review and founded his music ensemble, he was already grappling with the critical questions that arose from a too confident assertion of American separateness.

In pursuit of his future wife, and perhaps also in pursuit of a more nuanced context in which to work, he moved to London in 1985, and steadily established himself as an imported expert who knew more than the locals. Actually this, too, was an American tradition that went back as far as Henry James, T. S. Eliot and Ezra Pound, not to mention the Eighth Air Force during the Second World War, but his presence was refreshingly new to a whole generation of young British poets who came to his classes. The impact of his own collections of poetry might have been enough to pull them in, but his powers as a mentor kept them glued to their chairs. There was a paradox in that. Donaghy never ceased to warn against the menace of the 'creative writing' industry on either side of the Atlantic: hundreds of creative writing teachers with nothing useful to say, thousands of creative writing students publishing first collections that would go nowhere.

But his British students knew that they had found a teacher who transcended his own suspicions. At least a dozen gifted young poets benefited from his combination of a broad sympathy and a tight focus on language: if they are now a school without a name, it was because he taught them the merits of unbelonging. He had an even wider field of influence, however, through the pieces he wrote for such outlets as *Poetry Review*. Many of these pieces, undertaken as journeywork at the time but always lavished with the wealth of his knowledge and the best of his judgement, are collected in this book, and it is remarkable how they coalesce into the most articulate possible expression of a unified critical vision. He was a crucially important reviewer, and my chief concern here is to say why.

When reviewing another poet, Donaghy relied first and foremost on his ear for loose language. Devoid, on paper at least, of malice or professional jealousy, he could nevertheless quote a dud line with piercing effect. Robert Bly thought he was being profound when he wrote: 'There's a restless gloom in my mind.' Donaghy could tell that whatever was happening to Bly's mind at that moment, it wasn't profundity. But he made such judgements a starting point, not a death sentence. What had the same poet written that was better? Donaghy could quote that, too. He was always searching for the language that had reached a satisfactory compression and power of suggestion. (It didn't have to come from 'the tradition', or even from a poem: he was a close listener to song lyrics, playground rhymes, and street slang.) When he found it in a poem, he had his principles to help him explain it.

To his chief principle he gave the name 'negotiation'. A sufficiently tense diction, the alchemical pay-off, was, Donaghy argued, most likely to be obtained from a contest between what the poet aimed to say and the form in which he had chosen to say it. If the poet tied the creative process down to his initial commitment, with no formal pressure to force him to the unexpected, there was no contest; and a contest there had to be, no matter how loose the form. Always a great quoter, Donaghy, on this point, quoted Proust to telling effect: 'The tyranny of rhyme forces the poet to the discovery of his finest lines.' The tyranny didn't always have to be of rhyme, but there had to be some tyranny somewhere. Negotiation was Donaghy's touchstone concept, and lack of negotiation was the reason why he thought an informal poem was even more likely to slide into banality than a formal one. When he found intensity within an apparently formless work, it was because the author had imposed some kind of discipline upon himself, locally if not in general. He found a good example in C. K. Williams, whose ten-beat loose lines had, in Donaghy's opinion, an underlying formal drive, proving that something concrete had been negotiated even when the poem steered towards abstraction. This capacity to find practical merit even in what he was theoretically against was a precious virtue.

It was matched by an equal capacity to find the limitations even in what he was theoretically for. John Updike's poetry was as formally virtuose as might be wished, but Donaghy thought that too much of it was too much so. There were too many poems that 'almost made it before the skill took over'. The implication was that a display of skill should not be an end in itself, even though to eschew skill altogether was a bad way of avoiding the danger.

In this way, Donaghy left a door open so that he could get back to the informal spontaneity of American modernism after William Carlos Williams and praise it where praise was due. His openness to the possible strength of the informal poem lent him the authority to say that the rewards from a formal poem could be greater, just as long as they had been properly negotiated. But he was always certain that the informal poem had far more dangerous ways of going rotten than the formal one. When the formal tradition decayed, the result was, at worst, sclerosis: a malady whose chief symptom he neatly summed up as 'rhyming in your sleep'. But the informal tradition in decay was an infinitely adaptable virus which would always try to pass itself off as the next development of the avant-garde. Donaghy the mighty quoter liked to revisit his favourite quotations, and the one that he revisited most often was from Auden. 'Everything changes but the avant garde.' But the witticism isn't the whole truth. The avant-garde does change, in its scope: it continually increases its territorial claims. Logically it should have run out of steam when the ne plus ultra stood revealed as the reductio ad absurdum sometime during the reign of Dada, but here we are, almost a hundred years later, and there are still poems exploding all over a full page in the *London Review of Books* like fine shrapnel, just as if Apollinaire had never done anything similar.

Donaghy, not very neatly for once, referred to such abjectly pos-turing stuff as L-A-N-G-U-A-G-E poetry. He was borrowing the title of the busy movement's home-base magazine, but he might have done better just to call it poppycock. Large-heartedly, he found enough time for this tirelessly self-propagating fad in which to decide that it added up to nothing. (His rejections were seldom immediate, but they were always decisive when they came.) Donaghy's British acolytes were not encouraged to follow the example of those established poets, often well protected within the academy, whose poetry is beyond criticism because it is about nothing except language. Donaghy wanted his young hopefuls to write negotiated poems, which are never just about language even when they say they are. Some of his modern models were British, or at any rate Irish: he said he didn't mind being asked to talk about 'Auden & Co' as long as it was understood that the 'Co' meant MacNeice. There was a whole teaching programme hidden in that one remark, because it will always be true that a neophyte stands to learn more from MacNeice than from Auden: it is useful, if frustrating, to try copying MacNeice's strictness, but it is fatal to try copying Auden's apparent nonchalance.

But for his British students and readers, Donaghy's most provocative models for the accomplished poem were Americans. His range of examples drew from the two great lines of achievement leading on from Whitman and Emily Dickinson but he lent no credence to schools, only to the intensity of the individual talent. In one of his reviews, he ascribed to Richard Wilbur 'the most flawless command of musical phrase of any American poet'. It's a mark of the consistent authority of Donaghy's critical prose that the confidence of such a judgement sounds precise, instead of just like a puff on a jacket. In the quarter of a century before Donaghy became active as a reviewer, the outstanding critical voice in London had been Ian Hamilton. Nobody wrote a better argument than Hamilton, but not even once did he say something like that about Wilbur, or indeed about anybody. Hamilton was strongest when he found weakness. Donaghy, in so many ways the heir to Hamilton's seals of office, was no more forgiving to lax expression, but far less inhibited about communicating enjoyment, instead of just leaving it to be inferred.

Donaghy was not immediately famous as a critic in Britain, whose citadels fall slowly. But he was immediately understood: the broad sympathy of his view travelled well. Especially he was understood by his young admirers, to whom he gave, by his guidance of their reading, the modern American poetry that matters. Indeed he gave them America, with the result that some of the best poems about America in recent years were composed in Britain by young writers who had got their standards for highly charged and musically cadenced language from him. We all enjoy such a coup as Frank O'Hara's poem about Lana Turner, and even those of us who think that John Ashbery has turned into a factory get a kick out of his classic poem about Daffy

Duck. But not even O'Hara or Ashbery ever wrote anything quite as good about American popular culture as John Stammers's poem 'The Other Dozier'. Once it would have been a sign of cultural subjection for Britain to claim that some of the best American poetry is written here. Now it sounds more like a simple claim to truth: the Atlantic has become an exchange of energy, and Donaghy is partly responsible.

He was also responsible, and more than partly, for ensuring that some of the best American criticism would be written here. He might have found it harder to write it at home, where any critic who publishes a limiting judgement is thought to be an assassin. In a previous generation, the same had been thought of Randall Jarrell, but in fact Jarrell could be adventurous and generous in his praise: nobody, not even Galway Kinnell when introducing his indispensable selection from Whitman, could do a better job than Jarrell of showing why the best lines and phrases from *Leaves of Grass* defied belittlement even at their most naive. Jarrell's strength as an appreciator, however, depended on his powers of discrimination, and that dependency will always be regarded with suspicion in America, where a critic sins against democracy if he finds some poets more valuable than others. Donaghy, who had already committed the same offence, probably did well to head for less tolerant climes. And after all, he brought the best American criticism with him, just as he brought the best American poetry. Donaghy the great quoter always paid his fellow American critics the tribute, with due acknowledgement, of reproducing their best lines. Thus we came to hear Dana Gioia's opinion that ideas in the poetry of Ashbery are 'like the melodies in some jazz improvisation where the musicians have left out the original tune to avoid paying royalties'. Donaghy knew he couldn't beat that, so he quoted it. But there were many occasions on which he matched it. He could deliver judgements in a way that people remembered, and for anyone who is capable of doing that, it really matters if he is right or wrong.

In his theoretical work it mattered less. Quite a lot of Donaghy's writing on psychology is included here. The incidental remarks are frequently valuable, but in the end there is no settling some of the conundrums about the functioning of the brain: or anyway, if they ever are settled, it probably won't be by a poet. Perhaps partly because of the traditional nostalgia of the lapsed PhD, science always fascinated him. He not only admired Coleridge, he emulated him, producing pages of text in which various parts of the argument go on in various frames, rather as *The Rime of the Ancient Mariner* grew annotations in the margin. But such pretensions to complex simultaneity weren't what made Coleridge a genius, they were what ensured his genius would never be coherent. Donaghy was in no such danger, because he knew what came first: the sayable, memorable, living poem, and his living response to it. Science didn't even come second. His repudiated but never forgotten Catholicism would have a better claim to the silver medal. When he talks about poetic truth, he just can't help mentioning the Elevation of the Host. Ritual was deeply embedded in him, like music. They were formal resources. But every resource of his mind and memory was in service to language, of which, both creatively and critically, he was a master. Had he lived, he would surely have done such great things that he would have been universally recognized as one the voices of his time, not only in poetry but in the understanding of it. Some of the reasons we can be so sure are in this book.

Interlude

Like his predecessor T. S. Eliot, Michael Donaghy was an American literary figure in London, but unlike Eliot he felt no compulsion to blend in. For the Americans who changed countries, it was always a big decision whether or not to go native. For the Australians, the decision was less momentous, perhaps because the locals cared less; the British don't feel usurped when an Australian takes over the store. In the years between the wars, the Australian man of letters W. J. Turner established himself in London with such thoroughness that, by the time I came to hear of him, I didn't realize that he had ever been Australian at all. My friend Peter Porter never tried to disguise his origins, and often used them in his poetry; but he made it clear that his mental map was European. Treating even Britain as a mere province of Christendom, he was as much at home in a Florentine church as he had ever been in a Brisbane pub. In the earlier part of his London career, Australian critics tended to regard him a traitor because he went, and British critics as a carpetbagger because he stayed. Porter's way of being uncaring was to be equally impatient about nationalist pressure from either side, but it added up to what looked like nonchalance, and I was pleased to emulate it when I could. I was careful, though, to remember my poetic origins. A. D. Hope's commanding use of the argued formal stanza remained a model, and even in Cambridge I went on collecting his books, although in his later work he was seldom at his best. Having lost control of his line, he debarred himself from writing anything like Auden's poem 'The Shield of Achilles', which sums up a technical mastery developed through decades. Having ruled out his own life as a subject, Hope would have been unable to contemplate a truly mature work such as Thom Gunn's 'The Man with Night Sweats', even had his sexuality permitted the topic. When he was young, he attracted press attention by writing poems in which he featured as quite the stud, but afterwards he went respectable. The typical late poem by Hope features minor characters from the classical catalogue acting out scenarios hard to identify even from Bulfinch or Lemprière.

James McAuley, another Australian poet whose example loomed over my desk from the beginning, was just as eager as Hope to devote his later career to pious generalities. Where Hope's were about mythology, McAuley's were about Catholicism; but they were equally bloodless. McAuley, however, never let go of his technical skill, and on at least one occasion, making a rare reference to his personal history, he created a poem in which true candour and delicious music blended impeccably. His work wasn't always that attractive, but with poetry our memories play an unfair trick that works out well: the outstanding becomes the typical.

THERE YOU COME HOME

One of Australia's great artistic treasures, James McAuley's poem 'Because' is only a slight thing physically. Ten spare quatrains in total, swinging lithely along on a lattice of conversational iambic pentameter, it is over almost as soon as begun. Yet for some of us Australians who were born and raised while the poet was still alive, his miniature masterpiece, during the ensuing decades, has done the work that the tiny Amalienburg pavilion at Nymphenburg does for anyone who lingers in its network of reflections for a while – for as long as possible, usually – and then goes away reassured that there is an eternal value in perfect making. It's the way the poem is built, indeed, that transmits its aesthetic charge.

The poem's actual argument – if it could be reduced to its bare prosaic bones, we would find the poet blaming his unhappiness on his parents – I have always found to be as depressingly bleak as McAuley's brand of Catholicism: a convert's brand which had a way of condemning his own weaknesses while leaving him free to pursue them, just as long as he sounded strict enough. McAuley's devotedly anti-communist politics were useful at the time, but this tinge of Jesuit worldliness was never attractive, no matter how winningly he may have played a honky-tonk piano after dark. (In Australia in those wowser-ridden days, it was often the Jesuits who had read *Ulysses*: after all, they travelled.) Two of Australia's best critical minds, Leonie Kramer and Peter Coleman, later devoted slim volumes to McAuley without even once making you like him. I myself, in my Sydney University days, saw him deliver a lecture about the newly published *Doctor Zhivago* and wondered ever afterwards how he could have been so alkaline on such a vital topic. From his dress and manner I would have said he was an accountant, except that he wasn't having enough fun. But if you look at 'Because' long enough you start to wonder if he didn't have the kind of personality, not to say intellect, that depended on form for its focus.

The poem, a late work, starts off by being about his dead parents. In the first stanza we are already led to suspect that this is a soul-curdling subject for him. The phrase 'a kind of love' gives us the evidence straight away: a valuable lesson in dramatic tactics, because very few poets ever learn to start the action early, as soon as the finger has been inserted in the listener's buttonhole.

> My father and my mother never quarrelled.
> They were united in a kind of love
> As daily as the Sydney Morning Herald,
> Rather than like the eagle or the dove.

And they're racing at Randwick: the traditional Australian radio announcer's way of saying that the game's afoot. Since we already know that there was something wrong with the way his parents were united, the first three lines of the second stanza come as no surprise. But the third line gives us another lesson, in how to expand an argument by internalizing it – by bringing it home to the soul.

> I never saw them casually touch,
> Or show a moment's joy in one another.
> Why should this matter to me now so much?

Any trainee poet amongst his readership would have been impressed by the boldness of this démarche, where the story suddenly turns into a rhetorical question. (It matters so much, we soon find, because the father who could not show love to his mother couldn't show much of it to him either.) But the trainee poet would have been floored already, by the technique, which even down at the level of the single word is setting a high standard. I can well remember putting aside all feelings of self-congratulation about how far I had got with forming regular quatrains when I saw what McAuley could do when filling a strict form with free rhythms. Auden could do it too, of course: the big story, technically, of Australia's 'Great Generation' of poets wasn't about what they recovered from their studies of Australia's literary heritage, it was about what they felt bound to emulate in the heat of international literary competition. But Auden was in America. Seeing McAuley do this kind of thing right there in one's homeland was like watching a world champion high diver at the local baths. (In fact I first read this particular poem after I had sailed for London, but the best things in his earlier career had prepared me for its neatness, if not for its full coherence.) The way, in the first line of the stanza, that the word *casually* stretches three syllables over two stresses is the purest lyricism – try saying it without singing it – and the stress on *moment's* in the second line imbues a loose line of conversation with all the disciplined metrical strictness of English literary history. Later on, in England, when I saw the same kind of structures in the poetry of Philip Larkin, I thought always of this line: an example of how your receptivity, by example, gets imprinted early on with a range of possibilities.

So there are two dramas going on here, even this early in the poem. There is the story of the lack of love between his parents, with the consequence (as he sees it) of an emotional stunting for a child not often enough picked up.

> Having seen other fathers greet their sons,
> I put my childish face up to be kissed
> After an absence. The rebuff still stuns . . .

His mother did her best. They all did their best:

> People do what they can; they were good people,
> They cared for us and loved us . . .

And then there is the second story, the story of the poem building itself before your eyes. The sad first story having been told, McAuley begins the wind-up to the poem with another question: 'How can I judge without ingratitude?'

With this question placed adroitly near the end, a poem that was already flying brings in the second stage of its supercharger. The narrative is put aside – there was nothing more to be wrung out of it – and the tone suddenly becomes declarative. Young writers who were still learning about the freedoms that verse could allow them could learn from the poem's penultimate stanza that if you had got the build-up well enough detailed then you could form a climax out of generalities and sound sonorous instead of ponderous.

> Judgement is simply trying to reject
> A part of what we are because it hurts.
> The living cannot call the dead collect:
> They won't accept the charge, and it reverts.

A delicately paced wind-down follows, but the real work has already been done. The story of his upbringing has culminated in a great concentration of aphoristic summary. But it couldn't have done so without the second story, which is the story told by the poem's perfect construction. Whatever the childhood deprivation was, it helped bring him to this: a lyricism all the more musical for being free from any hint of standard beautification. In that regard, the poem is prosaic: its poetics are without poeticism. But a simpler way of putting it would be to say this is a poem made up out of the fullest possible intensity of prose. Good prose is an arrangement, and a great poem makes the arrangement part of the subject.

All kinds of implications follow, both for McAuley and for Australian poetry in general. For him, we can hazard that here is the secret of why so much of his prose is so chillingly pale. It had to be stretched on a melodic frame before it lit up. For Australian poetry, we can say that this poem was one of the many launching points for an adventure that returned European imperialism towards its origins: what had arrived as power went back as culture. Here was a language that had nothing especially Australian about it except confidence, but this time the confidence was not assertive: it simply took itself for granted. After this the Australian poetic language was ready for anything. It was ready for the world: a fact that Australian critics and cultural commentators were slow to spot, because it had not yet occurred to them that a new nation doesn't project itself to the world by flaunting its characteristics. It projects itself as a creative personality, which finally comes down to a tone of voice.

The paradox, or seeming paradox, of McAuley's poetic voice is that its enchantment can't be deduced from his personal history. It was generated only in his poems, and not always then. The less inhibited he was, the better: but he was hardly ever not inhibited. The hero in McAuley's poetry as a whole is not the poet engaged in an exploration of himself: it is Quirós, the world-explorer from the past who almost won the future nation for Catholicism. Reading McAuley's works in verse right through, it is hard to shake the impression that you are trapped in a *scriptorium* of the Counter-Reformation. A poem like 'Because' is not just a breakthrough, it's a break-out. To be so indulgent towards his own psychological needs was a rare event for a man who had given himself a national role, and pursued it with the zeal of a courier for Opus Dei.

But precisely there lay the misapprehension that Australian literature, of all the Australian arts, has been slowest to get over. A national role is the last part that a writer should want to play. The writer's role is to express the interior workings of the self, and achieve results that are less national than international, and less international than universal. That being done, a national artistic achievement joins the global conversation at the only level that counts. When McAuley wrote 'Because' he wrote a poem fit to conquer the world, and since then it has: or at any rate the tone of voice exemplified by it has become universally recognizable, without needing to be decorated with the properties that Barry Humphries called 'Austral'. Apart from the *Sydney Morning Herald*, there is nothing in the poem that would not be common property in Surbiton, or indeed Saskatoon. And this diminished dependency on local colour has gone on being true. In the poetry of Les Murray, a sandstorm could be taking place in any country that has sand.

It was a happy coincidence. Bitten in the conscience by guilt for colonialism, the Western nations were becoming one world at the very time when the Australian version of the English language had become ready to do its share in fulfilling a planetary scope. But there was also the factor of professionalism: usually the last thing that amateurs of any art want to hear about. Australian poetry after the Second World War produced a swathe of dedicated contenders, and some of them were bound to produce a few lines you could remember.

A. D. Hope, who could never count his syllables with the efficacious accuracy that McAuley found compulsory, still had an onrush to the big stanzas of his early poems that made him sound more majestic than his protégé. (Actually, in the real world, Hope was the protégé: for McAuley, dominance was the default mode.) You might argue plausibly that Nan McDonald could propel a line of pentameter even more sweetly than McAuley: her poem 'The Bus-Ride Home' is not one that he could have written even if his sympathies for his fellow passengers had been that generous.

David Campbell could talk about the women on the beach with a joyful longing that was never echoed by McAuley, who longed for them too but was too cramped to say so: his idea of letting himself go was to help cook up the Ern Malley hoax, a nasty episode which has served ever since as a dunce's cap for the kind of critic who would rather talk about literary events than about literature. (His irascible impatience with pseudo-modernist humbug helped lead him to the foundation of *Quadrant*, but the wrecking of Max Harris's career was a high price to pay: literary people should be slow to imagine that they can crucify a colleague without acquiring for themselves a lasting set of stigmata.)

On the whole, McAuley's poetry was a joy-free zone. But we have to remember that when we are talking about a nation's 'poetry' in general, or about somebody's 'poetry' in particular, we are talking shorthand, and have not yet reached the point. The point that matters is not poetry, but the poem. It's the poem that makes the impact, and gets remembered, even if only in pieces. For at least one reader, 'Because' still has its impact now.

And the impact resonates, as a voice in the head: a language. In another poem, 'Terra Australis', McAuley said that your Australia is within you, as a land of imagination: 'There you come home'. Armed with that language, you are always coming home, even when you stay away. A treasure more important than nationalism, a fully developed poetic language is the essence of the only patriotism that matters. It can do without red-back spiders and crocodiles, although those are nice too. What it can't do without, what it embodies, is a way of speaking about freedom and justice both at once. Not just by luck but by thought and endeavour, Australia is well placed to do that: so well placed that it often forgets its importance to the world, and thinks it has to go on proving itself, when the proof is already known to all. That important place was as much built as found; and McAuley's little poem was one of the things that built it.

Interlude

If you pick up an anthology of modern Australian verse and don't find McAuley's 'Because' in the list of contents, you will know that the anthologist is short of budget, if not short of brains. In the following chapter there are several anthologies mentioned, but perhaps I should here take a separate opportunity to say why I have always found anthologies a vital aid to study. They tend to get looked down on as if they were a short cut to profundity, a kind of mental K-ration. But really they are better thought of as a benevolent filtration system. In the editor's mind, at least, if in nobody else's, the poems in the book will be the outstanding works of his chosen authors. He is unlikely to be completely wrong about that, because there will be the pressure of opinion from his colleagues and friends to reinforce his instinctive choice. If the choice merely reflects a fashion, it will at least typify its time. But even at their least inspired, anthologies help to offset the most threatening fact about poetry: there are too many poems. This might not seem true of the far past, but any hint of a controlled output happened only because so much dull stuff got left out of the anthologies and miscellanies, thus leaving us with the illusion that a silver age once shone, or even a golden one. It is certainly true, however, of today. Sometimes you pray for a new generation of anthologists to set about stemming the tide, and you groan when the anthologists themselves turn out to be enthusiastic dullards or crazed theorists. But really the filtering has already begun, because the chosen poems were accepted for print in magazines, whereas all those others weren't, and vanished immediately into oblivion. In the age of the web, alas, every poem in the world will be 'out there'. I don't know what to say about that, except that I'd rather be in here.

INTERIOR MUSIC

An unusually successful example of that most easily mangled of verse genres, the philosophical disquisition made fully poetic, Robert Conquest's intricately argued poem 'A Problem' is in *The Penguin Book of Contemporary Verse*, an anthology that was always with me in the last few years before I left Australia in the early sixties. It's a long time ago now but I can still remember the thrill of reading, for the first time, the line that sums up what he was really after in that poem. On the face of it he takes a painterly approach, meticulously registering all the nuances of the Ligurian landscape, and how the light falls on it from the sky: falls and alters. But he also says that the shifting patterns of light are 'Like the complex, simple movement of great verse.'

We can call this prose if we like, but only if we wish that our own prose were as neatly suggestive, as rich in implication as it is authoritative in form – in other words, as complex yet simple, simple yet complex. The mere fact, however, that you have to say the same thing from two different directions is already proof that there is nothing dumb about the idea. Combined into a single oxymoronic phrase, the two words 'simple' and 'complex' not only collide, they explode. Once they touch and go off, each is riddled with the other's particular shrapnel. You can't have one without the other.

Is this seemingly simple notion – but so complex when you unpack it – really an appropriate measure for great verse? In those first years of mine as an appreciator of poetry, I found myself asking that very question when I started reading the later poems of Yeats. In Sydney I had already absorbed – or thought I had absorbed – Pound, Eliot, Auden, MacNeice, and Cummings, plus dozens of others among the avowedly modern – but with them I could always say, when I ran into a difficulty: well, that's modern art, complex and difficult. I could understand Henry Reed's 'Lessons of the War' perfectly, and thought they added up to a great work. I could understand the poems in Hart Crane's 'The Bridge' only intermittently, and thought they might add up to an even greater work, for that very reason. I could scarcely have been more receptive to a dash of obscurity. Tending to underrate intelligibility, I looked upon it as the poet's fallback position; a true simplicity with nothing complex about it: a life of ease that he might slip back into if he stopped trying. It never occurred to me then that an achieved clarity might be the apex of the craft; and might act as a vehicle for everything that the poet could not fully explain, just so long as he was clear about the fact that he couldn't. But in laying out the possibilities of choice like this – as if I had seen the choices but just hadn't yet done any choosing – I might appear to be retroactively giving myself credit for more acumen than I had at the time.

On the ship to England I took my first crack at the later Yeats. I sailed off for the territory beyond such earlier showstoppers as 'An Irish Airman Foresees His Death' and got myself into the territory where it seemed that the ageing wizard wanted to be plain as much as he wanted to be poetic. I caught on most quickly to the poems whose prose statements I knew I wasn't supposed to understand completely at first reading. Such lines as 'The blood-dimmed tide is loosed' were obviously meant to be clearer than their context. Byzantium was a destination in the mind, like the Land of Oo-Bla-Dee. None of it was supposed to check out: only to resonate. What threw me, and was to go on throwing me for years, was his use of the perfectly plain, apparently ordinary prose statement. Apart from its biblical rhythm and repetition, was the following moment poetic in any way at all?

> Man is in love and loves what vanishes,
> What more is there to say?

But the musical momentum of those words made them into an extraordinary statement anyway. And actually there was a lot more to say, and the reader, by trying to say it, must eventually arrive at the conclusion that this seemingly simple statement is complex in the extreme. First of all, man is quite likely to vanish before the thing he loves vanishes. If the thing he loves is a person – say, a beautiful woman – she will certainly vanish one day, but if the beautiful woman is painted by Botticelli, she won't. One can go on teasing out an argument endlessly, and this same attribute applies to almost every apparently plain statement that the fully mature Yeats ever made. Right up until the end, the simpler he sounds, the more complex he gets. So Conquest's formula is not invalidated: far from it.

That famous motto about the evanescence of man's love is an extreme case, but really a lot of Yeats's later work is like that. Some of the mystical rigmarole of the early work continues into the later work: there is no escaping 'the gyres! the gyres!'. But his big poems, such as 'Among School Children' and 'All Souls' Night', can mainly be read almost as if they were prose: it's one of their characteristics. The characteristic is deceptive because it can lead even the most acute critic into the delusion that Yeats in his advanced years was writing rhetoric rather than poetry. He didn't. What he did was to trim down the number of complicating factors. Sometimes there was little imagery and often there was none at all: just an argument. But even the most straightforward argument was made musical by the way it moved. In his spellbinder of a short poem 'The Cold Heaven', the 'rook-delighting heaven' is first of all a syntactically compressed way of saying that the sky delights the crows. But it is also a peal of music. (One night at a feast in King's College, Cambridge, when the late Frank Kermode was already older than I am now, he recited the poem to me in his soft voice, and I was breathless at the beauty of its switches and turns, its smooth linking of pause and glide.) To fill the straightforward with implication – to make the simple complex – brought Yeats to the height of his technique.

> Irish poets, learn your trade,
> Sing whatever is well made.
>   – from 'Under Ben Bulben'

In the early work there is frequent mention of mystical inspiration, but in the later work he is more likely to put the explicit emphasis on craft. We can be sure that he didn't think of craft as the lesser thing. It was the larger thing, embracing all the other mental activities going on in the mind of the artist.

Looking back on a long life of trying to get my feelings about poetry into order – a doomed task perhaps, but a compulsive one – I am shamed by the number of times that I did not catch on. The truth about my admiration for the later Yeats was that it took years to form. I was off the ship and in England for a long time before I followed up on the way Philip Larkin had provided latter-day mirror images for the big, sweeping stanzas of the last Yeats poems, and of how Dylan Thomas had said, while calling Hardy his favourite modern poet, that Yeats was the greatest by miles. When I read, in a preface by Larkin, that Thomas had said this, I didn't catch on about Hardy, but I was further encouraged into going on with Yeats.

•

I like to think that I finally did catch on about Hardy's poetry, but it was a shamefully recent revelation. There I was, shambling into oblivion, and I still hadn't learned to love the mass of Hardy's verse: that great bulk of finely made things so cherished by such connoisseurs as, well, Larkin. But catching on can have as much to do with the when as the how. Larkin, in contrast to his friend Kingsley Amis, thought that D. H. Lawrence was a valuable writer, even if overrated. Larkin wrote about Lawrence as if Lawrence had opened up the emotional world for him and helped deliver him from adolescence. I got to Lawrence too late in my life to feel that way: only a few years too late, but late enough to close off the possibility. When I was at Cambridge in the mid-sixties, not to be a worshipper of Lawrence's novels could make life tricky if there were any fans of F. R. Leavis about, but I had a get-out-of-jail free card: I genuinely admired Lawrence's poetry, and indeed his poem 'The Ship of Death' is still frequently in my mind today, especially as the skies ahead of me grow dark. I loved the way his verse moved; but if we spool forward a few decades I find that I still can't love the way most of Hardy's verse moves. For too much of the time he is concerned with making pretty patterns on the page, and it seems that he must fool with the syntax and the vocabulary in order to stick within the template. And yet I can quite see that his poem about the *Titanic* (cleverly, it talks about the iceberg rather than about the ship) is a startling feat of the historic imagination: one of the last of the Empire poems, and as ambiguous about imperial prestige as anything by Kipling. But what I want, and want perhaps too much, is a line that carries its load without contortion, a line simple in its complexity.

I heard such a line of Hardy's when I was starting off in Sydney. I was no more fit to seek Hardy out for myself than I was fit to seek out the music of Elgar, which always sent me back to Beethoven after only four bars. But Hardy, so to speak, sought me out. In our student days, we would be very choosy about the discs we played at parties. To sit beside the radiogram and load the discs was a position of power. It was an era when the female students were spraining their hips trying to dance to the title track of Dave Brubeck's hit album *Time Out*: a few minutes of gyrating in 5/4 time could have dire effects on a foundation garment. But there were discs of spoken poetry too; and the most favoured disc featured Dylan Thomas: and one of the tracks was 'Poem on His Birthday'. People demanded to hear it again and again. I knew what they meant. 'And my shining men no more alone / As I sail out to die.' I found that heroic, even if puzzling. (Wouldn't they be more alone?) But the track that I myself insisted on hearing again, sometimes against strong opposition, was his recital of Hardy's 'In Death Divided'. Thomas's speaking voice was so beautiful that he would have thrilled you if he had recited your death warrant, but he seemed to have been saving an extra dose of magic for the words of Hardy. What I liked best was the ending. After a twist of syntax in the second last line ('No eye will see') the poem ended with an unblemished directness to which Thomas's voice lent full power but which he had no need to distort. 'Stretching across the miles that sever you from me.' Really I should have caught on about Hardy right then, instead of decades later.

Because there it was: the simple statement made complex by its own interior music. Though it undoubtedly sounded all the better because Thomas was saying it, it still sounded pretty good even when I said it. It still does. There must be many more moments like it in Hardy's thick book of collected verse, which still daunts me with its heap of patterns, as if it were a code book for threading up looms in a cloth mill. But I shan't make the mistake of hunting about at random in all that. I'll go to the selections, of which I own several; and to those anthologies in which he is featured, starting with Larkin's *Oxford Book of Twentieth-Century English Verse*. Introducing you to a poet is one of the two best things an anthology can do. The other best thing is to introduce you to a single poem, as *The Penguin Book of Contemporary Verse* did for me when it gave me a line by Robert Conquest that I have been thinking of ever since.

•

When Yeats edited the *Oxford Book of Modern Verse* in 1936 he notoriously left Wilfred Owen's work out, thereby giving the impression that he did not find the most gifted English poet of the Great War quite poetic enough. (He left out the other war poets too, as if he thought war was not a fit subject. It is often necessary to remind oneself that the great man could be a tremendous fool.) At the time he edited the anthology Yeats had already made his own discoveries of just how poetic 'unpoetic' poetry could be. Indeed, he had only three more years to live; most of the body of work that we think of as constituting his later manner was already written; and Auden was all set to sing unforgettably over his grave. One of the phrases that rings most true in Auden's triumphal threnody for the departed Irish giant was 'You were silly like us.' In pretending that he had not seen Owen's unarguable poetic virtues, Yeats had been as silly as a man of letters can well get. Cruelly cut down when young, Owen had shown from the start the quality that Yeats arrived at only near the finish: the prosaically poetic, the simply complex. ('And each slow dusk a drawing-down of blinds': how could Yeats, even at his most batty, not have seen the genius in that line?) A gift for the clear statement that would be almost ordinary if it were not so alert with meaning is one of the things that lock Owen and Keith Douglas in their fearful historic symmetry. Owen, killed by one of the last bullets of the First World War, and Douglas, killed in Normandy in the Second World War, both had the secret. The loss was especially piquant in the case of Douglas because dozens of surrealists survived to help make a fashion of not knowing what they were talking about. Especially when they were subsumed under the blanket title of New Apocalyptics, surrealist poets were the plague of England in the war years. There were surrealist Americans too, but as the war wound down and the US took over as the dominant power in the West, no mishmash of meaning ever stood a chance against the brilliant clarities of Richard Wilbur, Anthony Hecht, and a dozen lesser figures who had seen service – some of them had even seen action – without letting the shock scramble their sense of logic. Not even Robert Lowell, who wanted to say everything at once, ever abandoned logical structure. But in Britain, the ideal of intelligible poetry had to be re-established. Robert Conquest's anthology *New Lines* was a key document in the struggle, which was like trying to lift a locomotive back onto the tracks. The job would have been a lot easier if Keith Douglas had come back from the fighting.

•

Complex simplicity means a phrase, a line, and sometimes a whole poem that makes a virtue out of incorporating its intellectual structure into its musical progression, and vice versa: it is always a two-way thing, a thermocouple of gold and platinum, but without the capacity of those two precious metals to give a precisely calculable effect.

On the contrary, a successful moment of poetry won't let you calculate anything. For as long as it lasts, it is a mental force that silences all the other mental forces. For any modern poets, the ability to transmit this quality seems to be an important factor in whether or not they will last. Perhaps not the determining factor: Dylan Thomas would probably still be with us even if all his poems had been as crowded with symbolism as 'Fern Hill'. But it certainly helped that he could also write

> The ball I threw while playing in the park
> Has not yet reached the ground.
>   – from 'Should Lanterns Shine'

Eventually we might have to decide whether the poetry of, say, John Ashbery is on its way to immortality or to the junkyard. But most of the great moderns have given us a larger proportion of intelligible statement to go on than he has done over the long span of his work. For what these titles are worth, Eliot and Frost are still fighting it out for the spot at the top of the rankings. Our first thought about Frost is that too often he was too plain: he could do a clinching line that courted banality. People employed the term 'cracker motto' and sometimes they were not wrong. But on second thoughts, and for many layers of thought thereafter, Frost was a master of organizing a prose argument into a poem. That brief but bewitching masterpiece 'The Silken Tent' is written in the most limpid of plain language throughout. It's a kind of level-headed dizzy spell. There was one academic – I forget which one – who thought that the mention of 'guys' meant men instead of ropes, but on the whole the poem's language is of a simplicity that not even an idiot with tenure could get wrong. And yet it is as complex as could be. Anyone who doubts that should try memorizing the poem. It defies memorization because of the complexity of its syntax.

Eliot wrote a smaller proportion of 'unpoetic' poetry but two examples might be usefully mentioned. Early on, in 'The Love Song of J. Alfred Prufrock', there is the passage that starts: 'No! I am not Prince Hamlet' and goes on into an astonishing sweep of deliberate prolixity. The fluent bravura of the structure is obviously meant to be one of the elements that produce the emotion – the 'art emotion' which Eliot said was separate from other emotions. When you search for details, you don't find details of imagery; you find details of syntax, and of how the phrases and sentences balance up. Thus, 'Politic, cautious, and meticulous' has a phonetic relationship, as well as a semantic one, to 'At times, indeed, almost ridiculous'. So effective that it can floor the first-time reader like an overcharged cocktail, this is poetry with very few of the usual poetic attributes. On the other hand, it is prose whose interior workings are calculated and refined to such a high standard that they turn incandescent. If it's simple, it's as simple as complexity can get.

Most of Eliot's poetry isn't like that. He struck a similar tone only much later, in *Four Quartets*, and we must remember that in each of the four constituent poems the texture is dictated by symbolism: not so deliberately tangled as in *The Waste Land*, perhaps, but still densely woven, and often oblique beyond analysis. An indicative moment is when the author completes an obscure lyrical flight and then starts his next verse paragraph with 'That was a way of putting it – not very satisfactory.' So he has admitted his own thirst for an alternative; but when he takes a different course, into plainness, it is only to floor us all over again, as he once did with the attendant lord who was not Hamlet. In 'Little Gidding' we get the long and rigorously unpoeticized passage that begins with how the poet and his interlocutor met each other before they 'trod the pavement in a dead patrol'. According to a mountain of scholarship, the poet's companion could be the shade of Yeats. Certainly the mysterious companion has overtones of Brunetto Latini, Dante's beloved teacher who turns up in the *Divine Comedy* to walk beside him. Towards the end of this sublime passage – there is no other adjective that will serve – even the most overtly poetic line, the line that sounds as if it could have been borrowed from Shakespeare, is a straight statement that you can take away and use in conversation. 'Then fools' approval stings, and honour stains.' Otherwise, at the end as at the beginning, the whole marvellous feat of versification is written as if it had no claims to the poetic beyond the surefootedness with which it is organized. Somewhere in the background you can hear the pulse of Dante's terza rima, but in fact Eliot's version doesn't even rhyme. The phonetic impetus is all provided by the arrange-ment of the syllables within each line, and the movement of each line against the next. It is a tour de force. But is it poetic?

Of course it is. And we can say that with rather more certainty than when we assure ourselves that a painting by Mark Rothko in his later manner is still a painting even though almost every standard painterly component has been suppressed at the deliberate wish of the artist. About a Rothko painting there will always be a question: it's one of the reasons why so many people have come to see it. But about this supreme moment in Eliot's verse there can be no question. We can tell that it is poetry by the way that we react.

•

I knew an English poet of my own age who was quietly mortified at being left out of Larkin's Oxford book. Since the poet in question was famous for his integrity and stoicism, this was a striking example of how anthologies count. The poet thought that being omitted would hurt his career. In the long run it didn't, but the long run was certainly made harder. Resentment at Larkin's policy of inclusion did not centre so much on the lavish space he gave to Hardy and Betjeman: everyone knew that he would serve his tastes. What cheesed people off was that he found room for poems written by sociable versifiers no longer in fashion, while thereby restricting his accommodation of current poets who were counting on making an appearance, however cursory. As my friend said, it hurt to give your life to the art of poetry and then find yourself crowded out by the resurrected corpse of a genteel scribbler such as Vita Sackville-West.

But we have to see the matter from Larkin's viewpoint. For all that he might have admired my friend's seriousness, he didn't think that the result was poetry: whereas he thought that Vita, even though a loquacious mediocrity whose work in verse could be measured by the square mile, had occasionally hit the mark. The inclusion of so much Betjeman was an obvious sign that Larkin's taste had triumphed: he had always seen Betjeman as an important poet and now he was in a position to assert it irrefutably. But the inclusion of even a little of Sackville-West was an even greater triumph of taste, if much less obvious. He was saying that something matters beyond the name and the reputation. What matters is the authoritative voice of the successful poem; a voice in which the poet might speak only once, but it is still a poem if it sounds like this –

> All craftsmen share a knowledge. They have held
> Reality down fluttering to a bench;
> Cut wood to their own purposes; compelled
> The growth of pattern with the patient shuttle;
> Drained acres to a trench.

After which she goes on to speak wonderfully about the rich subject she has opened up. Why couldn't she have written more poetry like that? The only possible answer is that she just didn't find it imperative. The idea that people might actually choose not to do more of their best thing is one that we are bound to find unsettling, but it is part of freedom. Robert Conquest, incidentally, has spent most of his literary career, when he has bothered with verse at all, cobbling squibs in rhyming form. In a long life he has written only a handful of serious poems. Sometimes to the dismay of his friends and admirers, the man who defined the simply complex has seldom pursued it. But his book *The Great Terror* helped to bring down the Soviet Union, so we owe him for other things.

PART II
OTHER ARTICLES
ABOUT POETRY

Interlude

During the few years in which I was writing and compiling the notes that form the main part of this book, I also, but not very often, wrote some articles in my usual manner, and for the usual primary reason: they were commissioned. They were, in other words, somebody else's initial idea. But, though I would really rather dream up my own projects, I have always tried to be grateful when an editor suggests a topic on which I might write. Even when the suggested topic seems too bizarre or banal to touch, the invitation is flattering, and sometimes the most acute reason to regret one's ebbing strength is that the debility removes the chance to make something useful out of a superficially lousy idea. Kingsley Amis was invited to write a regular short piece about poetry by one of the most horrible newspapers in Britain. Carrying the war to the enemy, he took up the commission, and wrote some wonderfully humane and quotable criticism. The fact that he was dealing with the kind of journalists who aren't talented enough to be terrorists served only to concentrate his wit.

In this next-to-last section of my book, the component pieces were brought into being on a more civilized basis than that. With the exception of the valedictory article on the poetry of John Updike, which was written at the invitation of the *New York Times*, they were all written to answer requests from publications in Britain, or, on one occasion, Australia: to that extent, the old Empire remained my stamping ground. This imbalance is fitting, I think, because in America poetry is something that happens to one side of the literary mainstream, whereas in the old Empire it happens in the middle of it. Even in Australia and New Zealand, countries where small population means being a poet depends so much on grants and prizes, poetry is still regarded as life's blood. Some of the poets mentioned in the main body of my notebook appear again here, treated with greater exclusivity: with, in a phrase, more focus. To that extent, any essay with a single topic must distort the picture, which is multiple, intertextual, endlessly complex. As the centuries accumulate, poems grow out of poems, and critical remarks out of critical remarks. (Would Hazlitt have spotted that Spenser had insufficient rhymes for his stanza, if Johnson had not first said that Pope sometimes failed to disguise that rhyme sounds were in sort supply?) A thousand names jostle to be remembered. A cautionary truism: any poet from the past whose name we remember once knew the names of all his contemporary poets who are now forgotten. Nothing is harder, in modern times, than for a new name to stand out longer than a little while. No surprise, then, that Robert Frost should occupy us again as the final topic in this section. He was there at the start of the book and he is still there as the book passes its half-way mark. There is no point protesting at such eminence: much as we might be suspicious of the long rule of a master, there is such a thing as a great name. Only twenty-four years old, Chidiock Tichborne wrote an uncannily good poem on the eve of his execution. But because the axe deprived him of the chance to write further, his name is hard to remember now. Sir Walter Raleigh, also, was beheaded, but at least he had had time to get a few things written, as well as having been the lover of Queen Elizabeth I. That last idea, however, was the invention of movie producers, and I'm afraid they were handing him a reward for his piracy, not for his poetry.

JOHN UPDIKE'S POETIC FINALITY

John Updike was always so careful not to make high claims for himself as a poet that he gave his more owlish critics the opportunity to say he wasn't a poet at all. They should have looked harder. Most of the poems he ever published in book form counted as light verse, but his light verse was dauntingly accomplished. Very few recognized poets could handle the formal element that well, and occasionally there was a serious poem with all the linguistic vigour of the prose that had made his novels compulsory reading.

Nevertheless, and despite a fairly large body of work as a poet, it was as a novelist that he was hailed. Clearly he had poetic qualities as a writer: he had the imagery, the observation, the rhythm, the delight in making words click into their ideal working order. But it was into his novels that he put these things, was it not? Nobody, and especially not other poets, wanted to think of him as a poet as well. Helpfully he appeared to think the same.

But this posthumous volume, *Endpoint*, tells a different story. Consisting entirely of poems he wrote in the last years of his life, it is a serious book indeed. The subject is his approaching death, and it turns out that he started treating it as a special poetic subject several years back. The 'Endpoint' poems, written at the rate of roughly one a year since 2002, deal with no other theme, and the 'Other Poems' in the book are plainly collected and grouped so as to reinforce the same theme from all directions, and especially from the direction of the past.

> The lawn's begun to green. Beyond the Bay —
> where I have watched, these twenty years, dim ships
> ply the horizon, feeding oil to Boston,

and blinking lights descend, night after night,
to land unseen at Logan — low land implies
a sprawl of other lives, beneath torn clouds.

In these 'Endpoint' summaries the Top Gun technician makes it easy
for himself from the mechanical angle: the forms are loose and un-
rhymed, held together only by the beat of the iambic pentameter. But
from the thematic angle there is a strict discipline in operation. Every
recollection has to be specific. If it passes that test, it can come from
as far back as early childhood.

The way that these poems search their author's early mind suggests that he has belatedly discovered a modus operandi that he might
have used all along. He used the novel instead, with results that we all
know. The Rabbit and the Bech novels placed him securely among the
high achievers of Team America, up there with Roth and Bellow, and
more substantially accredited, as a novelist, than Mailer, Vidal and
Salinger. Yet when it came to the last he chose another form.

In his early verse, Updike could be boastful about his sexual
prowess. One young woman was recorded as lying in his arms and
crying 'John!', so moved was she. Here, at the eleventh hour, he is
more regretful about his overmastering, though obviously masterful,
early lust.

I drank up women's tears and spat them out
as 10-point Janson, Roman and *ital.*

The typeface vocabulary is the tip-off to where those early feelings
of virile immortality came from. It was being a published writer that
turned him into Errol Flynn. (The priapic actor is tellingly invoked,
along with, for other qualities, Jack Benny, Fred Astaire and Lucian
Freud. The book is a gallery of role models.) At the *New Yorker*,
natural home of the Jewish upmarket wordsmiths, he was the go-to
Goy who could write anything. He revelled in the girl-getting fame.

Details of his earlier life are plentiful in the sequence, giving us a
touching counterpoint to the details of his life coming to an end. For

that second aspect, no detail is too grim to be recorded. Updike was always a clinical observer of his own body. Right to the wire, he took inventory: he had the mind of a regimental quartermaster. We find him planning the guest list for the last hours: 'My visitors, my kin.' And in the 'Other Poems', the famous names would clearly be invited too, if they had not already moved on. For the young Updike, Frankie Laine ranked with Flynn, Benny and Astaire as an incarnation of the all-male possibilities. Like a classical poet calling up a shade from the Halls of Dis, Updike addresses the singer's ghost through the teenage hormone-laden haze of the Sweet Shop in 1949:

> Your slick voice, nasal yet operatic, sliced
> and soared, assuring us of finding our
> desire, at our old rendezvous . . .

The famous faces and voices lay out the terms of the sexual drama that will be the writer's life. Doris Day bulks large, especially with regard to her bosom, which Updike in his first days of fact-based social research was pleased to discover was as ample as Marilyn Monroe's, just more discreetly reined in. The teen prodigy was mad about Doris Day and on his deathbed he still is. Philip Roth and Nicholson Baker would acknowledge the tone in which he speaks to her shade:

> Give me space to get over the idea of you—
> the thrilling silver voice,
> the gigantic silver screen. Go
> easy on me. *Cara*, let's take our time.

The phrase 'gigantic silver screen' is uncharacteristically automatic: in a novel he would not have permitted himself to be so ordinary. But poetry was his holiday. A pity, perhaps: though he would have had to live in a smaller house, he might have written the poetry that reported America. He could have given us a lot more about Doris Day. Frank O'Hara became a famous poet largely for a single mention of Lana Turner.

The poetic reporting of America began before Walt Whitman and in the twentieth century even the novelists were doing it. Not many recognized poets wrote as effectively about actual events as John Dos Passos did in the montage passages of his novel *U.S.A.*, the book which, for the future stars of Team America, made their mission clear. But Updike was unusually well qualified to write the kind of poem that gives a news event its historic dimension. Witness his bloodcurdling poem about the death of the golfer Payne Stewart in the private jet

> That rode the automatic pilot up and down
> like a blind man doing the breast stroke
> at forty thousand feet, for hours . . .

Updike could have reported the nation like this all his life, but he chose another method. Let there be no doubt, though, about the high quality of what he might have done. In a single poem, he did enough of it to prove that he not only had the whole tradition of English-speaking poetry in his head, he had the means to add to it. 'Bird Caught in My Deer Netting' deliberately and justifiably echoes Frost in its title, and in the body of the poem we can hear Gerard Manley Hopkins and John Crowe Ransom and . . . well, everyone, really, Jack Benny included.

> How many starved hours of struggle resumed
> in fits of life's irritation did it take
> to seal and sew shut the berry-bright eyes
> and untie the tiny wild knot of a heart?
> I cannot know, discovering this wad
> of junco-fluff, weightless and wordless
> in its corner of netting deer cannot chew through
> nor gravity-defying bird bones break.

It's a wonderful poem, but we shouldn't fool ourselves. He wrote very few like it, and usually, even on the comparatively rare occasions when he tried to give it everything, he was led towards frivolity by a fatal propensity for revelling in skill. But his very last book, a book of poems, proves that he always had what it took.

STEPHEN EDGAR STAYS PERFECT

Before writing a notice of Stephen Edgar's latest collection of poems, *History of the Day*, I should declare an interest, not to say a fascination. When I read his collection before last, *Lost in the Foreground*, and concluded that he was setting a new mark of accomplishment for the Australian formalist poets, I made immediate plans to meet him, if only to check up on whether he was a normally configured human being, and not a cyborg toting a large extra memory box for his vocabulary and range of technical skills. He turned out to look like what he is: a classicist who makes a crust by correcting the textual errors of other people, and writes poems on the side. Our first lunch at the Oyster Bar on Sydney's Circular Quay lasted until dusk, and we have been friends ever since. So the reader should allow for a possible bias. But the reader should first consider this:

> Above the cenotaph, stuck to the sky
> As though on long thin pins, the cut-out shapes
> Of kites tug at the wind and won't let go.

Placed arrestingly in a poem called 'Totenstadt', such an apparently elementary moment counts among the most basic building blocks of an Edgar stanza. Even the simplest registration raises a question of perception. You can see the kites, but you can also see how they might look as if they were stuck to the wind, and doing the tugging instead of being tugged. But a whole stanza can be a building block too, raising, on a larger scale, another question about perception. In 'Dreaming at the Speed of Light', the narrator is seeing the world from his viewpoint on a ray of light from Einstein.

The falling autumn leaves would stall
Above the lawn, their futile red
A stationary fire;
The dog erupting from the pond would spread
In hanging glints its diamanté shawl
Of shaken spray midair;
The blue arc of the wave would climb no higher,
A gauze of glare
And water that would neither break nor sprawl.

You might say that there are stretches of prose in Nicholson Baker's *The Fermata* that give the same freeze-frame effect, but Baker didn't do them in stanzaic form. And when we pull our own viewpoint back to see how Edgar's stanza is put together, we find that there are only four rhyme-sounds holding the fluent progress on course as it switches between four different iambic meters, the whole thing seeming so spontaneous that it might have been a one-off. But then, when we pull back to see the whole poem, all four of its stanzas are built on exactly the same pattern. Edgar often composes in free forms as well – he is a master of the blank verse paragraph – but an unpredictably varied yet precisely matching strophic construction is his characteristic approach.

When I first read Edgar, and realized he was making up these elaborate stanzas and then replicating them throughout the poem as if to prove that his idea of formal freedom was all discipline and vice versa, I thought immediately of Richard Wilbur in that sumptuous post-Second World War phase when he was producing the intricately articulated clarities of 'Piazza di Spagna, Early Morning' and 'A Baroque Wall-Fountain in the Villa Sciarra'. But at our first epic lunch the second bottle of Cloudy Bay had barely been broached before Edgar revealed that, much as he admired Wilbur, for him Anthony Hecht had been the Man.

Either way, a foreign technical influence had been the right kind to suspect. If Edgar had read neither Wilbur nor Hecht, he might still have got the idea from Larkin, who was making up stanza forms quite early in his career; and of course Larkin got it from Hardy and the later Yeats. Edgar might quite possibly have concocted the whole approach if he had read nothing but Keats's Odes. What is certain, however, is that there had been very little Australian poetry like it. If Edgar was getting his technical inspiration out of the air, it was out of the world's air, and not just the air of his own country.

The point needs stressing because in Australia the idea is firmly entrenched that any self-imposed formal requirement must be an inhibition to expression. The idea got a long way in America, where to argue the contrary seemed undemocratic; and has caught on in Britain, where it is thought to be a useful instrument in wresting the control of creativity from a privileged class; but in Australia it has attained the status of an orthodoxy. On the whole, by those who edit the anthologies and staff the prize committees, an apprehensible form is thought to be a repressive hangover from the old imperialism; and all too many of the poets think the same. The view is aided by the unarguable fact that Les Murray (whom Edgar admires, as we all do) usually doesn't write in apprehensible forms either.

But at least Murray knows what they are. It isn't his fault that the ruling majority of people concerned with poetry in Australia think that free verse is a requirement of liberty, and anything constructed to a pattern must be leaving something essential out. Edgar's steadily accumulating achievement has been of a quality too high to be buried by the attention of dunces, and he has attracted some excellent criticism. But it is still quite common for his work to be belittled as if there was something unAustralian about it.

Indeed there is. Though his work teems with specifically Australian details, much of it would be intelligible anywhere; and there is a lot more that is not tied to his country at all. Two of the poems in *History of the Day* are about the bad old days of lynch law in America, and one of them is among the best poems in the book. The poem is based on the notorious photograph taken at the lynching of Rubin Stacy in Fort Lauderdale, Florida, on 19 July 1935. As with so many of Edgar's poems, it is hard to tear a piece loose, but try this:

And then you see her. At the left she stands,
Behind the awful focus of suspense,
Her hands crossed, mimicking his handcuffed hands,
On her frocked crotch, her naked face intense
And lit up with a half-embarrassed leer,
A girl of twelve, too unaware
To mask her downward grin . . .

But Edgar doesn't need a non-Australian subject to be 'international'
in the sense that was once used so longingly. (There were commercials
that called John Newcombe an 'Australian International'.) There is a
little poem called 'All Rights Reserved' in which I would like to think
I play a key role, because it is set in the Oyster Bar, and I am Edgar's
opposite number in the story he narrates. This time it was dinner: but
the real subject, which goes right round the world, is the sky, which
adjusts to the sinking sun

Almost as though it hears itself discussed,
And flourishes its menu, from gold dust
Through peach to lazuli . . .

This range of colours at each end of the day is likely to be the first
attraction for a new reader of Edgar: dawns by Charles Conder link
to twilights by Whistler, with whole vistas assembled out of textures
and atmospherics. But there is nothing anachronistically fin de siècle
about his palette, or not that siècle anyway: Edgar's weather is the
weather of modern scientific observation, and quite often registered
in a vocabulary that sends you to the dictionary, although seldom
without first making you catch your breath at its luxuriance.

It's important to stress the enchantment of these subsidiary effects
because this volume is a bit lighter on his primary effects than his
previous one, *Other Summers*, which contained the sequence called
'Consume My Heart Away', whose constituent poems are generally
held to be his most intense things so far. Actually I think this is a false
trail, because there are magisterially personal poems, mainly to do with

the lingering anguish caused by the death of his first love, scattered everywhere in his work; but there is no denying that a poem like 'Man on the Moon' – which stands out even in the luminous cluster of 'Consume My Heart Away' – makes you wonder where he might go next if he ever decided again to give up some of his personal detachment.

He will never give up his control, which is of the essence in all his work; and he is unlikely to indulge in the confessional strain that Elizabeth Bishop was so right to find suspect in Robert Lowell, much though she admired him; but there can be no doubt that Edgar set a new standard for himself when he turned an interlude of heartbreak into a sequence of poems that cut unusually deep into his own equilibrium. So startling was the sequence that some of his critics have begun to use it as a stick with which to beat him, saying that the personal note put his earlier work in the shade.

But that view will not hold up, because his big stand-alone poems so often range as widely within his own psyche as can be imagined. The only possible objection to this collection would be that there are fewer of them than usual. But one of them is among his very best. Called 'The Red Sea', it is about three little girls playing with toy boats in the shallows of North West Bay, south of Hobart. I only wish I had space to take it apart with something of the same diligence he expended on putting it together. The task here, however, is not to lay bare the ghost in the machine, but to say what quality of ghost it is, as the children bend to their game.

> Hard to conceive that they should be
> Precisely who they are and here,
> Lost in the idle luxury of play.
> And hard to credit that the self-same sea
> That joins them in their idleness today,
> Careless of latitude and hemisphere,
> Blind with ubiquity,
>
> Churns elsewhere with a white uproar,
> Or wipes the Slave Coast clean of trees . . .

And so on, all around the globe, as the ocean threatens the idyll. A poem about how there can be no such thing as a local vision, no matter how particular and intense, it would alone be sufficient evidence that Stephen Edgar, in the fullness of his accomplishment, can be called an Australian poet only at the cost of slighting both adjective and noun. Even when his approach to a subject is oblique, you always get the sure sense that he is trying to light it up, and make you listen to the music of what he looks at. Models of plain speech even at their most eloquent, his poems are more sheerly beautiful from moment to moment than those of any other modern poet I can think of.

POETRY HEAVEN, ELECTION HELL

At the time of writing, in the first days of June 2009, it is still not clear why Arvind Krishna Mehrotra has not been declared winner of the election for the post of Oxford Professor of Poetry, the other two candidates having pulled out, one before the election, the other after. As the only surviving candidate, surely he should have been given the job automatically. Perhaps he himself resigned too quickly, having got the idea that resigning was the thing to do. The chair left vacant, the election was postponed until later in the year, and speculation has already started about who might run. Names have been put forward. One of them, startlingly, is mine. How did *that* happen?

It started happening a few days before the election, when I was being interviewed, nominally about my latest collection of essays, *The Revolt of the Pendulum*, a book I mention here because it wasn't mentioned in the interview even once. My interviewer, Decca Aitkenhead of the *Guardian*, was charming, so when she asked me a question I did the thing I always do when asked a question by a charming woman. I opened my mouth to its full extent and put my foot in it up to the knee. The question was about the Oxford Poetry Professorship election debacle. 'Would you like the job?' (Those might not have been her exact words, but that was the main thrust.) My answer (and these are far fewer than my exact words, but this is the thread) was: 'I would love it, but not if I had to run in an election.' She used only the first bit – that I would love to have the job – and the *Guardian* editors flagged it as 'Clive James throws his hat in the ring'.

In reality, Clive James had already made it clear that he would rather throw himself off a cliff. But the thing had been said, the Australian papers had the story next day, a Spanish paper, bizarrely, had the story the day after that, and within a week my supposed candidature in the postponed election was being discussed, with at least two pundits in the British broadsheet weekend press allowing that I might not be a bad choice, in the absence of William McGonagall, E. J. Thribb, the giftless bardic voice of *Private Eye*, or Baldur von Schirach, the Nazi youth leader who wrote a terza rima encomium to Adolf Hitler.

In my house on a Sunday morning, the major papers are read collectively by every female in the family including the cat, and very soon I was facing a tribunal. 'Please say that not even you could be that stupid.' 'You aren't thinking about it, are you?' '*You aren't.*' The cat was right: I wasn't thinking about it. Not in the sense of actually going for it. But I couldn't help thinking about the job itself.

It is always a doomed effort to say 'Let this cup pass from me' when you have already pronounced it attractive. And I do indeed find the Oxford Poetry Professorship just about the most attractive cup of its kind in existence. I would imagine that any poet who has spent his or her lifetime at the craft can only feel the same. The botched election might have made it a poisoned chalice, but what a chalice it is. You have only to think of the string of poets since the Second World War – Day Lewis, Auden, Graves, Blunden, Roy Fuller, John Wain, Heaney, Fenton, Muldoon – and think of how much you would have liked to hear them speak, summing up their knowledge, opening up whole fields of interest with the merest aside. You have only to think of how you would have quarrelled about them. Was Graves certifiable, or merely potty? Wasn't Blunden a dim bulb beside the candidate he beat into second place, Robert Lowell? (Perhaps: but it was Blunden who wrote *Undertones of War*.) How could such an uneven poet as Wain be so fine a critic? You have only to think of one book: Heaney's magnificent *The Redress of Poetry*, his richest critical work, and nearly all of it based on the lectures he gave while he held the office. In that book, he joined poetry to the world. Read it, students, and begin your adventure.

But wait a second, what's the name of John Jones doing in the list, as Poetry Professor between 1978 and 1983? Few remember him now, and certainly there is no lasting evidence that he ever wrote poems.

We should be fair to his literary competence and say that at least one of his books, a treatise called *The Egotistical Sublime*, was part of the general discussion for a while, and that he had a proven record as a professor of English. But that was just the trouble. They had elected, as Poetry Professor, an academic professor of English. How did it happen? Contemporary accounts remark on the campaigning skills of his wife. Apparently she knew how to win an election.

An alarm bell should have rung then, but most of us were probably not listening. Many of us were listening, however, when it rang again at Peter Porter's failure to win the post in a race against Christopher Ricks. Professor Ricks is a scholar, critic and lecturer of titanic prowess, and all are agreed that he did a mighty job. But he was not a poet. It could be said that he fell into the same hallowed category as erstwhile incumbents A. C. Bradley, J. W. Mackail, W. P. Ker and Maurice Bowra, who were not poets either, but knew an awful lot about it. (Lest you doubt his credentials, remember that it was Bowra who told Isaiah Berlin about Anna Akhmatova. Berlin had never heard of her. Bowra really had read everything.)

Knowing a lot about it, however, is not the same as doing it, and surely the importance of the post – the thing that makes it decisively different from all the other professorships of literature in Oxford – depends on its holder being a mature poet with some actual, concrete, hard-won stuff to impart about how poetry gets written. All kinds of people can read poetry, and more than a few of them can study it: but only a poet can write it. If poets write it for a long time, they find a lot out, not just about their own work but about all the work by other people, in all ages and languages, that they think is vital. They are well placed to say why they think it so, and when they get near the finishing line they are ideally placed. They speak not so much ex cathedra as ex atelier, as it were.

From that viewpoint, I thought both Fenton and Muldoon a bit young, and I might say at this point that I would rule myself out for the same reason: despite what the clock might say, I'm only just getting started. Peter Porter, however, when he ran for the office, was ready to sum up. At the risk of losing his friendship, I might hazard that he would not have been quite as practised a lecturer as Professor Ricks. But Peter Porter, quite apart from his stature as a poet, is a greatly learned man, a born educator, and a whole world of poetry and the arts is already in his mind, never needing to be mugged up, all ready to be brought out. (He would have been a master of the Poetry Professor's other, unofficial task, as exemplified by Auden and later by Heaney, which is to conduct the kind of informal tutorial that masquerades as a *tertulia*.) But the poet lost to a critic, because the critic had a superior campaign.

So there was already, to my mind at least, a prominent question mark over the electoral system before the recent election got started. But this time the press got into the act and the prominent question mark turned to vivid scarlet neon, wreathed in the smoke of hell-fire. When one of Ruth Padel's unwisely enthusiastic friends in the press informed the rest of the press of what it should have known already, namely that Walcott had a sexual harassment case in his past, the election for the Oxford Professorship of Poetry became an American presidential election in parodic miniature, with character as the only issue. It should have taken only a moment's thought to realize that character is just about the last parameter by which to measure the English poets, among whom the Earl of Rochester and Lord Byron are locked in contention for the title of most wicked and both are outdone for male chauvinism by Milton in fifty different passages of *Paradise Lost*. But nobody was thinking except Walcott.

It could be that he had a lot to think about. I have no idea. Or rather I have some idea, but it is based only on the publicly available documentation, which is not very extensive. I have met people who say they know more, but they always seem to have learned it from someone else who knows everything, and him I have yet to meet. Those who were glad to see Walcott hounded out of the race were not impressed by the arguments of those of us who said that he was un-likely, at the age of seventy-nine, to launch himself from the podium and fall ravenously on the young lovely in the third row, and I quite see their point. If he had indeed once done what he was rumoured to have done, then he was a villain. But there would still have been little relevance to his qualifications to be Oxford Professor of Poetry, a post for which you want the kind of man, or indeed woman, that people would flock to hear if he, or she, were lecturing from behind bars. Derek Walcott prudently retired before he could be scrutinized further, and Ruth Padel, gaining the office by default, resigned from it because her part in ensuring that her opponent should be scrutinized in the first place was itself scrutinized. The press decided the issue, and the third candidate, Arvind Krishna Mehrotra, might have been giving us his judgement on the whole pitiful business by resigning in his turn. How would he have found the post worth holding, if the press had started scrutinizing him? There might have been some unpleasantness about a disputed parking space back there in the University of Allahabad. Perhaps he had been photographed allowing his fond look to linger too long on the bare midriff of a Bollywood starlet while he was signing her well-thumbed copy of his collection *The Transfiguring Places*. And even if he had nothing to hide, why should he let himself be treated like an elected official?

The conclusion is inescapable. Since every future election will be subject to invigilation by the press, the only solution is to scrap the election system. This would probably need to be done even if the press could somehow reach an agreement to stay out of the lives of the candidates, because already the question of who should hold the post next is subject to the demands of social engineering, which are no doubt worthy but are entirely irrelevant. Derek Walcott wasn't running as the first black poet to aspire to the post. He was running as a great poet who happened to be black. If some time elapses before there is another great poet who happens to be black, then those are the breaks. There are no good reasons, only bad ones, for favouring P. Diddy as the next Oxford Professor of Poetry, just as there are no good reasons, only bad ones, for threatening a museum with a cut in its funds because not enough black people are coming to see the paintings. To think otherwise is just another way of patronizing people of colour, and a particularly insidious one.

The same applies to the view (we might call it the Winterson view) by which it is supposed to be a tragedy that a woman poet could not get the post. A truly accomplished woman poet, U. A. Fanthorpe, ran for the office in 1994, and lost. But if another female poet of equivalent stature were to appear, she could be appointed. Carol Ann Duffy, who revered Fanthorpe, should be of just about the right magnitude if her completed term as laureate is judged successful, or even if it isn't. But she would still be a bit young for the post. Kathleen Jamie, already impressive, should be magisterial by then; but she, too, will scarcely be ready to draw the conclusions of a lifetime. If either Duffy or Jamie gets hustled into an election ten years from now, it will be a bad sign. An appointments committee could make a principle of playing a long game.

Knowing what we know now, if we review the list of successive professorial terms in the modern era, there were times when Marianne Moore could have been appointed, or Elizabeth Bishop. But the reason to appoint them would have been that they were great and learned poets, and not because they were women. If they had run in elections, of course, they would probably have lost, because the electorate, all the graduates of Oxford, would have had to be persuaded that it was time for a woman.

The electorate is no doubt persuaded of that now, but what is the persuasion worth? It's all a matter of mediatized opinion, when what should count is well-informed opinion, as agreed on by a panel of people whose chief concern is poetry, and who rank poets by their achievement and vocational wisdom, and not by their membership of a group that is thought to be deprived. The group might very well be deprived, but it will be deprived still more if it is mined for a token.

How this board of experts should be constituted is beyond me. But before he was ever Oxford Professor, Seamus Heaney was a visiting professor at Harvard, an office to which he was not elected, but appointed, to the vast benefit of both Harvard and himself. So Harvard must know how to make a board system work. For the Oxford post, drafting all the surviving holders might not be a bad start, and then you could add in some critics and literary editors who know what they are talking about. Who those might be would itself be a matter of expert choice, so I can already see that there could be a welter of infighting and no clear course to a workable result. But we can be sure that the current system no longer works at all. Another election along the lines of the one we have just had will be a kamikaze convention, and we might as well have Ant and Dec presiding over the phone-in.

LES MURRAY'S PALATIAL NEW SHED

In the majesty of his years and accomplishments, Les Murray, sole author of the several increasingly massive editions of his *New Collected Poems* – one of the great books of the modern world – is in the position of a monarch who, having successfully constructed Versailles all on his own, is now pottering in the grounds building sheds. Six years ago *The Biplane Houses* was such a shed, and very prettily done. Now *Taller When Prone* is another. Perhaps I would not have had the idea of an enormous building and its satellite *bâtiments* if the first poem in the new book had not been about the Taj Mahal. The poem, called 'From a Tourist Journal' starts like this.

> In a precinct of liver stone, high
> on its dais, the Taj seems bloc hail.

Immediately he's got you in. He has always been able to do that. The way he can register, in words nobody else would quite choose, a perception nobody else could quite have, is at the centre of his art, ensuring almost infallibly that a poem will work like a lucky charm for as long as he pours in the images. A Taj made of hail: you and I might say that we would have seen that to be true eventually, and we might even argue learnedly that the word 'Mahal' phonically suggested the word 'hail' (points for an essay there), but the daunting truth is that he doesn't just think that way, he sees that way.

Murray sees the things of this world *mis à nu*, like Baudelaire's heart. (More points for an essay.) The charm is infinite because the universe goes on forever, and he would have something unique to say about every bit of it if he could go on sailing long enough through its eternity of transparencies. That's why, I've just decided, the Versailles analogy won't quite do for the big book of poems. Versailles is as charmless as the Escorial. There is nothing delicious about it. The Hermitage in Petersburg is a better bet, because you always want to break off a bit of plaster moulding and taste the quality of eighteenth-century Italian sugar dipped in Russian winter air.

Such world-girdling analogies, however, are invariably appropriate as to scope, even when they err in their field of resonance. No poet has ever travelled like this one, whether in reality or just in his mind. This poet will show up wherever a specific quality comes to light, whether made by God or made by man – who is made by God too, who was man-made.

> Perfection as a factory making depth,
> Pearl chimneys of the Taj Mahal.

When Shah Jahan built the Taj to express his grief, his religion was concentrated into love, and one could say the same of the boy from Bunyah. Australia might seem like an unlikely place for all the religions in the history of the world to be combined in a single literary expression, but what the hell, the man who split the atom came from New Zealand. Intelligence of this intensity doesn't have a single home. It belongs anywhere – anywhere that the pearl chimneys spill their depth.

In my dreams I see the ideal poetry teacher, nearly always a woman, giving personal instruction to the ideal pupil, nearly always a girl (the boys stay so thick so long, do they not? Although some of them sharpen up later, in their tediously competitive way), and the teacher says: 'With Les Murray, you have to get the *speed*. As soon as the first image strikes, the poem is always on its way to somewhere else. He never elaborates without covering distance, so you have to keep your skates on.'

In 'As Country Was Slow' the new high-speed road is seen through what would be our eyes if they had enough supporting electronic equipment.

Our new motorway
Is a cross-country fort
And we reinforcements
Speed between earthworks
Water-sumps and counterscarps,
Breaking out on side glimpses,
Flying the overpasses

But by the third stanza the viewpoint has switched to beneath the road, and animals are doing the viewing.

Wildlife crossings underneath
The superglued pavement
Are jeep size: beasts must see
Nature restart beyond

Galway Kinnell once put a poem's point of view inside a cow's head, from which it could see rocks going by below on an endless conveyor belt. I wonder if Murray ever saw that poem but I don't wonder very hard. I have never caught him borrowing anything except a range of possibility, and any good poet will borrow one of those. They aren't, after all, nailed down. For all I know, Murray got the idea for talking about life in the bush when he first noticed how Shakespeare talked about life in a hedgerow. It's something an exemplar can provide: you can break through to subject matter that lay so close you didn't notice. At home everywhere, Murray doesn't always tell you that the poem is not set in Australia, although sometimes the title tips you off that he has crossed the world. It seems a fair guess that 'Midi' is set in France, unless there's a town called Midi somewhere near Murwillumbah.

Muscles and torsos of cloud
Ascended over the mountains.
The fields looked like high speed
So new mown was the hay.

The men in the creative writing class spot the hay laid out like a comic-book illustrator's speed lines, but it takes one of the women present to wonder aloud what a stilted word like 'ascended' is doing there. My ideal teacher raises the possibility that Murray is thinking of the ascending Christ in some of the last drawings of Michelangelo. She will remember, as we all must remember, that Murray has got a lot of artistic history in his head. He doesn't have to dial it up. It goes with him. Art, however, or let it be the knowledge of art, never clogs the basic work of perception, as unblunted with him as with an autistic child – burdened with family reasons for treating that subject, he is blessed with the ability to do so – or with a bat. (In one of my dream-ings about Murray, a cave full of bats have a book club and study 'Bats' Ultrasound' on a continuous basis. This guy, they squeal, *gets it*.)

The bats see with sound. Murray sees so keenly that even his most attentive readers can forget he sometimes works a trick – or, to speak more grandly, points out a connection – with sound alone. In 'Nursing Home' the clinching benediction of the last line comes purely through noise,

> As bees summarise the garden.

You could call such an effect a nucleus in Murray's total atomic effort. He starts small. But the speed of expansion can spread sonic precision to a whole topic. In 'Eucalyptus for Exile', the dangerously combustible propensities of Australia's most globally popular tree are all there in a single word, 'craquelure'. You don't even have to look it up: just savour it, while wondering whether it was ever really a good idea to restore the English garden around your house to its native state.

> Standing around among shed limbs
> And loose craquelure of bark
> Is home-country stuff
> But fire is ingrained.
> They explode the mansions of Malibu
> Because to be eucalypts
> They have to shower sometimes in Hell.

A lecture about Murray's politics could start with that stanza. He is too much of a man of the bush ever to favour a Green ideology. In one of the many classic moments of his earlier poetry, the felled tree that dropped along its own shadow was earning a living for the loggers. Like almost all agrarian writers, Murray retains an element of conservatism that no amount of bien pensant gush from his readers can ever wish away. (Too long to quote here, and needing to be quoted in it entirety, 'The 41st Year of 1968' is a sharp rebuke to ageing hippies who imagine themselves to be in sympathy with Gaia.) Mainly the steady show of recalcitrant realism – not the purpose of his total effort, but nearly always its undertone – springs from the fact that the poet, like all the people mentioned in his poems, works for a living. Luckily for his box office figures, he doesn't make the business of observation sound always like hard yakka. Even when close to home in the bush, you can sometimes, as in 'The Cowladder Stanzas', just look.

> Not from a weather direction
> Black cockatoos come crying over
> Unflapping as Bleriot monoplanes
> To crash in pine tops for the cones.

The monoplanes were in at the start of the transportation revolution that would give the Australian poets the world for an oyster. Famous for having never left home, Murray has left home over and over, piling up the languages and the air-miles in a quietly successful quest for world citizenship. He might not have any money in Switzerland, but during the long flight he knows which leg to sleep on when 'Visiting Geneva'.

> I arrived in spring when
> The Ferraris came out.

Some day soon perhaps, a jet will take him to Stockholm. Only occasionally changing its personnel and never changing its dark suits, the Nobel Prize committee has seldom been a good judge of poetry, but once in a blue moon they get it right, and Murray's world currency is hard to miss. The question of why this should be so is always worth asking. There are poets, even Australian poets, as universal in their scope and even more learned: Peter Porter is only one of them. But Murray's international appeal works on the assumption that he speaks a lingua franca. The assumption is not quite so absurd as it might at first seem. When you get right down to it, he does. The perceptions and connections would show up in any language that could find the verbal equivalents. The trick, from the Stockholm angle, lies in the translation. The translator needs not only to be a master of his own language, he needs to be terrific in English. One can imagine Murray's Japanese translator consumed for a full year – the time needed to anneal the blade of a good sword – in finding the equivalent for that half line in 'The Buladelah-Taree Holiday Song Cycle' when the ibises, having arrived at their place of work, get busy.

> Pronging the earth, they make little socket noises.

But it could be done, because first and foremost so much of Murray's inventive force is antecedent to language. Seeing the shape or hearing the sound of one thing in another, he finds forms. A world of forms is what Picasso inhabited, and when he started painting the pictures to prove it, he left the world of immediate charm. Murray has never done that, although lately he has shown signs. There are poems in this book that are hard to figure out, which isn't like him. For all his career, close reading has been rewarded with meaning. The implication that meaning might be beyond reach is rare for him, and really something new. Perhaps he's getting ready to start again. Perhaps the Versailles-Hermitage was only a shed, and now he wants to build the real palace. There might not appear to be much time, but he wrote *Fredy Neptune* in no time at all. Nevertheless it's hard to abandon the idea that one of the great merits of his outstanding body of achievement is its intelligibility. To make its first impact on the new reader, it doesn't really need a preliminary lecture, or an essay, or even the ideal teacher. It just needs you, the visitor to the 'Southern

Hemisphere Gardens', ready to wait patiently while the beauty comes welling up.

> The nankeen heron has moved to Japan
> But ink-blue waterhens preen long feet
> Or, flashing undertail
> Like feathers of the queen protea, run
> Each other round the brimming rain dam
> Where inner sky is black below shine
> As if Space were closer, down.

Even before you look up 'protea', you know for sure where this is that he's taken you. It's heaven, for which Space is just another name, another word.

TALKING TO POSTERITY
PETER PORTER 1929–2010

If the eternal life in which Peter Porter did not believe had granted him permission to look down and check out the action shortly after his demise, he would have been interested in his obituaries. Self-deprecation having been his characteristic mode both in his art and in his life, he was always reluctant to claim a victory even when weighed down by the arrival of yet another van-load of laurels. But he might have been pleased to see how, in both Britain and Australia, those deputed in the media to lament his passing nearly all hailed him not just as an Australian poet, but as a poet of the English language. With his two nationalities blending into a global significance, a matter of contention had finally been settled, simply because he had spent so long being the man and artist that he was. His early poetry was so brilliant that the argument should have been over immediately, but sometimes the obvious answer can take a lifetime to become common wisdom.

He had spent much of his career caught in a fork, punished in Australia for trying to please the Poms, and punished in the UK for being an Aussie expatriate with a frame of reference above his station. Later on, he won acceptance in both camps, and by the time of his death he was a living example of the old country's culture reinforcing itself with the energy of the new, and of the new country's culture gaining scope from an expanded context. From the Australian viewpoint, if Les Murray was still the king of the stay-at-homes, Peter Porter was the king of the stay-aways, the position of expatriate artist having at last come to be seen as a contribution rather than a betrayal. For the British, his work and stature added up to a powerful reminder that the old Empire lived on as an intellectual event. In both countries, after his death, those who wrote about him awarded him so much admiration that even he would have been obliged to believe it, although undoubtedly he would have described it as part of a scheme to have his estate taxed twice.

Born in Queensland to a family in reduced circumstances, the young Peter was shunted off to a boot-camp boarding school just to get him out of the way, and was denied any university education because in those days if your father couldn't pay, you couldn't go. (A bit later on, the often mocked conservative prime minister R. G. Menzies changed all that with the Commonwealth Scholarship scheme, but too late to save Peter from discovering Brisbane's shortcomings as a cosmopolitan metropolis.) His upbringing was scarcely the blacking factory, but he couldn't be blamed for looking back on it as a non-event. To a painful extent, his character was shaped by what didn't happen: nobody, as he later complained, was ever kissed less often. From that experience, or lack of it, grew his strange conviction that women found him negligible. (He was notorious for saying that there really *were* two nations, but they were the attractive and the unattractive.) He was too nice to notice that women found him adorable. At several stages in his life, before the advent of his second wife, Christine, removed his credibility as a victim of deprivation, I knew plenty of women who complained that they would have very much liked to kiss him but he wouldn't stop telling them about Scarlatti.

Thus habituated from his earliest years to believing that even his good luck must be bad luck in disguise, Peter, established in London, had the grace to turn his own mental disposition into a joke, and many of us who knew him were glad to join in, sometimes making stuff up to boost the legend. He would come back to London from some Australian literary festival and recount how the Australian headliner poet had been given the luxury hotel's penthouse suite with resident chef and dancing girls, whereas he, Porter, had been allotted a motel room on the fringe of town with one towel and a stale cheese sandwich. Glad to be at the same rocking table, we evoked, with his delighted participation, what would happen when he was awarded the Nobel Prize for Literature. Instead of receiving it from the hands of King Carl XVI Gustaf in Stockholm, he would be asked to pick it up from Sweden's assistant cultural attaché in the car park of Stevenage railway station.

Possibly he took too much pleasure in running himself down. When you are speaking to the media, the trouble with modesty is that the reporters tend to agree with it, just as, when someone has a high opinion of himself, the reporters tend to agree with that. As I tried to tell him by way of a parable, a certain famous writer who wore dark glasses indoors did the right thing when he assured a journalist it was because his nervous system was so sensitive. The famous writer's putative sensitivity had been the first characteristic discussed in any profile written about him ever since. A lover of literary gossip, Peter revelled in this information, but did not change his ways. Speaking to an interviewer concerned with the eternal non-question of which of his two nations he felt nationalistic about, Peter said 'patriotism and allegiance are small matters in comparison with my egotism'. He was lucky that 'Aussie Poet Admits Ego' was not the headline of the piece.

In truth, he had very little egotism, and might have been better off if he'd had more. Instead, at the heart of his nature was generosity, to the extent that it sometimes threatened to be his undoing. Though his financial position was always parlous and could scarcely be saved by his industry as a first-string critic for the *TLS*, the *Observer* and the BBC – only a culture gets enriched by that kind of effort, not the contributor – he would give time he didn't have to any demands from the poetic world, immolating his energies in symposia, conferences and doomed readings in the upstairs rooms of penniless literary societies. This particular form of generosity would often extend to inviting Australian poets visiting London to billet themselves in his flat. Apart from judging a poetry competition, I myself couldn't think of anything more likely to ruin the concentration necessary to write poetry. Peter, however, didn't think that way. He had no idea of rationing his energies, and anyway, as his prolific output of verse proved, he didn't believe in the jealous nurturing of a few fine things, Flaubert-style. Indeed his role models weren't from literature at all: they were from music. He was fond of saying that Bach's cantatas would have been no more marvellous had there been fewer of them.

Peter already knew a lot about classical music before he first left home and he wasn't far into his London residency before he had learned everything. The geology of the flat in Cleveland Square altered in recent years when the ranks and banks of LPs were supplemented by rows of CDs. But though he often told interviewers that he rated music above literature, it is important, once again, for us to watch his words. He loved literature as much as anyone can who takes pains in adding to it. At our last meeting, during that strange period when the sky was silent and we were all ruled by the moods of an Icelandic volcano, he was typically eloquent about the arts, about which he had always had the rare gift of speaking with unapologetic enthusiasm. He was frail, and sometimes his speech came slowly, but we still had our usual fight about the later Wallace Stevens, whom Peter revered and I find suspect, and somewhere in the conversation, casually but strikingly, he let slip the remark that he thought nothing could beat the feeling of writing a poem at that moment when the poem takes over and starts to write itself.

Even though there would clearly be not much more of it, this was magic talk of the kind that I, like all his friends, had grown so used to over the years that we tended to take it for granted. I often had to remind myself that hardly anyone could speak like this. Alive a long time and active all over the cultural map, Peter joined several literary groups together, but in one of them I was lucky enough to be included, and when the gang now known as the Friday Lunch used to meet each week, often he and I would be the last two left at the end, and the subject of the conversation was almost always the arts. He was a walking university, except that you rarely encounter that kind of range in a university. As time went by I got better at playing feedman in a routine that I could see was a stage-show in the making. This was proved true one year at the Melbourne Festival, when, at short notice, Peter and I were pushed on stage by the tridents of the organizers, having been told to improvise an hour's conversation. As usual we both quoted reams of poetry from memory. It caused a sensation among the young people in the audience, not because what we remembered was so unusual, but because for them it was so unusual to find someone remembering anything.

The ABC arts producer Jill Kitson was in the audience and she suggested that we might, when we got back to London, go into the ABC's studio in Great Portland Street and record a set of six broadcasts along the same lines. Eventually there were six seasons of them recorded at the rate of one season a year, and in Australia they became a staple of arts broadcasting, with Peter's knowledge and easy eloquence remarked on by thousands of listeners. Though he never knew, in my opinion, how to read his own poetry aloud, Peter was an ace broadcaster from a script. But he was even better off the cuff, and in those shows he is at his dazzling best, as fluent and entertaining as he was in real life. On behalf of his reputation, if not of mine, I might suggest that it would be good if the BBC could pick them up. They are all on my website (an enterprise he rather approved of, because it took endless labour and made no money, a pattern he recognized) but his contribution deserves a far wider audience that that.

The forthcoming book of selected poems, *The Rest on the Flight*, will doubtless provide the core of his heritage. I hope it will sell the way Larkin's *Collected Poems* did, like snow-cones in the Sahara. Wedded to tumultuous simultaneity and sometimes, it seemed to me, to outright obscurity, Peter was rarely as approachable as Larkin, but he shared the gift of the phrase that lodged in the reader's head. At its best, his poetry spoke the way he did. 'Auden didn't love God, he just found him attractive.' I can hear him saying it now. In the broadcasts, he proved that he could say things like that all the time. Dr Johnson might have talked for victory, but Peter seemed to talk for posterity.

When we last met, it was the only thing I said that was good enough to match him. Complaining away as hilariously as usual about the injustice of the literary world, he said he didn't care about posterity. 'You don't have to,' I said. 'For you, it's already here.' Surely I was right for once. While he yet lived, so many people thought he was great that not even he could have believed they were in league to do him down. But he could never have played the hero, because for him it was creativity itself that had the heroic status, beyond politics, beyond patriotism, beyond even personal happiness. It's the reason why his work is like that. His poetry, so wonderful when it is really flying, isn't trying to tell you how much he knows. It's giving thanks for how much there is to be known.

ELEGANCE IN OVERALLS:
THE AMERICAN PASTORAL OF
CHRISTIAN WIMAN

Not yet fifty years old, the American poet Christian Wiman has recently been stricken with a serious illness. At the moment his doctors say that he is likely to survive it, but for anyone in doubt about the magnitude of the possible loss, one glance at his latest collection, *Every Riven Thing*, should serve to state the case. In a poem called 'Sitting Down to Breakfast Alone' he remembers the Longhorn Diner:

> steam spiriting out of black coffee,
> the scorched pores of toast, a bowl
> of apple butter like edible soil,
> bald cloth, knifelight, the lip of a glass,
> my plate's gleaming, teeming emptiness.

The risk for any American poet following Robert Frost into a pastoral mode is to sound the way Norman Rockwell looked. It's not the worst fate, but the aspirant was after something less comfortable and more intense. Wiman attains intensity often enough to remind you of just how great Frost was, and often there is a touch of another of his masters, Richard Wilbur: the apple butter like edible soil might have been on the menu if Wilbur had ever written a poem about a cheap American eatery.

But the best thing to say about Wiman is not that he reminds you of previous poets: it's that he makes you forget them. His rural landscapes might start off by sounding like Seamus Heaney with more machinery, but soon they are all his. Wiman's poem 'Five Houses Down', which caused such a stir when it came out in the *New Yorker* last year, is a piece of American Gothic so sharply seen that it brings back, for any reader in the English-speaking world, that eccentric junk-buff who lived nearby. If he never did, he does now.

> I loved the eyesore opulence
> of his five partial cars, the wonder-cluttered porch
> with its oilspill plumage, tools
> cauled in oil, the dark
> clockwork of disassembled engines

Wiman has retained his childhood fascination with the disassembled engines, to the point where, though well capable of strict forms, he would rather take them apart and leave the pieces in approximate touch. Though an outstanding poem, an instant classic, 'Five Houses Down' is only one of his many backyard masterpieces, as if the Wright Brothers were still turning out flying machines at home. Actually the brothers had a flourishing bicycle business and Wiman is the powerful editor of *Poetry* (Chicago), but once those wide open spaces start to work their magic it's hard to shake the impression that every complex mechanism in America was invented in a barn, up to and including moon rockets.

Rangy and soft-spoken in real life, definitely a Sam Shepard type, Wiman seems ideal casting for a would-be rocketeer raised in the flyover (he was born in West Texas), as long as we remember that only an extreme technical sophistication can produce such simplicity. He knows all about having more. You need to know that if you are plausibly to long for less.

> Welcome to the hell of having everything:
> one repentant politician on sixty screens,
> van-sized vats of crabgrass toxin,
> a solid quarter mile of disposable diapers,
> all our impossibles pluralled.

Here one of his illustrious predecessors, Randall Jarrell, would have recognized a fellow sufferer, a sad heart at the supermarket. But

Wiman can go only so far towards despair, because he has God for solace. On the rare occasions that I find a Wiman poem less than profound, it's because it claims profundity, usually by employing an ellipsis . . . those deadly three dots that indicate a thought too deep to be dealt with just now. Such gestures towards the unsayable mark his religious poetry, which he might think of as his strongest, at this time when the threat of death is so real.

But we must hope that what this fine poet faces is more life, and the obligation to go on with redoubled force. In which case, the poems he writes will be among the best written by anybody, at this favourable time for poetry, when everything is against it – in the same way that the wind, blowing against the bows of the aircraft carrier, lifts the aircraft into the air. If one so often thinks of being airborne when reading Wiman's work, it could be because he seems to be thinking that way too.

> There comes a time when time is not enough:
> a hand takes hold or a hand lets go; cells swarm,
> cease; high and cryless a white bird blazes beyond
> itself, to be itself, burning unconsumed.

Those lines are a fragment from 'The Reservoir': the longest single poem in the book and an indication of where his work might go next, towards larger constructions. It would be a welcome development, although not without its dangers. Even in 'The Reservoir', which I find enviably fluent, the ineffable looms. It's so hard for a poet to be clear that anyone who can manage it should embrace his duty never to be any other way. More power, less smoke! But that's the kind of thing we shout only at the greatly gifted, as they go flashing by.

MICHAEL LONGLEY BLENDS IN

Michael Longley started out in Northern Ireland at about the same time as Seamus Heaney. But Longley, over the course of a long career, has done a steadily more effective job of not doing what Heaney did. By now, with Heaney so firmly established on the international scene that he makes the secretary general of the United Nations look like a filing clerk on a short contract, Longley remains such a local poet that one would not be surprised to hear of his beard being taken over by squatting leprechauns.

There is still a serious gift, however, lurking among the shrubbery of his localized vocabulary. His new collection, *A Hundred Doors*, gives us a small poem that should settle any doubts about the intensity of the lyrical talent we are dealing with. It is called 'Twayblade'.

> Twayblade. We find it together,
> The two of us, inconspicuous
> With greeny petals in long grass,
> Lips forked like a man, two leaves
> Some call sweethearts, our plant today,
> Fed on snowmelt and wood shadows.

For a while there, early in the poem, the reader must wrestle with the possibility that it is not the tiny plant, but the poet and his interlocutor, who are inconspicuous with greeny petals in long grass. But the last line is delectable, written as if meant to be remembered. If, however, you take memorability as a desirable criterion for any poem, many of Longley's later things seem designed to circumvent it by itemizing the landscape with a thoroughness which would surely bring weariness

even to a naturalist. A naturalist, after all, must occasionally rest, and
see what's on television.

Longley, when naming names, is rarely off the case. The Carrigs-
keewaun area was already present near the end of his *Collected Poems*
(2006). Here it is again, with all its plants and animals. 'Otters are
crossing from Dooaghtry to Corragaun.' Do they later cross back
from Corragaun to Dooaghtry? Luckily, we trust him: 'How snugly
the meadow pipit fits the merlin's foot.'

And that's just the first poem in the book. As we delve deeper,
we approach the landscape always more closely, and find the poet
tangled up in it. This was already happening in the *Collected Poems*
but by now he blends into the shrubbery like a sniper laying up for an
ambush, or Dick Cheney out hunting his friends.

> Firewood for winter when
> I shall not be here – wild
> Fig perhaps – white sap
> For curing warts, scrotum-
> Concealing leaves . . .

Good to know that the scrotum is safe from detection. Pretty phrases,
though, keep popping up in the seed catalogue. All the children get
at least one poem each, and a girl called Catherine will now always
be remembered as 'the harbour seal'. What a sweet notion. There
is an appropriately well-wrought little poem about Chidiock Tichborne (not the famous claimant) who wrote a masterpiece before he
was torn apart, and very lovely it is: 'And now I live, and now my life
is done.' One of the great lyric poems in English, it can't, of course,
be matched, but Longley sensibly makes a subject out of its deeply
underlying mystery: how on earth did Tichborne concentrate on
the fabrication of so exquisite a thing when he knew that he himself
would soon be dismantled?

> A smile on his face, surely,
> As he found the syllables
> And the breathing spaces.

All poets will acknowledge that Longley is on to something here. The delights of composition are indeed wonderful. If Longley has a drawback – or if he has arrived at one after decades of detour – it is that he writes poetry more often than he writes poems. The self-contained, stand-alone thing has become more and more rare in his work. Back when the Irish boys were all starting off, some of them thought they would make it as singers. They had the towering example of Yeats looming behind them, but they were more impressed by his fey gush than chastened by his sculptural monumentality. One of the reasons that Seamus Feamus (it was my joke, so let me use it) broke into the clear was that he put the poem before poetry. James Simmons, movingly lamented by Longley, was only one of the poets who found out the hard way that a tone of voice wasn't quite enough. The hard way tended to be spread over the long run, and that made it harder.

But Longley himself is ever cheerful, perhaps because the land of his birth, always within reach, is a natural world that will never cease to move him to a phrase. In 'A Swan's Egg' he handles a 'century-old / Alabaster emptiness' and notes the 'collector's particulars' that are written around the black hole in its surface. The display cabinet is 'Brimming with bird silences.' We know that the egg's history is safe with him. He isn't going to drop it. Here is a wealth of noticing and sympathy in one little poem, 'A swan's egg among wren / Pearls and kingfisher pearls.' The tactile tact, as it were, is uniquely his: a big man with a light touch.

Spectator Diary

This month has been the launching season for my new collection of poems, *Nefertiti in the Flak Tower*. Not many younger people, I have been discovering, know what a flak tower is, or was. Perhaps I should have called the book something else. One of the poems in the book is called 'Whitman and the Moth': it might have been wiser to call the book that. Early in the launching season I was asked to read the poem aloud on that excellent radio programme *Front Row*. The poem is a meditation on the old poet at the point of his death and I'm afraid I found the right voice for it exactly.

•

I have been exhausted for more than two years now, by illness. Leukaemia is practically the least of my ailments. In a lull between bad stretches the Saturday edition of the *Telegraph* kindly asked me to review television. That was about a year ago and we have now completed my first year on the case, so this month has been my first annual holiday. I tried to time it so that the book launch could fit into the slot. When you are short of energy you have to ration it. So far I have managed to look busy by doing one thing at a time. Put it all together and it's a decent fraction of the work I did before I fell ill. I still feel guilty, however, that hours go by when I don't touch the keyboard.

•

I doubt if illness improves the concentration. Though its individual perceptions take thought, a critical column is comparatively easy to construct because it is cumulative. This column you are reading now counts as a general column and it will have to have an argument. In a general column you have to tackle a subject, and my subject, by force of circumstance, must be about how I have been so sick that almost nothing else has happened to me.

•

Or not much that shows. So far I've been lucky that way. Various clinics stick needles in me but I look reasonably intact. The major action is going on in the soul. Everything has become personal. Famously productive until his death, my old friend Christopher Hitchens had a memorial service in New York. Almost everyone I knew was there. I would have been there too but I was not allowed to fly. I was envious of them. Even less nobly, I was envious of him. I read his obituaries: he had attracted so much love. What would be said of me when I was gone? I almost was. Why not devote myself to the form of writing that has always mattered to me most?

•

But poems don't necessarily come to you when you ask them. It is more than six months since I have had a poem in the works. I suspect the direct reason is one of the drugs I am on, but there is an equal chance that I am simply in a dry patch. I was drugged to the nines when I lay in New York's Mount Sinai hospital last year and wrote 'Whitman and the Moth'. I pride myself on that poem's nifty construction. When poetry doesn't come, the first thing that doesn't come, as it were, is a structure. The combinative capacity isn't there. It might be there for prose, but with prose you know what happens next. With a poem, only the poem knows what happens next, and you must wait for it to speak. It can take years.

•

Near the very end of his life, Hitchens wrote a brilliant piece about Philip Larkin. Some of his recent American admirers were surprised by how literature mattered to the Hitch but those of us who had known him longer knew that his love for the language was his bedrock. I was not convinced, though, by some of those editors among his American obituarists who wrote of how he would take home a huge new book and read it and review it in a single evening. I think he probably just reviewed it in a single evening.

•

The Hitch's afflictions hurt badly and he was brave to bear them so well. Those of us less painfully stricken are obliged to be of good cheer. The whole process of being kept alive against such relentless natural forces is, after all, very interesting. It takes all the science in the world. Most writers don't see much adventure after they become successful. Well, here is their chance. The hospital that looks after me, Addenbrooke's in Cambridge, might as well be CERN. And in addition to the luxury of being the centre of so much attention, one is contributing information to the last and greatest battle, between mankind and nature. Even as we waste away, the measurements of decline go to swell the data bank. One is thus less useless than one feels. My scientist daughter caught me making a bad joke about the failure of the proposed NHS central computer. She explained that such a computer would be an essential tool for the future. So there is a politics to one's demise, like it or not.

BUILDING THE SOUND OF SENSE

While its subject was still alive, the first two volumes of Lawrance Thompson's relentlessly hostile biography of Robert Frost had already come out, creating a lasting image of the simple poet as a manipulator without conscience. Journalists of all altitudes loved that image because it made for easy copy: cracker-motto bard envied real poets, etc. After Frost died, a third volume of the biography finished the job. On the basis of the complete trilogy of dud scholarship, published between 1966 and 1977, the opinion formed that the gap between Frost's achievement and his real life was too glaring to be tolerated. Helen Vendler, justifiably regarded in the US as a guru in matters of poetry, pronounced Frost to be a monster of egotism.

When I last heard of her, Helen Vendler was proclaiming the virtues of John Ashbery's circular poem *Self-Portrait in a Convex Mirror*, which has been published in a limited edition circular book. While she deals with the vital critical question of whether the reader should turn the book around, or take a turn around the book, we can assume that if there is any further correcting to be done to Frost's reputation as a monstrous egotist, it probably won't be done by Helen Vendler. Too good a critic to be completely deaf to Frost's poetic quality, she published, in 2012, an essay that praised his lyricism, but the essay did not do much to make up for her 1996 *Paris Review* interview in which she lavishly name-checked dozens of her touchstone American poets while mentioning Frost exactly once, and only in passing.

Luckily not even America – still a puritan culture in which an artist's integrity must be sufficiently unblemished to impress Oprah Winfrey – has proved entirely devoid of critics and academics who can handle the proposition that the creator of perfect art might be a less than perfect person. Though Thompson's hostility was a power-fully attractive theme for the kind of dabblers who would always rather read blame than praise, it could not quite offset the praise from such an expert witness as, say, Randall Jarrell. In his mighty little book *Poetry and the Age*, Jarrell showed for all time just how Frost worked the miracle of disguising the complicated as the elementary.

But although Frost's artistic greatness is nowadays more widely acknowledged, it is still generally thought to be the output of some kind of simpleton. There have been further, and less crass, biog-raphies since Lawrance Thompson's, but they have had to fight a hard battle, as for a town already reduced to rubble. The damage that was done by Thompson still lingers. Deaf to a tone that made him the living echo of Iago, Thompson wrote to Frost: 'The simple truth is that I love you.' God help any artist who acquires so passionate a lover. Onlookers, thirsty for gossip, will always think that there must have been something in it. To put Frost's proper renown back on track, what's needed is the re-emergence of common sense.

The new collection of Frost's letters should help. Eventually there will be three volumes, but the first volume is already enough to prove, if proof were needed, that Frost was anything but the shit-kicking fireside verse-whittler of legend. When not actually practising his art, he thought about it so long and hard that it was a wonder he had time for anything else. His detractors would like to think that he found plenty of time to suborn editors, sabotage rival poets and practise infinite cruelties on his wife and family, but even his detractors must have noticed that he got quite a lot of meticulously crafted poems written. These letters are proof that his working methods and prin-ciples were the product of a mental preoccupation that began very early. Right from the start he had an idea of what a poem should do.

He wrote his first poems at home in America, but did not get as far along towards an acknowledged status as he had a right to expect. Eventually, when he was already thirty-eight years old – a late age to become an expatriate – he sought a more hospitable literary environ-ment in England. But before he crossed the Atlantic in 1912, he was already regaling his American editors and poetic acquaintances with his considered ideas about poetry: ideas that add up to a conception of modernism still pertinent today. He talked of 'skilfully breaking the sounds of sense with all their irregularity of accent across the regular beat of the metre'. This was an early occurrence of a key phrase: the sounds of sense, or the sound of sense, went on cropping up in his writings, lectures, letters and conversations to the very end of his life.

It was a true idea, not just an easy motto. Implicit in the idea was that the spoken language supplies the poet with a store of rhythms which he can, and indeed must, fit in counterpoint to the set frame of the metre. A hundred years later, very few poets want to face the labour involved in doing this.

But those few are the ones we tend to notice. What we notice is their musicality, and conjuring music out of spoken words was an aim that Frost made explicit. He was ready to suffer neglect as long as he could pursue that aim. Having safely arrived in England, Frost wrote to an American friend: 'Poetry is not a living. It is not even a reputation today. It is at best a reputation next year or the year after.' Does that sound like a master manipulator hustling for position?

Of course it doesn't. But he was justifiably concerned with getting his work put in front of the public; all the more justifiably because he was, in his own schooled and studious opinion, pretty good. 'A little of the success I have waited for so long won't hurt me. I rather think I deserve it.' In England, he was able to bring out the first few slim collections that could somehow never find a publisher back in America. In England, his self-esteem was augmented by esteem from others, with a familiar result: he was able to worry less about the awkward necessity to blow his own trumpet. And anyway, some of his new fans could blow a trumpet at the level of a military bugler announcing the next dawn.

Ezra Pound admired him, and told the literary world. Prominent writers listened to Pound because they had no choice: he got into their heads like an earwig. We can deduce two main reasons for Pound being impressed by Frost. The first is merely persuasive: Frost really was at home in Latin and Greek, whereas Pound only pretended to be. But Pound, armed with an infinite intellectual arrogance, was not easily made to feel ignorant by anybody. The second reason is decisive: Pound could see – or, better to say, hear – that Frost was a supreme technician, a bearer of the modern torch. Frost's advocacy of a language 'absolutely unliterary', of a 'war on clichés', was catnip to Pound, who had long favoured just such a campaign himself. The fact that Frost was better equipped than himself to pursue it was not one that crossed Pound's mind; or if it did, he was not inhibited in his determination to jump up and down on Frost's behalf.

Frost, a lifelong enemy of all arty pretension, thought that Pound dressed the part of the poet. But Frost never disparaged Pound's antics, even when they worked to his, Frost's, detriment in the very area which his English sojourn was meant to ameliorate: his standing at home. Pound not only proclaimed Frost's virtues, he insisted on announcing, at the top of his voice, that those virtues had been beyond the comprehension of American editors. Frost, who had always been polite to editors even when they rejected him, was appalled. Quite apart from the question of elementary courtesy, Frost knew that he would have to go home some day soon, and at this rate the earth would be scorched before he got there. He and Pound fell out. But it was after they fell out, and not before, that Frost told a friend: 'Pound is the most generous of mortals'. A poet who is out to sabotage his rivals – a monster of egotism – doesn't say things like that.

Frost rated Pound highly but Yeats even higher: 'the man of the last 20 years'. Amiable and clearly decent, Frost was welcomed into all the right groups of literati; 'the allurements of the London literary crowd'. But he was allured only up to a point. He seldom gave his whole admiration to anyone. He was glad to have the company of the Georgian poets but his praise for their work was generalized. His praise for W. H. Davies was specific but limited: 'those flashes in a line'. He was unequivocal only about Edward Thomas, his fellow late-starter. Here, surely, is the certain and final proof that Frost, from the career angle, was at least as much a giver as a taker. He did everything he could to help Thomas along as a poet, and when Thomas was killed on the Western Front, Frost's grief was terrible.

Despite the loss of a true soulmate, however, Frost's invasion of

Europe had been an early version of D-Day. Success was achieved and made secure. But there was nothing easy about the process, and a close reading of these letters will reveal that England, despite its traditional congeniality for an idealistic literary class, was just as rich a source as America for chumps, cheats and fools. Booby-traps were made more deadly for Frost by his accursed virtue of honouring a bargain. There was a woman called Mrs Nutt who got hold of some of his best copyrights and used them to screw him around for years. He should have had her bumped off. (Later in his life, he should have lowered the boom on Lawrance Thompson, but nobody could persuade Frost against honouring a promise even if it killed him, and that one damned near did.)

Back in America, he could take pride in the success of his plan to build up a reputation offshore. It had worked, and he had become thought of, at long last, as a prominent American poet. But poetry, in the material sense, was still not a living. He worked hard to make a go of farming, thereby providing himself with the store of imagery that lent the substance to nearly all of his most memorable work. But in the long run he could not make farming pay the rent. Farming is a full-time job, and perhaps Frost spent too much time with his mind on other things – poetic masterpieces, for example.

And as always, when he was not actually writing, he was thinking about how to do it. Thinking about the local rhythm of a phrase within the grand rhythm of a sentence might not have been the best thing to have on his mind while trying to plough a straight furrow, but it was good preparation for teaching. Though his image in our minds is of a taciturn rustic artisan stacking stones to form a wall, he actually spent most of his life giving lectures. He had a gift for prose, but that was where the gift went to: it was talked out across a lectern. Though the duties and skills of tending the land were always present in his imagination, he was quite proud of his knack for holding an urban audience. 'I am a much better teacher than farmer,' he said.

Scanning the addresses from which the later letters in this volume were sent, the reader will find that Frost was often on the road. A born performer, and doubly blessed because he performed his own stuff, he was in demand in distant colleges for the kind of evening in which the poet gives what amounts to a one-man show. Frost was inventing the poetry circuit; the blessed device which nowadays, both here and in America, helps to keep the best poets alive – as well, unfortunately, as some of the worst. Frost soft-pedals all questions of stipend, but it's a fair guess that his share of the gate made the trips worthwhile. No wonder Thompson hated him. Frost was self-sufficient, and a true acolyte can allow the object of his worship any virtue but that. Helpers want to be needed.

Frost made no apology for collecting his rewards. 'Nothing is quite honest that is not commercial.' If what he did had been subsidized, he wouldn't have felt that it was proper work. You could call it a right-wing view. He was conservative in many ways, but none of them matter except one: he was a die-hard believer in art as a discipline, and not as a mere indulgence. For him, there could be no such thing as 'the literature of irresponsible, boy-again, freedom'. But even while he still lived, we were already surrounded by the literature of boy-again freedom, and girl-again freedom too. Today, freedom rules, and the rules are nowhere.

Yet some of the thousands of our current poets might harbour the secret urge to take their work seriously. They might be like those bad boys in the Anthony Burgess novel who sat in the back of the class surreptitiously teaching themselves Latin. In view of that possibility, there is plenty that a clueless but hungry young tyro can learn from Frost, and the learning would be made more palatable by the fact that there was at least one kind of freedom that Frost believed in all the way.

Frost was the man, even more than Eliot and Pound, who both formulated and demonstrated the modernist principle of listening for the rhythms of poetry in the language around us: 'We must go out into the vernacular for tones that haven't been brought to book.' In our day as in his, the privilege of bringing vernacular tones to book is a freedom beyond price. Our tyro might find this privilege reassuringly near to his own propensity for bunging down anything that comes into his head, but he might as well start from a position of comfort, because he faces a mountain of hard work. Among the many things that poetry essentially is, poetry is essentially the business of finding a form by fitting things into it. Frost, in this respect not conservative at all, thought, or said he thought, that the resultant form should be equally non-threatening to everybody. 'I want to be a poet for all sorts and kinds,' he said. 'I want to reach out.'

His most formidable detractors think that his reaching out was too often a folksy grab at the lapels. The truth of the matter is that the typical, seemingly unambitious little Frostian poem is a wonder of sophisticated construction: no other poet could have done it. Our tyro – Coleridge would have called him a nursling – will soon find that Frost's poetry, even at its most approachable, is the product of craft at a level that it takes sweat even to analyse, let alone to emulate. Frost could tell you what made an English vowel long or short; it was as if he had transported the tools of a quantitative language, Latin, into a new language, English, that was not supposed to have quantities, only stresses. But Frost had studied how the metre and the intonation formed an interplay which, on the page, would stabilize the rhythms of a conversation overheard from the next room; a conversation whose specific meaning might be a mystery but whose drift was detectable from how the speech rose, fell, sped and slowed. It was a version of Eliot's electrifying proposition that poetry in a foreign language could communicate before it was understood.

Eliot, the man of the century, respected Frost. I myself, who have never stopped reading Eliot since I was a student in Sydney in the late 1950s, have often stopped reading Frost – not, I think, because he daunts me, but because his vast barn of country reference is not congruent with my personal experience. Most Australians, including the literary people, are city-bred. (Les Murray is almost unique in his closeness to the land; the main reason, I think, why he sometimes reminds us of Frost.)

So I keep on having to rediscover Frost, but I am delighted each time I do. Whatever else they reveal about him – perhaps he stole cars – the next two volumes of letters are bound to go on showing that he was as thoughtful and hard-working as an artist can get: further evidence that the best of modernism is a way for the classical to keep going.

Interlude

While I continued to write articles and book reviews about poetry, I necessarily had a last chapter of my poetry notebook in mind, because my declining health told me that it might be wise to wrap things up. The trouble was, there was still so much to say. It's in the nature of the subject. Poetry is finite – from all of its history, only some of it is of the first concern – but it is also limitless. In music, you don't have to hear Beethoven's late quartets very often before you realize that you will never stop responding to them. And in music, unless you are musician, your response is not complicated by technical questions. With poetry, there is not only the appreciation of a successful work, there are all the questions of how it got that way. It would be easier if the enjoyment of a poem put your mind to sleep. Instead, you are woken up. That degree of mental excitement can be awkward when your physical strength has begun to flag. The old urge to get everything said should by rights be stymied by the awareness that time is running out, but instead there is a renewed determination, entirely inappropriate to the resources available. 'Old men ought to be explorers' said Eliot in 'East Coker'. That line has always given me the picture of some buffer tottering under the weight of an enormous backpack topped off with a collapsible canoe.

No, the time comes to let go. And anyway, what we say about a poem is a small part of its point. The large part is what the poem says about us. In his 'Secular Masque' of 1700, Dryden wrote:

> All, all of a piece throughout;
> Thy chase had a beast in view;
> Thy wars brought nothing about;

Thy lovers were all untrue.
'Tis well an old age is out,
And time to begin anew.

We could talk forever about the easy pomp of those lines, but the first thing to do is to submit to them. Even if we won some of our wars and our lovers were as true as angels, the old age is bound to go out, and someone else will begin the new one. There is grief in all poetry, even when it is light-hearted. Poetry holds itself together, and eventually we ourselves do not. I started this book by recalling some of my young reactions. Since then, a lot has changed in the sociology of the art form that I chose, or that chose me. Women now exercise unquestioned the equality that once they had to fight for. Where once there were only hundreds of would-be poets, now there are thousands. But poetry remains what it has always been: the thing that hardly anyone can do. Most of the contenders are aware of that, but go on trying anyway. Since there are such thin rewards even for success, and no rewards at all for failure, we might as well say that they do it from instinct, and call the instinct divine. And besides, there will be no lingering embarrassment from failing to make one's mark: a poem that doesn't work will be forgotten even while it is being set down. When Keats said that his name was written in water, he was right about almost every poet except himself.

PART III

FINALE TO A NOTEBOOK

TRUMPETS AT SUNSET

When I was young, cartoons by James Thurber were so widely known that people would refer to them in conversation just by quoting the captions. I remember not quite understanding the reference in one caption: 'I said the hounds of spring are on winter's traces – but let it pass, let it pass.' I thought the line very funny at the time but I didn't know that Thurber was quoting Swinburne's 'Atalanta in Calydon'. You don't need to get the reference to get the joke; but the joke eventually got me to Swinburne, who would gradually turn out to be the most accomplished poet that I couldn't stand. Spenser, in *The Faerie Queene*, would occasionally throw in an alliterative line for effect ('Sober he seemde, and very sagely sad') but Swinburne wanted the whole poem to be that way: a meal of popcorn. Sometimes, in his blizzard of alliteration, he failed to notice that he had written an identity rhyme instead of a rhyme:

> And time remembered is grief forgotten,
> And frosts are slain and flowers begotten . . .

Perhaps he noticed but thought we wouldn't, intoxicated as we were bound to be by his sonic hurtle. But for a poet to be all sound is nearly as bad as for a painter to be all paint. After several attempts over the years to detect any signs of an underlying strength, I still find that a Swinburne poem affects me like a painting by John Bratby: there is so much impasto that the only tension lies in your wondering whether it will slide off the picture and fall on the floor. I have to give up on Swinburne; there is no time to go on quarrelling; and besides, there are problematic poets with whom one can quarrel to more purpose.

•

A dangerous point arrives when you tell yourself that you are still proud of your memory. It means that your memory is failing. Nowadays there is always Google, but that huge and dumb storage facility can't always make up the difference. As far as I can tell, the phrase 'trumpets at sunset' is one I thought of, but perhaps I lifted it from someone else. Always, during my time as a writer, I made it a rule never to use unacknowledged a phrase that was not my own: but perhaps my subconscious, in its old age, has taken to making its own rules. If I did lift this phrase, I hope it was from someone serious, like Kipling. But if I had seen the phrase on the page, surely I or Google would remember that; besides, I make marks in books, and often a phrase or line that strikes me as outstanding gets copied into the end-papers, so eventually I come across the moment of treasure again. More likely, if I didn't borrow the words, I borrowed the mood. Scott Fitzgerald called the last of his short-story collections *Taps at Reveille*. Though his plangent title needs translation – 'Taps' for 'Last Post' is strictly an American usage, and in America 'Reveille' rhymes with 'Beverly' – you can't miss the threnodic complaint that the end has come too early.

Dorothy Parker, however, is the most probable victim of any urge to emulate that I might happen to have had. She called one of her little collections *Sunset Gun*. There is no time-twisting paradox in that title, but there is an aching beauty. Leaving aside Dorothea Mackellar (in school we all read her great hymn to Australia, 'My Country'), Dorothy Parker was my first woman poet. But although I enjoyed the witty carpentry of her poems and even memorized a few of them, I was never touched by her use of language, except for that one title. By the phonetic coupling of those two words, 'sunset gun', I was bowled over, and for life. Their rhythm became for me, so early on in my writing career, a part of the tread of passing time, the grander rhythm to which I'm afraid that I now have better access when I write: afraid, because you don't hear that music properly unless you are already on your way into the empty regions. Sunset *gun*. The sound of a slamming door, but it's behind you.

•

As one's time runs out, the mind is weighed down with a guilty mountain of the critical duties that won't be attended to. There is barely time to read Elizabeth Bishop's poems again and pay them a less stinted praise. When I first wrote about her, thirty years ago, I tried to be clever. It was a failure in judgement: she was the clever one. Still conceited enough to think that even so illustrious a reputation as hers could benefit from my recommendation, I should try to put things right. Any young student who has not yet discovered Elizabeth Bishop simply must be told about 'The Man Moth', 'his shadow dragging like a photographer's cloth behind him', or about the 'Sandpiper' walking along the beach, taking for granted 'the roaring alongside'. And her famous poem 'The Fish' deserves more fame yet. I still hold by my original opinion that its tactics are bad: her final decision to 'let the fish go' is bound to elicit the wrong kind of smile when the reader considers how long she kept the fish in the boat while she was describing it. The pictures within her general picture of the fish, however, brook no belittlement. 'I thought of the coarse white flesh / Packed in like feathers . . .' Not just an eye for texture: an ear for it.

But how many hours will I have for, say, Leonie Adams? In her time, she was America's poet laureate. In my time, I tried a couple of her collections and found that her poems fell into the fatal category of polite but pale. Now, while shelving books, I open Louis Untermeyer's venerable anthology *The Collins Albatross Book of Living Verse* (1933, updated in 1960) and find a poem by Leonie Adams near the back of the book, among the moderns. She describes how Hesperus, the wishing star, 'Is risen only finger-far'.

But that's a bit better than polite, and not entirely pale: you can see her with her finger held up to her eye, measuring. Unfortunately she doesn't tell you whether the distance is covered by the length of the finger, or by the width. One assumes it's the width, but it would have been better to be told for sure: her precision is not quite precise enough. So there, I have my excuse not to chase up the rest of her work. It's not a very good excuse, though, and at some time in the near future I can see myself breaking my recent rule of buying no more books. I'll be leafing through a full collection of her poems, just to allay the suspicion that I might have failed to report a noble attempt, even though not one of her poems emerges that is as intense throughout as its best phrase.

Sometimes a late search can be more rewarding. Anyone whose attention has been caught by U. A. Fanthorpe's 'Not My Best Side' will find that her *Selected Poems* of 2013 has many other tightly integrated things. It wasn't that she wrote one thing that put everything else in the shade. Though she had been awarded, very quietly in 2003, the Queen's Medal for Poetry, her whole output was in the shade, and then suddenly it all came to light at once: at the very end of her life, and partly because Carol Ann Duffy, who has a gift for fame, was an admirer of hers. Thus Fanthorpe's gift for obscurity was overcome: until then, despite her having published several volumes with a faithful minor publishing house, she was read mainly by her devotees, and it is one of the laws of poetry and the arts in general that the instructed are an insufficient audience: one must break through to the uninstructed. One would like to see every talented female poet winning through to general favour. God knows enough talentless female poets do.

•

I realize that the talentless female poets are still outnumbered by the talentless male poets. Nevertheless, the business of poetry is much more equally distributed between the genders than it was even in the period after the Second World War, when women seemed to be taking up poetry as if it were a new kind of swing shift, the equivalent of putting the wiring into silver bombers. There had always been women poets, from Sappho onwards; and a few, like Juana Inés de la Cruz, defined their place and time; but in English poetry, a small eighteenth-century triumph like Anne, Countess of Winchelsea's poem 'The Soldier's Death' did little to remind the male literati of the immediate future that there could be such a thing as a poet in skirts. They might remember the poem, but they didn't remember her. True equality really began in the nineteenth century: Christina Rossetti, for example, wrote poems of an accomplishment that no sensitive male critic could ignore, no matter how prejudiced he was. (There were insensitive male critics who ignored it, and patronized her as a cot-case: but the tin-eared reviewer is an eternal type.) Elizabeth Barrett Browning was spoken of in the same breath as her husband. He was the greater, perhaps even the greatest: but nobody except devout misogynists doubted that she was in the same game.

In the twentieth century, Marianne Moore achieved the same sort of unarguable status: she was acknowledged to be weighty even by those who thought she was fey. In Sydney in the late 1950s, the poets of my circle would make a habit of reciting by heart from Edith Sitwell's *Façade*, but still we all thought that she was some kind of echolalic succubus, and that a more typical English woman poet was, say, Anne Ridler: polite but pale. I would listen to an all-poetry LP that included Marianne Moore reciting 'Distrust of Merits' and come away convinced that she had the strength to make seriousness sound the way it should. When she said 'The world's an orphans' home' I thought hers was the woman's voice that took the measure of the war in which the men had just been fighting to the death. Judith Wright spoke on the same theme to a far less resonant phonetic effect: she was a big Australian name but I could find only two or three self-sustaining poems in all her body of work. Today, I find only one or two: as an environmentalist she was a tough operator who saved the Great Barrier Reef from the mining companies, but as a poet she let her language drift towards the merely conceptual, until, in her later phase, it was like fluff. Another Australian female poet in Wright's generation was, however, a better guardian of real meaning: Gwen Harwood. I should have spotted her at the time, but I was too caught up with the Americans.

Leaving Emily Dickinson aside – after all, she never found the public, the public had to find her – Marianne Moore would have been enough on her own to make women's poetry seem like an American thing. She was a Special Forces operative in a black tricorne hat. But there was also Edna St Vincent Millay, whose sonnets, despite their wilfully traditionalist structure and diction, looked more and more original to me as time went on, to the point where, in my mind, I was casting the movie about her love affair with Edmund Wilson. My choice for the starring role was Gwyneth Paltrow, on the basis not just of how well she had played Sylvia Plath, but of how well she recited blank verse in *Shakespeare in Love*. Philip Seymour Hoffman would have made the ideal Edmund Wilson: Hoffman even had the physical bulk. The Edna–Edmund double act could easily have become as famous as Ted and Sylvia, if not for one vital factor: Plath was the formative woman poet for whole generations throughout the English-speaking world, whereas Millay has never really caught on. But then, not even Marianne Moore has ever caught on like Plath. In the whole of literature's long history, Plath must be the supreme example of a poet breaking through to masses of people who know nothing about poetry at all. The young readers who went mad for Byron had all read verse before.

But if we look only for a big impact, we are treating women's poetry as a commodity. And what should please us is that women's poetry has joined men's poetry in the harsh realm of art, where nothing except quality can survive the perpetual bushfire of time. Elinor Wylie's finely fashioned poem 'Wild Peaches' glitters among the ashes, and some of the ashes are the remains of her other work: there is quite a lot of it, but it won't be coming back. The main reason that the bulk of her poetic achievement will stay absent is the intensity of 'Wild Peaches' in its role as an outlier, a strange attractor: packed with fully observed and realized images, it is so well organized that the organization becomes part of its texture, and not just part of its driving force.

Donne, in one of his regrettably few statements about how 'Metricall compositions' are made, referred to the putting together of a poem as 'the shutting up'. An unfortunate term, and we could use a better one; because there can't be much doubt that the shaping of a poem is also a pressure, in which the binding energy of the poem brings everything inside its perimeter to incandescence. If that were not the prize, then the great women poets of our time might not have worked so hard to join the men.

•

By now it's quite possible to look forward to a time when women will dominate the art. But in my time, men still did. Throughout my career as a critic, I did my best to say that women had contributed vitally to the heritage, but here at the final reckoning it bothers me that I might not have done enough, and that my critical work, if any of it is still consulted after I am gone, will make me look like a chauvinist. I sincerely believe that I was not, but in these matters it is not enough to believe, you have to behave. Will I get myself off the hook just by saying that I ended up with almost as many lines by Elizabeth Bishop in my head as by Robert Lowell? What one feels bound to acknowledge fully is her artistic stature. Of her moral stature there can be no question. The big book of her letters, *One Art*, is a mind-expanding picture of a difficult yet dedicated life, and a smaller book of letters, *Words in Air*, by collecting her correspondence with Lowell, defines the ethics of an historic moment: a moment when poetry, queen of the humanities, took a step towards the opportunistic privileges of totalitarianism. Lowell wanted her endorsement for his bizarre temerity in stealing Elizabeth Hardwick's letters to use unchanged in his poetry. Bishop refused to approve, and surely she was right. She didn't much like the idea of confessional poetry anyway – if she had, she would probably have written some – but clearly she thought that if it had to be done, it should be done within the bounds of civilization. Students in the future who are set the task of writing an essay about the limits of art could start right there, at the moment when one great poet told another to quit fooling himself.

•

Look into Chapman's Homer and you can see what alliteration once did, long before Swinburne arrived to overdo it. Agamemnon kits himself out before going into battle:

> Then took he up his weighty shield, that round about him cast
> Defensive shadows; ten bright zones of gold-affecting brass
> Were driven about it, and of tin, as full of gloss as glass,
> Swelled twenty bosses out of it . . .

While the 'defensive shadows' are good, 'as full of gloss as glass' is beyond good: it's brilliant. Just don't let Swinburne hear about it. But you can't stop poets finding inspiration in the heritage; and no doubt to be as learned as possible is not just a duty, but a good thing. Still, you can't help wishing that some of the learned poets since Shakespeare had been blessed with the knack of forgetting what they had read. For much of his life, Milton needed his memory because he couldn't see. When he considered how his light was spent, he didn't complain about being too often driven back into his remembered books. Perhaps he didn't see the problem. But my quarrel with *Paradise Lost* – man against mountain! – begins with how Milton's beaver-dams of learning turn streams of invention into stagnant ponds. One of the several Miltonians among my friends kindly goes on telling me that the displays of learning were part of the invention. Milton obviously believed that to be true. But here I am, once more submitting myself to *Paradise Lost* in the hope of being caught up; and once more realizing that the famous clash between T. S. Eliot and F. R. Leavis on the subject of Milton (Leavis did most of the clashing) was not a quarrel about nothing. It was really about a monumental example of poetic genius defeating itself; because the question of the possible insufficiency of his single most important work would never have arisen if it did not seem to pride itself on undoing things that Milton well knew how to do. A consummate lyricist faced with his biggest opportunity, he strained every muscle to be bad. Let one illustration serve, from Book Ninth, line 385 onwards. Eve has just spoken, and now she is described:

> Thus saying, from her Husbands hand her hand
> Soft she withdrew, and, like a Wood-Nymph light,
> *Oread* or *Dryad*, or of Delia's *Traine*,

Betook her to the groves, but *Delia's* self
In gait surpassed and Goddess-like deport,
Though not as shee with Bow and Quiver armed,
But with such Gardning Tools as Art, yet rude,
Guiltless of fire had formed, or Angels brought.
To *Pales*, or *Pomona*, thus adorned,
Likest she seemed – *Pomona* when she fled
Vertumnus – or to *Ceres* in her prime,
Yet virgin of *Proserpina* from *Jove* . . .

But enough. Such passages, and there are scores of them, are impoverished by their riches: erudition distorts the picture, whose effect divides into the poetic and the encyclopaedic. Johnson, though he despised *Lycidas*, was keen to find virtues in *Paradise Lost*, and a grand sweep of intertextual didacticism was high among the virtues that he found. But Johnson, who was also keen to tell the unadorned truth, said of Milton's great masterpiece: 'None ever wished it longer than it is.' The burden of learning helps to make it long. In mitigation, we should note that this element of Miltonics can be called uniquely Milton's only because he did the most of it: in fact, it's a hardy perennial. In the previous century, Spenser had been often at it, as when he loaded a library on top of his two swans in 'Prothalamion':

Two fairer birds I yet did never see:
The snow which doth the top of *Pindus* strew,
Did never whiter shew,
Nor *Jove* himself when he a Swan would be
For love of *Leda* . . .

Even those among his readers who knew nothing about Greece might possibly have known that Pindus was its principal mountain range, and everybody knew about shape-changing Jove and his priapic attentions to Leda. Similarly, readers of Marvell's 'Bermudas' probably knew that Ormus – still in business at the time, although soon to decline and vanish – was a kingdom notable for wealth:

> He hangs in shades the Orange bright
> Like golden Lamps in a green Night.
> And does in the Pomegranates close,
> Jewels more rich than *Ormus* show's.

But here we see where the trouble with this aspect of Miltonics really starts: when an encyclopaedic reference is outclassed by its poetic surroundings, like a fake jewel in a fine setting. The line about the lamps in the green night is one of Marvell's best things, and poor old Ormus pales beside it. (Milton, too, dragged Ormus in, and to even less effect.) One hesitates to rhapsodize about the pure spring of inspiration, but there is such a thing as clogging the pipes. The awful thing about the apparent success of Milton's unyielding stretches of leaden erudition was that the plumbing of English poetry was affected far into the future. Without Milton's example, would Matthew Arnold have taken such pains to burden his 'Philomela' with this lumbering mention of a naiad nymph and her habitat?

> Lone Daulis, and the high Cephissian vale?
> Listen, Eugenia . . .

But surely Eugenia has stopped listening, and is checking the menu for room service. At least we can say, however, that Arnold, by perpetrating such a blunder, helped to define what makes 'Dover Beach' so wonderful: in its clear cascade of distilled but unstrained speech, nobody from classical times except Sophocles makes a credited appearance, and even his bit is part of the argument, not just a classical adjunct parked on top of the edifice like a misplaced metope or triglyph. Milton, of course, schooled himself well in the trick of pulling a learned reference into the narrative texture, but all too often, no matter how smoothly the job is done, the most you can say of it is that it sounds good.

•

But sounding good can't even be called a requirement. It's a description. A poet who can't make the language sing doesn't start. Hence the shortage of real poems amongst the global planktonic field of duds. In the countries of the Anglosphere, the poet's first relationship is with the English language even when the poet is indigenous. There is therefore no mystery, although there is some sadness, about the shortage of Australian Aboriginal poets: the pseudo-progressive idea dies hard that there is something imperialistic about making it compulsory for Aboriginal youngsters to study the language of the white invader. Until the corrective opinion of such inspired Aboriginal leaders as Noel Pearson prevails, it will go on being true that too few people of Aboriginal origin are masters of the country's principal language. Published in 2009, the Macquarie PEN Anthology of Australian Literature attempted to compensate for this imbalance artificially by including anything in English from an Aboriginal writer that might conceivably be construed as a poem, even if it was a political manifesto. It wasn't the first attempt in Australian literary history to give Aboriginal culture a boost into the mainstream. Back in the 1930s to 1950s, the Jindyworobak movement did the same, with whitefella poets rendering themselves unreadable by using as many of the blackfella's totemic terms as possible. New Zealand might have been in the same position with regard to the Maoris (nowadays known as the Maori, for purposes of confusion), had it not been for the advent of Hone Tuwhare (1922–2008), in whose poem 'To a Maori Figure Cast in Bronze Outside the Chief Post Office, Auckland' the bronze figure speaks thus:

> I hate being stuck up here, glaciated, hard all over
> and with my guts removed: my old lady is not going
> to like it . . .

After twenty-five lines of brilliantly articulated bitching, the statue signs off:

> Somebody give me a drink; I can't stand it.

Tuwhare was himself a Maori, so the argument was over. Finally it is the vitality of language that decides everything, and this hard fact becomes adamantine as one's own vitality ebbs. Nevertheless, I still make plans to live forever: there are too many critical questions still to be raised. Most of them can never be settled, which is the best reason for raising them. For instance, who needs a smooth technique after hearing Hopkins praise 'All things counter, original, spare, strange'? Well, everyone does, because what Hopkins does with the language depends on the mastery of mastery, and first you must have the mastery. And how can we write as innocently now as Shakespeare did when he gave Mercutio the speech about Queen Mab, or as Herrick did when he wrote 'Oberon's Feast', or even as Pope did, for all his show of craft, when he summoned the denizens of the air to attend Belinda in Canto II of *The Rape of the Lock*? Well, we certainly can't do it through ignorance, so there goes the idea of starting from nowhere. Better to think back on all the poems you have ever loved, and to realize what they have in common: the life you soon must lose.

PROVENANCE OF CHAPTERS

Part I

Listening to the Flavour: *Poetry* (Chicago), December 2006

Five Favourite Poetry Books: *Wall Street Journal*, 6 January 2007

The Arrow Has Not Two Points: *Poetry* (Chicago), December 2007

Meeting MacNeice: commissioned by the Reading for Life project, 2006

Little Low Heavens: *Poetry* (Chicago), October 2008

On a Second Reading: *Poetry* (Chicago), December 2008

The Necessary Minimum: *Poetry* (Chicago), August 2009

A Deeper Consideration: *Poetry* (Chicago), September 2010

Product Placement in Modern Poetry: *Poetry* (Chicago), May 2011

Technique's Marginal Centrality: *Poetry* (Chicago), January 2012

A Stretch of Verse: *Poetry* (Chicago), November 2012

The Donaghy Negotiation (first published as an introduction to
    Michael Donaghy's collected critical writings, *The Shape of the
    Dance*, 2009)

There You Come Home, *Quadrant*, April 2011

Interior Music: *Poetry* (Chicago), September 2013

Part II

John Updike's Poetic Finality: *New York Times Book Review*, 3 May
    2009

Stephen Edgar Stays Perfect: *TLS*, 4 September 2009

Poetry Heaven, Election Hell: *Standpoint*, July/August 2009

Les Murray's Palatial New Shed: *Monthly*, April 2010

Talking to Posterity: Peter Porter 1929–2010: *TLS*, 14 May 2010

Elegance in Overalls: The American Pastoral of Christian Wiman:
    Financial Times, 12 November 2010

Michael Longley Blends In: *Financial Times*, 18 March 2011
Spectator Diary: *Spectator*, 26 May 2012
Building the Sound of Sense: *Prospect*, January 2014

Part III

Trumpets at Sunset: *TLS*, 16 May 2014

CREDITS

Kingsley Amis: from "Bed and Breakfast" from *Collected Poems 1944-1979* (Penguin Books, 1980), copyright © Kingsley Amis, 1979.

John Ashbery: from "Daffy Duck in Hollywood" from *Houseboat Days* (Viking, 1977), © 1975, 1976, 1977 by John Ashbery.

W. H. Auden: from "XXX" from *On This Island* by W. H. Auden, copyright © 1937 and renewed 1962 by Random House. Used by permission of Random House, an imprint and division of Random House LLC. All rights reserved. From "The Fall of Rome," copyright © 1947 by W. H. Auden and renewed 1975 by the The Estate of W. H. Auden, from *W. H. Auden Collected Poems* by W. H. Auden. Used by permission of Random House, an imprint and division of Random House LLC. All rights reserved. From "Through the Looking-Glass" from *Collected Shorter Poems 1927-1957* (Faber & Faber, 1966).

John Betjeman: from "On Seeing an Old Poet in the Café Royal" and "Invasion Exercises in the Poultry Farm" from *Collected Poems* (John Murray, 1972), © John Betjeman 1958.

Elizabeth Bishop: from "The Fish" from *The Complete Poems, 1927-1979*, © Elizabeth Bishop, copyright renewed © 1974, 1976 by Elizabeth Bishop, copyright © 1983 by Alice Helen Methfessel.

Daniel Brown: from "On Being Asked by Our Receptionist If I Liked the Flowers" from *Taking the Occasion* (New Criterion Series, 2008), reprinted by permission of Rowman & Littlefield.

Amy Clampitt: from "Good Friday" from *The Kingfisher* (Faber & Faber, 1984).

Hart Crane: from "Voyages" from *The Complete Poems and Selected Letters and Prose* (Liveright Publishing Corp., 1966).

E. E. Cummings: from "Poem, or Beauty Hurts Mr Vinal." Copyright 1926, 1954, © 1991 by the Trustees for the E. E.Cummings Trust. Copyright © 1985 by George James Firmage, from *Complete Poems: 1904-1962* by E. E. Cummings, edited by George J. Firmage. Used by permission of Liveright Publishing Corporation.

Michael Donaghy: "Shibboleth" from *Shibboleth* (Oxford Poets, 1988).

Stephen Edgar: from "Totenstadt," "In Dreaming at the Speed of Light," and "The Red Sea" from *History of the Day* (Black Pepper, 2009); from "Man on the Moon" from *Other Summers* (Black Pepper, 2006), all reprinted by permission of Black Pepper Publishing (blackpepperpublishing.com). All rights reserved.

T. S. Eliot: from "Morning at the Window" from *Collected Poems 1909–1962* (Faber & Faber, 1974), copyright © 1991 by Esme Valerie Eliot. Reprinted by permission of Houghton Mifflin Harcourt Publishing Company. All rights reserved.

William Empson: from "Just a Smack at Auden" from *The Complete Poems*, edited by John Haffenden (Penguin Modern Classics, 2001).

Robert Frost: from "At Woodward's Gardens" and "Snow" from *Selected Poems*, edited by Ian Hamilton (The Penguin Poets, 1973).

Seamus Heaney: from "Shore Woman" from *Selected Poems 1965–1975* (Faber & Faber, 1980).

Geoffrey Hill: from "The Eve of St Mark" from "An Apology for the Revival of Christian Architecture in England" from *New and Collected Poems, 1952–1992* (Houghton Mifflin Company, 1994), copyright © 1994 by Geoffrey Hill.

Ted Hughes: from "The Jaguar" from *The Hawk in the Rain* (Faber & Faber, 1957).

Kenneth Koch: from "The Art of Love" from *The Art of Love: Poems* (Vintage Books, 1975).

R. F. Langley: from "The Upshot" from *Collected Poems* (Carcanet Press, 2000), reprinted by permission of the publisher.

Philip Larkin: from "Sunny Prestatyn" and "The Whitsun Weddings" from *The Complete Poems of Philip Larkin*, edited by Archie Burnett, copyright © 2012 by The Estate of Philip Larkin. Reprinted by permission of Farrar, Straus and Giroux, LLC.

Michael Longley: "Twayblade" and from "Firewood" from *A Hundred Doors* (Jonathan Cape/Wake Forest University Press, 2011), reprinted by permission of the publisher.

Louis MacNeice: from "London Rain" and "Meeting Point" from *Collected Poems* (Faber & Faber, 1979).

James McAuley: from "Because" from *Collected Poems 1936–1970* (Angus & Robertson, 1985).

Samuel Menashe: "Beachhead" and "Cargo" from *New and Selected Poems* (Bloodaxe Books, 2009), reprinted by permission of the publisher.

James Merrill: from "The Broken Home" from *Collected Poems* (Alfred A. Knopf, 2001).

Les Murray: from "From a Tourist Journal," "As Country Was Slow," "Midi," "Nursing Home," "Eucalpyts in Exile," "The Cowladder Stanzas," "Visiting Geneva," "The Buladelah-Farce Holiday Song Cycle," and "Southern Hemisphere Gardens" from *New Selected Poems* (Farrar, Straus and Giroux, 2014) copyright © 2007, 2012, 2014 by Les Murray. Reprinted by permission of Farrar, Straus and Giroux, LLC.

Vladimir Nabakov: from *Pale Fire* (Vintage International, 1989).

Charles Olson: from "Sixth Song" from *The Maximus Poems* (University of California Press, 1985).

Ezra Pound: from "Canto XVII" and "Canto XXI" from *The Cantos of Ezra Pound*, copyright © 1934 by Ezra Pound. Reprinted by permission of New Directions Publishing Corp. From "Canto XLVI" from *The Cantos of Ezra Pound*, copyright © 1937 by Ezra Pound. Reprinted by permission of New Directions Publishing Corp. From "Canto LII" from *The Cantos of Ezra Pound*, copyright © 1940 by Ezra Pound. Reprinted by permission of New Directions Publishing Corp. From "Canto CIII," "Canto LXXIV," "Canto LXXVIII," "Canto LXXXI," and "Rock-Drill de los Cantares LXXXV–XCV" from *The Cantos of Ezra Pound*, copyright © 1948 by Ezra Pound. Reprinted by permission of New Directions Publishing Corp. From "Canto CX" from *The Cantos of Ezra Pound*, copyright © 1962 by Ezra Pound. Reprinted by permission of New Directions Publishing Corp.

Peter Redgrove: from "Travelogue" from *The Harper* (Cape Poetry/Jonathan Cape, 2006).

Vita Sackville-West: from *The Land* (William Heinemann, 1926), copyright Vita Sackville West 1926.

Frederick Seidel: from "Morphine" from *Poems 1959–2009* (Farrar, Straus & Giroux, 2010).

Anne Sexton: from "The Fortress" from *Selected Poems of Anne Sexton* (Farrar, Straus & Giroux, 2010).

L. E. Sissman: from "Pursuit of Honor" from *Hello Darkness: The Collected Poems of L. E. Sissman* (Little Brown, 1971), reprinted by permission of Houghton Library, Harvard University. From "New York: A Summer Funeral" from *The New Yorker* (August 27, 1973).

Dylan Thomas: from "Poem on His Birthday" from *Collected Poems 1934–1952* (J. M. Dent/Everyman Paperback, 1977); from "Should Lanterns Shine" from *The Poems of Dylan Thomas*, copyright © 1939 by New Directions Publishing Corp. Reprinted by permission of New Directions Publishing Corp.

Dunstan Thompson: from "Seascape with Edwardian Figures" and "Valley of the Kings" from *Poems 1950–1974* (Paradigm Press, 1975); from "Largo" from *A Little Treasury of Modern Poetry*, edited by Oscar Williams (Scribner, 1946).

W. J. Turner: from "Mystery" from *Landscape of Cytherea* (Chatto & Windus, 1923); from "Hymn to Her Unknown" from *A Little Treasury of Modern Poetry*, edited by Oscar Williams (Scribner, 1952).

Hone Tuwhare: from "To a Maori Figure Cast in Bronze Outside the Chief Post Office" from *Small Holes in the Silence: Collected Works* (Random House NZ, 2011), reproduced by permission of Rob Tuwhare, on behalf of The Estate of Hone Tuwhare.

John Updike: from "Frankie Laine," "Endpoint," "Her Coy Lover Sings Out," "Elegy for a Real Golfer," and "Bird Caught in My Deer Netting" from *Endpoint and Other Poems* by John Updike, copyright © 2009 by The Estate of John Updike. Used by permission of Alfred A. Knopf, an imprint of the Knopf Doubleday Publishing Group, a division of Random House LLC. All rights reserved.

Richard Wilbur: from "A Baroque Wall—Fountain Wall in the Villa Sciarra" from *Collected Poems 1943–2004* (Harvest Book/Harcourt Inc., 2006), copyright © 2004 by Richard Wilbur.

Christian Wiman: from "Sitting Down to Breakfast Alone," "Five Houses Down," and "The Reservoir" from *Every Riven Thing* (Farrar, Straus and Giroux, 2010), copyright © 2010 by Christian Wiman. Reprinted by permission of the author. All rights reserved.

W. B. Yeats: from "The Tower," "Byzantium," and "Under Ben Bulben" from *Collected Poems* (Picador, 1990).

Every effort has been made to trace copyright holders of the poems published in this book. The author and publisher apologize if any material has been included without permission or without the appropriate acknowledgement, and would be glad to be told of anyone who has not been consulted.